Washington Irving
Seville April 23ʳ 1828.

PORTRAIT OF IRVING BY DAVID WILKIE

WASHINGTON IRVING, ESQUIRE

AMBASSADOR AT LARGE FROM THE NEW WORLD TO THE OLD

by GEORGE S. HELLMAN

*Illustrated with old engravings; facsimiles
of Irving's letters and manuscripts;
and sketches by himself*

NEW YORK : ALFRED · A · KNOPF
MCMXXV

PS
2081
A4

H

17728

This book is Dedicated

Prefatory Note

Biographies of Washington Irving since the appearance, in 1862, of the "Life and Letters" edited by his nephew, Pierre M. Irving, have followed closely along the lines of that publication, to which the present volume is also in many ways indebted. During the last ten years, however, there has been discovered, or, in some instances, re-discovered a very considerable amount of original Irving material making possible a new visualization of that talented, lazy, pleasure-loving, charming man who was not only the first American author of international reputation but also the best beloved American during the first seventy-five years of our republic. A large group of Irving journals and notebooks ranging from the year 1804 to 1842; unpublished letters of Irving in the Library of Congress and in the files of the State Department at Washington; the entire correspondence between Irving and his best friend, Henry Brevoort; books and private papers at Sunnyside; unpublished journals of Irving's contemporaries—these are but some of the sources from which new information has been gathered for the pages of this biography.

To many persons I am indebted for courtesies in the course of this work, and I record with grateful appreciation the names of Mrs. Robert Sedgwick, Mr. and Mrs. L. DuPont Irving, Mrs. Isaac N. Seligman, Mr. Henry H. Harper, Mr. Gouverneur Kemble, Miss Elisabeth Brill, Mrs. Alfred A. Scheffer, Mr. James K. Hackett, Prof. Brander Matthews, Prof. Arthur H. Nason, Mrs. G. R. C. Conybeare, Dr. S. L. Rowe, Mr. J. Butler Wright, Mr. W. A. Slade, Mr. Horatio S. Krans, Mr. William R. Langfeld, Mr. Clayton Hamilton, Mr. Philip Boyer, Prof.

PREFATORY NOTE

George C. D. Odell, Mr. Edward M. Herzog, Mr. James
Branch Cabell, Prof. Gilbert Chinard, Prof. Fred Lewis Pattee,
Mr. Henry L. Savage, and Prof. W. P. Trent.

On the jacket of this book are shown three of the windows in
the Washington Irving Memorial Chapel, Sleepy Hollow Cemetery. Messrs. Hardman & Co., of London, designed these windows, and Messrs. R. B. & A. Ware, of New York, were the
architects of the chapel. Mr. Arthur Ware very kindly made
these designs available.

I am also under a very considerable debt to the Bibliophile
Society of Boston, the Grolier Club, Messrs. G. P. Putnam's
Sons, the Department of State, the Library of Congress, the
New York Public Library, and the New York Historical Society.
From all these sources, from all the men and women who have
been named above, there has flown into my labour that spirit
of generous helpfulness which was so predominantly a trait of
Washington Irving.

G. S. H.

Upper Saranac Lake
September, 1924

Contents

Illustrations

WASHINGTON IRVING
ESQUIRE

Chapter I

THE DEACON'S SON

LEWIS MORRIS had come from Philadelphia, bringing great news. The Articles of the Preliminaries of Peace between Great Britain and France had been signed on the 20th of January. Some seven weeks earlier, in November, 1782, John Adams, Benjamin Franklin, John Jay and Henry Laurens, the American Commissioners, had agreed with Richard Oswald, the Commissioner of George III, on terms which should become part of the final Treaty to be concluded after France and Great Britain had come to an agreement. The tidings brought by Lewis Morris were thus confirmation that the War of Independence was about to come to an end in the field of diplomacy, and that the City of New York would soon be disinvested of its British military rulers.

Lewis Morris had not alone been a signer of the Declaration, and a member of the Continental Congress, but his opposition to the British had continued of so determined a character that much of his property was destroyed by the British army in way of revenge. He had given up his seat in Congress to make place for his brilliant young half-brother, Gouverneur Morris, and was now serving as Major-General of the New York State Militia. The capitulation of his British Majesty thus had for him a flavour of peculiar satisfaction, and he lost no time in making the news available to Hugh Gaine, the publisher of *The New York Gazette and the Weekly Mercury*. Within a few hours Gaine had the details of "this happy and glorious event" set up in type, and they appeared in the first column of the issue for the week ending April 5th. In this same week, on the 3rd of April, was born Washington Irving.

3

WASHINGTON IRVING ESQUIRE

In all our annals what happier coincidence? The Treaty whose preliminary articles thus appeared for the delighted edification of the American people, established, it is true, the basis for conditions which led to the rapid growth of our Republic and those relations between the United States and Great Britain which, despite the backward impulse of the War of 1812, were gradually to develop from friction into friendship; and if there is any one man who deserves most credit for cementing, if not actually for creating good-will among the English-speaking peoples, it is the son who, as, so to speak, her eleventh edition, was published by Mrs. William Irving in that memorable week.

New York, when Washington Irving made his entry at 131 William Street, was just emerging from its lowest state. For seven years it had been in the possession of the British, and during this period its commerce had declined to a point where hundreds of vessels lay idle in the harbour and its population had dwindled to less than twenty thousand. The British authorities had allowed wharves to crumble, streets to get into miserable condition, portions of the town wrecked by fire to remain unrestored. Public buildings of learning and of worship the British troops had taken over for barracks, for prisons, for hospitals; and private buildings had been impressed into similar service by military rulers who treated the patriotic element of the population with rigour and disdain. Revenues were largely uncollectable, and for reasons of business as well as of sentiment thousands of persons had departed from the city.

William Irving was among the merchants who left in the early days of the Revolutionary War, but when his new home at Rahway in New Jersey was taken over by the British troops, and he and his wife and their already numerous children were forced to sleep in the garret, he decided to return to New York. A strong character this William Irving, with much of the tenacity of his Scotch forbears; a man of uncompromising probity, whether in trade or home life, but hardly the kind of man to win affection. For the lovable traits in Washington

4

Irving we must have recourse, if the theory of inheritance be our sign-post, to the mother, Sarah Sanders, granddaughter of an English curate. She was very gentle with the children, and with Washington most of all. There were William and Ann, and Peter and Catherine, (and three had died in infancy,) and there were Ebenezer and John and Sarah and Washington. Their father sought to hold them with such tight reins that, with the exception of Ann, one and all reacted from his religious instructions, some even to the point of departing from the Church of the Covenanters. Especially in the case of Washington, who in early youth had himself secretly confirmed at Trinity Church, did the relation between father and son bear a resemblance to the conditions that existed in that other severely Scotch Presbyterian household where, seventy-five years later, Robert Louis Stevenson rebelled from his father's rule. Irving did not indulge in dissipation equal to that which characterized the youth of the Edinburgh boy, but his surreptitious amusements, his neglect of study, his light attitude towards the religious exercises that were so distressingly frequently presided over by his father the Deacon, were similarly due in part, at least, to excessive parental discipline.

What an uncompromising man William Irving must have been! On Washington Irving's desk at Sunnyside in Irvington there still rests the family Bible in which the father inscribed the names, the very hour of birth, and, of those who died during his lifetime, the date of death of each of his children. A son who was to have been called William Irving Jr. was born before the parents left England, and died in a few hours. In America two years later (approximately every two years, for nearly a quarter of a century, Sarah Irving brought forth a child) another son was born, and was named William Irving Jr. He passed away in infancy, less than a year old. The third child was again a son, and again called William Irving Jr.; and if this child, too, had died before the advent of the next male offspring, doubtless William Irving would have continued in his determination to have his oldest living son bear his

5

name. To yield, even in a matter of nomenclature, was not in his inflexible nature.

There has, in recent years, been an increasing realization of the importance of childhood and adolescent experiences in the biographical consideration of the ambitions and activities, the moods, the failures, and the accomplishments of later life. Irving's career well illustrates the theory that manhood fulfils the tendencies brought into being by the circumstances of childhood and that the deepest of later emotional experiences are the incisive repetition of the earlier outline. From this point of view episodes and inclinations of Irving's boyhood and youth are weighted with a significance that has hitherto remained unemphasized. The preponderant influence in the Irving household was that of the father. It was oppressive to such an extent that, according to Irving, the Deacon led his children to believe all pleasures were wicked. The children resorted to strategies to taste enjoyments. Irving as a lad would steal away from the atmosphere of his father's home, which not even the native gaiety and sweetness of his mother could make congenial, and wander about the streets of the little town, finding his way to the piers where he would look out upon the sail boats and the frigates, and dream of exciting adventures on seas remote. He would stay away so long and so late that more than once the town-crier would accost passersby with queries as to the missing child of the Deacon. So strong was the passion to get away from home that Washington tried to accustom himself to the odious diet of salt pork, and to sleeping on the bare boards of his room, so as to harden himself for experiences as a sailor before the mast. A little more determination of will, a little more robustness, and Washington would no doubt have run away from his father's roof; and that for so great a number of his years he was the wanderer is largely explained by these early longings intensified by paternal rigour.

But the most significant phase of the Deacon's influence, both before his death in 1807 and throughout the more than half a century till Washington Irving himself came into the rest that comes to all, has to do with the absence of any deep religious motivation in the life of his famous son. Throughout the years, both at home and abroad, Irving had recurrent periods of depression amounting at times almost to melancholia, but there was little recourse to the sustaining comfort of religious faith. Seldom did he attend divine services until he had reached the age of fifty, and none of the three chief sorrows of his life was followed by any attempt to find solace through religion. When his beloved Matilda Hoffman died, Irving left New York and went to the country place of his friend Judge Van Ness at Kinderhook, where he threw himself into the labour of completing "Knickerbocker's History." When, in 1817, his mother died, he went on, unhappy but brave, under the shadow of commercial disaster. The flute, not the church organ, brought him comfort then. When, in 1823, he suffered the greatest disappointment of his maturer years through Emily Foster's refusal of his offer of marriage, he sought in literary work and in the relaxation of the drama, surcease from the harassments of mind and heart. His diaries show no evidence of any resort to the consolations of religion. In the language of present day psychologists his was a "complex" where his earthly father stood between him and his Heavenly Father. And that, during the final period of his life, Irving, after formally becoming an Episcopalian, was a vestryman in the church at Tarrytown may be regarded as partially a gracious compliance with the wishes of his neighbours, partially a willing concession to religion, life drawing towards its close in the quiet harbour of his retreat on the Hudson. And yet, in his attitude toward his fellow men his was ever the gentle spirit of Jesus.

In order to get as close as possible to Washington Irving in the formative years of his boyhood let us envisage not alone his home life but also the life of the little town in which he grew up. And indeed it was only a little town, not much more than a mile in length, although its growth in prosperity and population increased so rapidly that, by the time of the Deacon's death in 1807, its outgoing vessels carrying iron, timber and oil, wheat,

7

flour and corn, and its incoming vessels with woollen and linen from England, mahogany and indigo from the Spanish Main, wines and silks and other luxuries from France, Spain and Portugal, rum and molasses from the West Indies, brought affluence to the merchants and led to a trebling of the population that had clung to the little city in the dark days of British rule. When George Washington entered New York in November, 1783, on the evacuation of the King's forces, he passed by streets that had the irregularity of country lanes, that were, in fact, the old country lanes of Dutch days now sufficiently well paved. Through the centre of some of these would run gutters, but of course of the modern system of sewers, or of water supply within the house, there was not even a suggestion. Public pumps served some of the purposes of the household and were available, all too inadequately, when fire broke out. When Washington Irving was a lad the housewives obtained their tea water from carts that had been driven down from the outlying portions of Manhattan Island.

Architecturally the city rises to the reminiscent eye as a combination largely English and part Dutch. The style of the brick buildings, as well as of the houses built of wood, was preponderantly English, but the general neatness and trimness were pleasantly evocative of the atmosphere of Holland. Some three or four thousand houses constituted the town of Irving's younger days, and if mention is made of the City Hall, Columbia College, the Governor's Palace, the Barracks, the Alms House, the Jail, and the Merchants Exchange (known as Tontine's because the fund for its construction had been raised by life annuities), there remain only the churches, theatres and the markets to complete the list of public or semi-public buildings.

The public markets were meeting places for the housewives, and Sarah Irving often had her little boy with her while she selected the meats and vegetables. There was only one servant in the Irving household at 128 William Street—the house to which the family removed the year after Irving's birth at 131— and while the elder children were at school, the care of the youngest often fell on the mother. It was a period without canned fruits, without cold storage, without those thousand and one edibles which now make daily marketing less necessitous. Though ladies of even high degree made their own preserves and head cheese, the selection of food at the public markets was an important duty of daily feminine life. And here we fancy young Washington watching some of the butchers ending up their parades of beef and sheep that, with a band of music to attract attention, had been led through the city streets as their own most effective advertisement.

The residential and the business district being one and the same—indeed a man's residence serving often as his place of business, whether mercantile, financial, or legal—there were few restaurants in New York during the first decade or two of the nineteenth century, unless one cares to dignify with that name the little rooms, more often cellars, on the river front. The first hotel worthy of recording was not erected until Washington Irving was nineteen years old, and it had neither bath rooms nor gas. The lamps that lighted the streets at night were regulated by the almanac, the moon being thriftily impressed into as much service as possible. Literary and educational societies existed, but there was no purely social club with its own club house. Apart from the daily gatherings after luncheon in the Tontine Coffee House, where business was the main topic, the male element assembled for its rare banquets and special patriotic celebrations at Fraunces' Tavern where Washington had taken farewell of his generals or, later, at the City Hotel, where Washington Irving himself was, in 1832, the great guest of honour. Not until 1815 did the Frenchman, Guerin, open the first confectionery shop in New York; when the city could at the same time boast of two billiard rooms and a well attended dancing school.

Children as well as grown-ups were called upon to be industrious, and with the exception of a week in April and again a week in September, there were no school vacations; yet apart from its theatres, New York had its relaxations. There was a

9

great love for horses, with much driving and some racing. Skating was enjoyed by young and old. Cock fights and bull baiting offered excitement to those thus inclined. Public executions were a more drastic form of thrilling entertainment. Along milder lines we have the occasional exhibition of wax figures, and of unusual animals. Leopards, elks and electrical fish were among the precursors of the animal shows in the circuses of to-day. The streets themselves were entertaining with their occasional music, their cries of the vendors, their booths and wagons where people paused for buns and oysters and gossip. And socially most important of all were the Gardens, such as the Columbia Gardens at the corner of Broadway and Prince Street, where trees had lamps twinkling through them, where fountains played, where coloured lights were strung in festoons, where statuary of Cupid, hunter of men, and Diana, huntress of beasts, and other figures of mythology added to the decorativeness. In these Gardens there were frequent concerts, and the young fellows treated the young girls to ice cream in the intervals of music. The Gardens themselves were surrounded by circular buildings, two or three stories in height, made up of little rooms and boxes with tables and chairs. From these boxes the observers, while sipping their refreshments, would watch the gay life below, with, presumably, keenly interested glance at the swings just large enough for two.

How predominantly, however, commerce and politics, and not leisure or cultural pursuits, held the forefront of the stage becomes most readily apparent in turning to the newspapers of the day. The first thing that may strike the reader is that under the name of such a journal as, for instance, *The New York Gazette,* appears no weather forecast, as nowadays, but a table of the tides. At what time a vessel could enter the harbour, or sail up the North River, or weigh anchor was a fact more significantly affecting the life of the entire town than whether there would be rain or sunshine, heat or cold. The citizens of New York, both men and women, in that early period which was commercially as well as politically so critical, had to have much of the spirit of the pioneer. Nor did the columns of New York's few newspapers give any appreciable space to notices concerning public entertainment, gossipy or scandalous news of one's neighbours, or even of accidents. A search through many issues of the *Gazette* reveals as the sole recorded accident the tragic mishap of a young boy crushed between the logs of a sawmill. Excitement, pleasure, sensationalism, had little place in the public prints where, however, political news from Philadelphia, and later from Washington when that city became the Capital, and political tidings from England and the Continent were accorded considerable space as affecting both the governmental and the commercial affairs of the young Republic.

And then, too, one observes how essentially these early newspapers were written for the male portion of the population, even as to advertisements. There are innumerable notices concerning vessels whose owners, on the payment of forty dollars a year, had available as much space as they might desire. Incoming cargoes are advertised at length; and here we meet with many quaint and aromatic names of eastern products. True, in such lists one finds items of feminine appeal, yet answering for the most part to the simpler needs of women's apparel and the necessities and very minor luxuries of the housewife. Swords, when swords were used not only for dress wear but for duelling; pistols and fowling-pieces on an island where partridge and quail and hares tempted young and old to go a-gunning; horses and wagons; wines and liquors of all kinds; hardware of all kinds; real estate for the affluent or the speculative; these, with frequent notices concerning runaway slaves, formed the bulk of newspaper advertisements.

Deacon William Irving, for all his limitations, may be thought of as honourably representing the masculine, sternly persevering, mercantile aspect of the city of his adoption. Washington Irving, for all his virtues, or, rather, perhaps, because of many of these virtues, suggests the gayer, the more cultural, and very decidedly the feministic phase of our city's development. There was nothing of the woman in the father, much in his son. The

Deacon was intolerant of pleasures to the point of hatred; Washington Irving, his life long, was, though never in a degraded sense, a devotee of pleasure, and if his kindly nature, whether as boy or as man, ever could be worked up to an emotion of hatred it would be alone a hatred of intolerance.

From early infancy Washington Irving was tended by women who naturally adored the family baby, and to this circumstance he owes his continual longing to bask in the sunshine of feminine affection. The first songs that he heard were from the lips of his mother and the old Highland songs sung to him by Lizzie, the general household servant who was also the little boy's nurse. The lovely tunes of Scotland, the sentimental and romantic words that Robert Burns had fitted to many of them, were never to be forgotten, and how enwrought they were in his heart and mind the man Washington Irving was later to indicate when he wrote of his visit to Walter Scott at Abbotsford, and the effect of those old songs on hearing them sung in the land of Robert Burns. Burns himself had died when Washington Irving was three years old; and the little boy in New York had assuredly already heard his Scottish nurse sing "Scots Wha Hae Wi' Wallace Bled," the stirring poem celebrating that battle of Bannockburn where Washington Irving's earliest recorded ancestor was the armour bearer of Robert Bruce.

Then too, there were the sisters to sing to him—Ann, in especial, who used to call her youngest brother "a little rack of bones." It was she who sang to him the pathetic ballad beginning "The moon had climbed the highest hill," a song that, though it made him weep, the five-year old lad wished to hear again and again.

Lizzie figures in an anecdote which no biographer of Irving has ever omitted. That worthy Scotch woman, with the infant Washington in her arms, had followed the Father of our Country into a shop and said to him: "Please, your Honour, here's a bairn named after you"; or, according to another version, George Washington was on horseback in front of a shop when Lizzie held up her little charge for the interested attention of

the great man. In either case we have Irving's own testimony
to the fact that the General placed his hand upon the head of
his future biographer and gave him his blessing, thus happily
concluding an episode whose main interest for us lies in its evidence of the self-confidence and courageous character of Lizzie.
She seems to have been in no awe of the reserved and august
personage.

But neither the capable Scotchwoman, nor the stern Deacon—
and of course not the indulgent mother—could do much with
Washington's namesake as the youngest of the Irving boys passed
from infancy into boyhood and from young boyhood into
adolescence. His frail health accounts in some measure for
the leniency with which his mother treated him. "Oh, Washington, if you only were good," is the severest of her rebukes
recorded in the family annals; and there is no escaping the fact
that Washington Irving, never bad in any bad sense, was certainly not good from a schoolmaster's, or a Deacon's, point of
view. He was lazy, and would study only those subjects which
interested him. In the eleven years of his school life he was at
four different schools but manifestly did not accumulate sufficient knowledge, or sufficient desire for further education, to
enter Columbia College which his elder brothers, Peter and
John, had attended. At the school where he stayed the longest,
and whose principal, Benjamin Romaine, formerly a soldier in
the Revolution, took a great liking to the young Washington because his propensity for telling the truth was even more marked
than his laziness and mischievousness, Irving effected a tidy arrangement with his classmates: they did his sums while he wrote
their compositions. A touch of Latin, a few lessons in music,
instruction in dancing carefully kept from the knowledge of his
father the Deacon, and there is little left worthy of special note
in Irving's education prior to his entrance into a law office at the
age of sixteen. Little, that is, of a regular nature; but there
still remain to be considered the books which, whether openly
or furtively, the young boy read.

The Deacon's library contained, in addition to its theological volumes, the more serious classics of English poetry, and Shakespeare and Milton were favourites of Washington Irving when he was still in his teens. Of prose volumes, "Pilgrim's Progress" made a special appeal to his imagination, much as later it became the cherished companion of young Nathaniel Hawthorne in the days when he still spelled his name Hathorne, and when he would carry Bunyan's volume around with him in fields and woods. But while Hawthorne, whose early style was largely influenced by the writings of Irving, reacted so strongly to "Pilgrim's Progress" because of its spiritual and symbolical character, the lure centred for Irving in its adventurous quality. For the same reason "Robin Hood," "Sindbad the Sailor," "Robinson Crusoe" and "Orlando Furioso" thrilled the Deacon's son; yet probably most influential of all was the series of twenty volumes, quaint in their woodcuts, entitled "The World Displayed." These were the books that he carried to school, reading them when the teacher was not looking; reading them late at night when all candles should have been out; reading them on Roosevelt's Dock and Dey's Dock and Messier's Dock and the other wharfs and pier heads of the city where he dreamed those dreams to which he refers in "The Sketch Book." When Irving was almost seventy years old he received from an old friend and admirer, Philip J. Forbes, a volume of "The World Displayed," and in his letter of thanks he wrote that he had never been more fascinated by any course in reading than by these books of voyages which were more delightful to him than a fairy tale, and which he had read "slyly to the great neglect of my lessons." He informed the donor that "it was your good father that first put this series of little volumes in my hand," and one wonders whether the elder Forbes was not the gunmaker, Gilbert Forbes, who, in 1775, advertised his shop "opposite Hull Tavern in Broad Way." Irving's boyhood adventures led him into that Hudson River country which he was later to make famed in literature when "Rip Van Winkle" and the "Legend of Sleepy Hollow" established the romantic charm of American literature, and it was with gun in hand that he explored the loveliness of Westchester County. With a gun that he may have bought from Gilbert Forbes he went after hares and partridge; nor, more than thirty years later, when he visited the Indian tribes of our Western prairies, was he averse to bringing down a bison; but the ardour of the hunter was never his, for too gentle and kindly a nature had Washington Irving for much zest in the taking of life. As a young child his recoilment from the infliction of pain was so intense that he would beg the headmaster to let him leave school with the girls when the afternoon hour came for the severe chastisement, in exposed manner, of the delinquent boys.

Tales of adventure and travel, imaginative and actual, were thus the main mental stimulus of Irving's youth. School lessons themselves making very little impression on the lad, and the exhortations and religious instruction of the Deacon having an antagonistic rather than a constructive effect, other influences that moulded him intellectually must be sought, partially by surmise, in the activities of those elder brothers to whom Washington Irving was ever so closely joined by ties of unusual sympathy.

William Irving, Jr. was Washington's senior by seventeen years and was really regarded by the youngest as somewhat of a father as well as much of a brother. When Washington was four years old William was already active as a trader with the Indians in the wilder parts of New York State, and Washington's continued interest in the American Indian (a theme that evoked his most fearless and noble writing) had its inception in William's adventures. Later on this interest was revived when Irving's lifelong friend Henry Brevoort sent him lengthy letters concerning the tribulations as well as the customs of the Indians at the time when Brevoort was associated with John Jacob Astor in the fur trade. William, as also Peter, the second of the Deacon's five sons, had very decidedly the literary flair, and the example and predilections of these two brothers had a potent influence over the youngest boy long before Washington was associated with William in the publication of *Salmagundi,* and

15

with Peter in the initial stage of "Knickerbocker's History of New York." The manuscript journal of the proceedings of the Calliopean, a literary society started in 1788, shows that William Irving, its Second Vice President in the year 1792, was on a committee to purchase books, and not long thereafter we find Peter active in the affairs of this organization whose members included a considerable group of young fellows of intellect. The society was constantly adding to its library. These books (often having to do with voyages, such as Warvill's "Travels in Arabia and Egypt"), were no doubt borrowed, whether with or without permission, by young Washington between the ages of eleven and fifteen. Then too, at the family table, he heard William and Peter tell of what took place at the weekly meetings of the Calliopean. This group of boys—we note such well known New York names as de Peyster, Moore, Dodge, Davis, Van Kleeck among the membership—originally divided themselves into four classes. One class would prepare the debate—the "disputation"—for the next meeting; a second would write compositions; a third framed the questions for subsequent debates, while a fourth had in charge the oratory of the evening. Criticism of the compositions was one of the most amusing functions of the members, although the debates themselves seem to us, as we study the manuscript records of this early literary society, to have been its most engaging element. Is virtue or vice more natural to man? Is it probable that the present generation in France will receive more benefit than injury from the Revolution? Should any crime besides murder be punished with death? Are literary pursuits or rural employment most productive of happiness to the individual? Are the fine arts conducive to morality? Would it not be to the advantage of society if the term of marriage between persons of less than thirty-five years of age was restricted to seven years, allowing them at the expiration of that term, if agreeable to both parties, to renew the contract; the man in all cases to support his children? Is it lawful and right to eat swine's flesh? Is the

16

How these singular barbarians turned out to be notorious squatters. How they build air castles, ~~together with their~~ ~~misunderstandings on the borders of river dead woods.~~ How the ~~renowned~~ ~~western fellow in a~~ ~~deep~~ ~~performed doubt and how~~ finally ~~co-operated and how they~~ attempted to initiate the Nederlanders in the mystery of ~~funding.~~

In ^the^ ~~my~~ last chapter, I have ~~faithfully~~ ~~and with~~ ~~scrupulous~~ ~~candour~~ ~~given~~ my honest little reader, I have given thee a faithful and ^unprejudiced^ ~~candid~~ account, of the origin of that singular race of people, inhabiting the country eastward of the ^the^ ~~new~~ Nederlands; but I have yet to mention certain ^peculiar^ habits ~~familiar to them~~, which rendered them exceeingly obnoxious to our ~~most~~ ^own^ honoured dutch ancestors.

The most prominent of these was a certain rambling propensity, with which, like the sons of Ishmael, they seem to have been gifted by heaven, and which continually goad them on to shift their residence from place to place. ~~so that their~~ ~~acting the~~ ~~so that their life is a constant~~ ~~scene~~ ~~of change and they may be literally termed~~ ~~strangers and~~ ~~sojourners in the land~~ So that a Yankey farmer is in a constant state of migration; tarrying occasionally here and there, clearing lands for other people to ~~cultivate~~ enjoy, building houses for others to inhabit, & in a manner may be considered the wandering arab of america.

His first thought on coming to the years of manhood, is to settle himself in the world — which means nothing more or less than to begin his rambles. To this end he takes unto himself for a wife, some strapping country Heiress. that is to say, a buxom rosy cheeked wench, possessing such a rich

PAGE OF ORIGINAL MANUSCRIPT OF
"KNICKERBOCKER'S HISTORY OF NEW YORK"

period of youth or of old age most productive of happiness? Has the discovery of the art of distilling ardent spirits been of advantage to mankind? (This was won by the affirmative.) Is the imprisonment for debtors consistent with the interests of a republican government? Is polygamy useful to society? (This, we hasten to say, was decided in the negative.) Are large commercial states dangerous to the liberties of republics founded on principles of equality? Such were the subjects of debate in which Washington Irving's brothers took part. And with them, now reciting Hamlet's Soliloquy, and again criticizing William Irving's composition entitled "On the Pleasure of Wine," was James K. Paulding, William's young brother-in-law who formed with Washington and William the trio that was later to catch the fancy of New York when the foibles of the town were satirized in the pages of *Salmagundi.*

Another companion of Irving's and a hitherto unknown influence over him in the days of his boyhood is revealed in the pages of an unpublished diary owned by the New York Historical Society. John Anderson (Washington's senior by ten years, and the elder brother of Dr. Alexander Anderson, America's first noted wood engraver), began in 1794 a diary continued until his death in the yellow fever epidemic of 1798. An appealing record of a patently fine young fellow whose practice of law did not dim his interest in art and music, the manuscript wins prophetic pathos from the Greek and Latin and English inscriptions on its title page, setting forth the fact that "the life of man is an empty shadow, and a vapour." But in 1794 John Anderson was a happy young fellow, much in love with Washington's elder sister, Catherine, who appears frequently in his diary as "Miss Kitty" or simply "Kitty." With the usual strategy of the suitor, the twenty-one year old John was very friendly toward Kitty's favourite brother, and we find in an entry for January 25th: "Washington Irving spent the afternoon with me. Gave him some of my drawing books to look over, and presented him with a small one; play on the violin

17

for him. He stayed to tea. Shew'd him the copy of my old journals and let him read part. Went home with him as it was dark—set a few minutes at his Papa's."

Here we have the first recorded evidence of Irving's interest in drawing and in music, and it may well be that John Anderson, who so often went sketching with his brother Alexander and who himself painted so delightfully on silk, and who was so fond of playing on the violin, led Irving to take up the pencil of the artist and, with whatever hesitating fingers, the flute.

A few days later John again had Washington around in the afternoon after school hours and again took the boy home at dark, and "set for a few minutes with Mrs. Irving and Kitty." The next week, on February 7, there is the following entry: "Miss Kitty Irving drank tea with us in the afternoon. Waited on her to Dr. Roger's lecture . . . I partly opened my mind to Miss Kitty on a subject that I have long wished to inform her of."—After that there are numerous mentions of various members of the Irving family. Catherine and Sarah come to see John's mother; he walks with Sarah and John Irving on the Bowery; Washington continues to come in for tea and sometimes spends part of the evening. John Anderson drops in to "set awhile" in the Irving living room, and on one occasion, in the store of the old Deacon, the stern father of his "Dulcinea." But whether because they were too near of age, Kitty being already twenty, or whether because she had already met Daniel Paris, the young lawyer who was to become her husband, Washington's second sister said (or suggested) "no" to the suit of the talented son of doughty John Anderson, whose pro-colonist sentiments as publisher of the *Constitutional Gazette* had, in 1775, won him the title of "the Rebel."

For the student of autographs there is a special interest in comparing the handwritings of Washington Irving when he was twenty-one, and John Anderson, Jr. when he was twenty-one. So similar are they that it would seem as if not only in the direction of music and of art young Anderson had influenced Kitty's brother.

18

Thus as Irving grew up the inhibitive influence of the Deacon was counteracted by the gentleness and innate, though subdued, gaiety of his mother; by the liberal tastes of such young men as his elder brothers and John Anderson; and also by the sympathetic companionship of his sisters and of Ebenezer and John, John being his particular companion in the games of mimic warfare that took place in the yard of the William Street home. Irving's education had been so sporadic, that when he entered a law office he was, in those days when a part of the duty of the junior clerks consisted in sweeping the offices, more efficient with the broom than with the pen of argument. Not proficiency but the lovableness of the boy carried him through many of the difficulties in which his laziness and his fondness for mischief involved him at home, at school, in the law office; this, and the increasing fragility of his health which, as he approached manhood, seemed to forebode an early grave.

Chapter II

FIRST TASTE OF EUROPE

THE coast of Spain, that country wherein he was some forty years later to hold the high office of American Minister, afforded Irving his initial glimpse of the Old World, but it was at Bordeaux, after five days of quarantine in the mouth of the Gironde, that the feet of the young traveller for the first time touched the soil of Europe.

The journal begun by Irving at Bordeaux on the first of July, 1804, together with other diaries recording travels during the next two years, formed the treasury of events on which he drew for lengthy letters to the folks at home. These letters, rather than the journal itself, were used by Pierre M. Irving, his uncle's literary executor and first biographer, but some years ago the Bordeaux journal and its followers, the earliest of Irving's sustained attempts as a writer, were published by the Grolier Club, under the illuminating editorship of Professor W. P. Trent. These diaries of travel became available for the enjoyment of a few hundred members of a private society of book lovers, but to the public at large they still remain practically unknown. So important are they for the fuller understanding of Irving's life, character, and art that they call for intense study in a biography of their author.

An outstanding fact in considering the life and work of Irving is, that in contradistinction to far the greater number of our representative authors, he had in him nothing of the Puritan strain. Emerson, Thoreau, Lowell, Longfellow, Whittier, Bryant, the genial Curtis and the witty Holmes, whether or not of Puritan ancestry, all carried on that New England tradition which includes an emphatic interest in reform, in moralizing, or in the general relationship of instruction to entertainment. Irving, on the other hand, believed in enjoying life and in making life as pleasant as possible for others. He was not the exponent of morality but the proponent of good will. He was an observer, not a teacher; and he cared much more to observe and to enjoy than to be taught.

How marked was this predilection in the young fellow who roamed through various countries of Europe in the years 1804 to 1806, his first biographer was well aware. Pierre M. Irving did not omit references to evidences of this perfectly normal, and from the point of view of American progress, decidedly valuable phase of his uncle's nature, but he did, by drawing mainly on home letters where this phase is naturally less accentuated, and by largely passing by the early journals themselves, fail to give the truest picture of Irving in this important formative period.

The fact is that our young hero soon regulated his itinerary with an eye less to churches and picture galleries than to the more obvious pleasures of youth. He was fond of dancing and of masquerades; passionately fond of the theatre, and pleasantly fond of flirtation. He was much more interested in people than in institutions, in the personal than in the typical—as, indeed, his later writings were to show. The spirit of sentiment, of romance, was his, and his keenness of observation was in the direction of the picturesque, not of the philosophically analytical. His early journals reveal him as the potential author of "The Sketch Book" and of "Bracebridge Hall" (books whose chapters evolve an idealized picture of English life and customs); but not as the potential author of such a volume as Emerson's "English Traits."

While still in the harbour of Bordeaux Irving had heard of the declaration of Napoleon as Emperor, little imagining how vitally his own career was to be affected by the ambitions of Bonaparte. The struggle between the conqueror of the Continent and the forces of the British Empire was to involve the United States in that War of 1812 whose aftermath of economic disaster bankrupted the firm in which Irving's brothers had given him a financial interest without business responsibility. This bankruptcy forced Irving to engage upon literature as a means of livelihood.

Although Irving arrived in France at a time so big with historical happenings, his comments on world affairs are (in part, perhaps, as a matter of caution,) few and far between. He does indeed note, at Bordeaux, that criticism of Napoleon is permitted in private circles; at Marseilles, where Irving witnesses a balloon ascension of Blanchard (whose unsuccessful attempt in New York he recalls), he observes, in passing, the lighthearted ways of the French who—the whole town caught up with the balloon mania—seem to forget their national calamities in any new amusement; at the small town of Fréjus he jots down (though with his frequently faulty spelling) that when Bonaparte landed there on his return from the Egyptian campaign, "he debarked without performing Quarentine, a crime punishable with death according to the laws of the country which were very strict on vessels from Levante." He records having witnessed the entrance of the English fleet into the harbour of Messina, headed by the Victory, the flagship of Lord Nelson who was then, in June, 1805, in search of the French fleet which had shortly before sailed out of Toulon. But nowhere in these diaries can one find indication that either the military happenings or the politics of a France at war engaged anything more than his most superficial attention. What we do find, however, is that the state of belligerency between Great Britain and France, while it occasioned young Irving some inconvenience when his passports were considered unsatisfactory and when, on one occasion, he had been denounced as an English spy, brought him into an exciting, and on the whole, enjoyable experience when, off the coast of Sicily, the ship on which he was voyaging was attacked in pirate fashion by a privateer. Further, it offered him delectable opportunities to win the sympathy of some young French peasant girls by posing as a British prisoner of war.

22

Wherever Irving went he was, in these young days, especially observant of women and their ways. He was rather disappointed at the outset in finding so few handsome women in Bordeaux. He did not like their manner of fixing their hair which "they torture into unnatural twists and ringlets and lard it over with a profusion of ancient oil." He prefers the "light fanciful ringlets of hair dry and elastic, that play with every zephyr," such as he was used to among his young girl acquaintances in New York. The dress of the ladies of Bordeaux likewise failed to arouse his admiration though he was to some extent prepared for the disclosures of French style by "the light robes of our *transparent elegantes.*" At Montpellier Irving sees "more pretty faces in proportion among the girls than as yet anywhere else in France." Of the Genoese women he writes that they are "generally well made with handsome features and with very fine black eyes. They are infinitely superior in my opinion to the French women in respect to personal charms. They are much given to intrigue, exceeding amorous and in case of neglect it is said revengeful." He observes (with an exclamation point closing the italicized last three words of his observation), that in the main theatre of Genoa the stage alone is illuminated "as the ladies complain that lights placed in the other part of the theatre *hurt their eyes!*" He learns, no doubt with personal regret, that the Italian young women are, "like the French, kept under great restraint," and that "such a thing as a young gentleman gallanting a young lady along the street would be looked upon as exceedingly singular." In Irving's youthful opinion this restriction causes both the Italian and French girls to "rush into matrimony without having any affection for their husbands. They merely consider it as a privileged state where they can indulge themselves with greater freedom." He then goes on to suggest that the unfaithfulness of Italian women is in some degree due to the fact that the husbands "do not confide implicitly in her virtue," whereupon the wife thinks herself "no longer bound in honour" to observe the marital vows.

In the smaller villages, as in the larger cities, Irving pursues

23

his interested study of the women.   Paraphrasing Virgil's line, one might say that milkmaid and Countess alike are treated by him with fairness.   If, at Velletri, a little town between Naples and Rome, he is displeased at the "large clumsy stays that project out before in a grotesque manner," he is as quick to commend the lace or muslin or calico veil that falls so enticingly over the head and shoulders of a pretty woman.   "I have seen a pair of languishing blue eyes from under one of them give the countenance the air of a beautiful Madonna."   So susceptible is he to feminine charm that he cannot refuse to buy, at what he knows is too high a price, the peaches and grapes offered him by a group of girls in a little village near Paris, his sufficient and excellent reason for this extravagance being that some of the girls "were very pretty."   Nor does our young traveller confine his attention to peasantry and nobility.   At the Convent of Sacred Cheer at Syracuse we find him with Captain Hall, Wadsworth Baker and Lieutenant Cargill, three other young Americans, quite frankly flirting with the nuns.   Ignorance of the Italian language prevented much verbal conversation, but there was the language of the eyes, the delightful interchange of laughter, and the kissing of hands to one another.   One of the novices Irving thinks "the most lovely girl that I have seen in Italy," and he reflects on the unfortunate circumstance of numerous Sicilian families where the father's comparative poverty leads him to place his younger daughters in a convent.   "It is a painful sight," writes Irving after having spoken in broken Italian with this "most lovely girl," "to behold young females—endowed with all the graces of person and charms of countenance that can render a woman lovely— with apparent sensibility of mind—sprightliness of manner and susceptibility of heart—shut up forever from the world." Four days later he and his friends visit another convent, that of the Benedictines, but the Abbess who greets them "had taken care to send the handsome nuns out of sight."   One wonders whether the other Abbess had given her a hint.

In later life Irving's stoutness accentuated his lack of height—

he was only five feet, seven inches—but even then the geniality of his countenance made him pleasant to look upon. In youth, when he was slender, his grey-blue eyes, his well-set though slightly longish nose, his medium sized mouth, his chestnut coloured hair, his high forehead and the oval shape of his face rendered him, with the sparkle and kindliness of his expression, a decidedly attractive looking young fellow. But it was ever his ways of courtesy and of gaiety, often with a touch of melancholy in the background, that made him most winning to women in all stations of life. However, neither in youth nor in later years, was Irving the libertine. There is no more candid expression of masculine interest in the other sex than in that entry of his diary of days at Rome where he writes: "As I have often leisure time on hand I now and then stroll into the churches to see the faces of the ladies and to see the church ceremonies performed." The precedence given to the faces of the ladies is significant, connoting Irving's interest in the picturesqueness of religious ritual as a secondary affair, but more inescapable in the statement is its naive frankness. Irving was always fond of women, yet if this phase of Irving's nature, as shown forth so often in these early journals, be frequently observed in this volume, it is not only because of its inherent importance and because his first biographer (in whose footsteps all later biographers have followed) took care to scamp the subject throughout Irving's life, but also because Irving's interest and sympathy with women and their ways are related to that vein of femininity in his writings which affected the entire course of American literature in the era preceding the Civil War.

On several occasions in October and November, 1804, Irving enjoyed the hospitality of Mrs. Bird, the wife of the English Consul at Genoa, whose charming residence at Sestri had among its younger inmates not only her three daughters but also the two daughters of a Mrs. W. All these seven women enter into Irving's notes, but especially worth observing are the felicity with which he characterizes his hostess and the attitude of mind that colours his comment on Mrs. W. "Mrs. Bird," he writes, "is a charming woman. Polite without ceremony—attentive and hospitable without being officious and possessed of good sense without the ostentation of it." As to "Mrs. W." "she is one of those *knowing, notable* kind of women. Has read considerable and sets up for a *woman of learning*—a dangerous character for a woman to sustain who has not strength of head or delicacy of face and judgement sufficient to support it."

Such good times did Irving and his New York friend of boyhood days, Hall Storm, have at Mrs. Bird's, with excursions in the day time and dancing or playing games in the evening, or in songs and the music of the harpsichord, that these two young fellows would generally sleep at a hotel in Sestri, not getting back to their rooms in Genoa till late the next day. The gaiety of their actions was such that "the sober Italians stared at us often with surprise and called us the *wild Americans.*"

On one of their rambles in the neighbourhood of Sestri Irving and Storm, and a Scotch painter, Wilson by name, came to the cottage of a peasant couple with three handsome daughters. "One in particular, had a blooming complexion, fine black eyes a beautiful set of teeth and when she smiled, two of the prettiest dimples imaginable." This was Angelina. She acted as their guide to a high place from which entrancing views could be had on every side. The young fellows plied her with many questions to which she answered "with much simplicity and good humour. She had all the artlessness of nature and amused us much with her replies." The Scotch painter desired to know if she had any sweetheart, and unhesitatingly she answered "that she loved Iacimo, and that Iacimo loved her likewise and that they were to be married in about a year." She saw him frequently, during the week, and always on Sundays at church. "Uno Amabillessimo Giovinotto." She blushed and smiled whenever she mentioned Iacimo's name; and it was Angelina and her parents, her brothers and her sisters, with the "good humour and content" that "seem to reign in this happy family" who afforded Irving the first realization in Europe of, as he says, the many poetic pictures he had read of rustic felicity.

The French and Italian journals, notably the latter, are not lacking in those passages of topographical and architectural description and historic data inevitable in a record of first travel in Europe, and no doubt Brother William and the rest of the family were gratified and duly instructed by the information which Washington's letters gave them concerning the history and appearance of the various cities he visited. In this phase of his journals, where Irving is indebted partially to guide books, and partially has recourse to his own quick powers of observation, we confess we are not hugely interested. It may be dismissed with the comment that his record, adequate and quite unpriggish or stilted, has a certain historical significance in the annals of American literature as the first description of its kind from the pen of an American man of letters. Longfellow, Motley, Emerson, Bayard Taylor and many others were to follow Irving in the narration of European travels; but Europe is a subject too familiar to the myriads of ocean-goers, or of motion-picture-goers, of to-day to admit of any interesting exposition of Irving's achievement as the recording traveller per se. These passages, when copied into the letters that he mailed to William Street were, in a manner of speaking, the grateful payment of a debt to the generous brothers who had agreed to the financing (partially by their now aged and paralytic father) of Washington's trip abroad; yet it is significant that when he obtained his first book in Bordeaux he quotes from this "Cronique Bourdelaise" only the kind of fact that especially appealed to him, a fact relating not to a statesman or a warrior but to a man, a bon vivant, accused of sorcery and condemned to death for knowing, as Irving supposes, "too much for the common run of folks." And so, too, although now and again churches are described in the orthodox manner, Irving, in visiting cathedrals, frequently shows that in part romantic, in part ultra-sensible approach characterizing his attitude towards subjects whose interpretation involves both the imagination and the reason. At the Cathedral of St. André in Bordeaux he had his first introduction to a beautiful Gothic structure. What he writes after that occasion proves that Irving had come into touch with the romantic literature of Europe before he had left America. "Our ascent" (of one of its towers) "was quite intricate and reminded me of some of those winding and perplexed passages through which some of the heroes of modern romances wander when prowling about the interior of an old castle." Horace Walpole's "The Castle of Otranto," published in 1764, and the forerunner of similar works in France and Germany as well as in England, was undoubtedly in Irving's mind. The glamour and excitement of this kind of "Gothic" literature enhanced Irving's enjoyment of the cathedrals, as, similarly, Mrs. Radcliffe's "The Mysteries of Udolpho," first published when Irving was a boy of eleven, increased his interest in ruined castles. On the way from Bordeaux to Toulouse, on seeing such a castle, he writes: "It had a most picturesque appearance as the first glimpse of morning fell on its mouldering Towers. It stood on the brow of a high bank of the River which glittered at its Base. The descriptions of Mrs. Radcliffe were brought immediately to my reccollection."

Consider one of these descriptions no doubt recalled by Irving—that of the Castle of Udolpho. "The sun had just sunk below the top of the mountains, whose long shadows stretched athwart the valley; but his sloping rays, shooting through an opening of the cliffs, touched with a yellow gleam the summits of the forest that hung upon the opposite steeps, and streamed in full splendour upon the towers and battlements of a castle that spread its extensive ramparts along the brow of a precipice above." Now, this is much the kind of writing that may be found in the pages of Irving himself, and not only in subject matter, but in style, the influence of Mrs. Radcliffe on Irving is worth pondering; though Irving would have written "across," and not "athwart." So well equipped an historian of American literature in general as Professor Fred Lewis Pattee suggests (without, of course, these early journals to guide him) that Irving's interest in the romantic and highly coloured European literature found its first strong incentive in the works of

28

Walter Scott. No doubt it was Scott who gave a further pro-
pulsion to Irving's interest, but its inception may, it would now
seem, be accepted as having taken place with such writers as
Walpole and Mrs. Radcliffe whose volumes, one feels quite
certain, were *not* bought by Deacon Irving for the library in
William Street. And to Walpole and Mrs. Radcliffe one may
assuredly add the name of M. G. Lewis, whose novel "The
Monk" had such an enormous vogue in the days of Irving's boyhood—Lewis "the boldest of hobgoblin writers," whose themes
revolving around enchantments, the Inquisition, romances of
Spanish cavaliers, the legend of the Wandering Jew, and Satan
himself were later to be the themes to which Irving's own pen
was directed.

However receptive to the picturesque and the extraordinary
Irving was, both in these early days, and some fifteen years
later when, with "The Sketch Book," he entered upon his own
noted series of legendary and romantic writings, his good common sense always saved him from any easy acceptance of supernatural phenomena. When he visited the Cathedral of St.
Lawrence at Genoa, among whose chief treasures were said to
be the bones of St. John the Baptist, and an emerald dish
"pretended by some to have been the same dish out of which
our Saviour eat at the Last Supper," he characteristically adds:
"If I recollect right the Supper was eaten at an inn where
it is not likely they would serve their guests in Emerald dishes."
So, too, of a church in Syracuse, a church through whose roof
a bomb shell had fallen, in the days when the Spaniards were
besieging the town. According to the legend an old woman
in the terrified congregation "saw the ghost of Lucia a very
pious young lady who had died some time before run to the
bomb shell and put out the fuse." Lucia had been made a
guardian Saint of the city; but even so could not command sufficient reverence from Irving for her brave and valuable services
to lead him to refrain from commenting: "Such is the origin
of Catholic Saints and reminds one forcibly of the manner in
which gods and goddesses of the Ancients originated." When,

again, at Syracuse, he is asked to believe the marvellous tale concerning the Fountain of Arethusa—the tale of a cup of one of the Olympic Games thrown into the Fountain of Arethusa in Greece and later thrown out of a fountain in Syracuse—instead of accepting this as in accordance with the goddess Diana's fluid fusion of Alpheus and the nymph, he merely caustically observes: "Priesthood has been the same in all ages and scruples at no falsehood or contrivance to support its impositions." Thus Irving, hardly more than a boy, reveals (perhaps too emphatically) the clarity of his reasoning processes, proving that this greatest of all American writers of legends was later to be intrigued by the sentiment, the excitement, the humour, and, as in "Rip Van Winkle," the appealing humanity of his themes, without personal concession on the side of either supernatural or spiritualistic belief.

Irving's sense and sensibility, the stark genuineness of his quiet mind and the susceptibility of his emotional nature, sometimes in conflict and again happily merged, find illustration in other passages from these notebooks. If, in one place, he writes with undisguised impatience of a ceremony where a Cardinal washes the feet of a group of humble men representing the Apostles, contrasting the haughtiness of that high dignitary with the essential humbleness of spirit which should characterize his task, he still cannot forbear writing on another occasion that "there is certainly something very solemn and impressive in the ceremonies of the Roman Church. Unwilling as we may be to acknowledge it we cannot deny that forms and ceremonies have a great effect on the feelings in matters of religion."

The consideration of Irving's sentimentalism suggests the interesting reflection that the name of the English author appearing more frequently than that of any other one author in these early journals is Laurence Sterne. In no index to any biography of Irving can Sterne's name be found, but it is now quite obvious that Irving had read "The Sentimental Journey," and it was largely in the mood of the literary Sterne (the selfish, licentious, cold-hearted English clergyman being very different, in actual

30

life, from the engaging man of letters) that Irving travelled through France and Italy. "A quiet journey of the heart in pursuit of Nature, and those affections which arise out of her," Sterne called his tour; and, in accounting for his lack of interest in those objects which crowd humanity out of the guide books, Sterne wrote: "I have not seen the Palais Royal, nor the Luxembourg, nor the Façade of the Louvre; nor have attempted to swell the catalogues we have of pictures, statues and churches. I conceive every fair being as a temple, and would rather enter in and see the original drawings and loose sketches hung up in it, than the Transfiguration of Raphael himself."

Irving's first mention of Laurence Sterne has to do with an episode at Fourves, a village on the road from Aix to Nice, a loathesome town, he calls it, vile with the smell of manure. Its inn, despite the coats-of-arms on silver spoons presumably stolen from some despoiled castle, was dirty and uncomfortable, but Irving, accustomed by his trip the previous summer to the Canadian wilds, was prepared to rough it. "For my part," he writes with that philosophy which was one of his mainstays in a none too happy life, "I try to take things as they come, with cheerfulness, and when I cannot get a dinner to suit my taste I endeavour to get a taste to suit my dinner." As long as the master and mistress of an inn show a disposition to serve him, then, "as Sterne says—'it is enough for Heaven, and ought to be enough for me.'" It is with this enunciation of a very human point of view, supported by Divine authority, that Irving refers to his dislike of all Smelfungii, Smelfungus being that character in Sterne's "Sentimental Journey" "for whom every object was discoloured or distorted," and who, when he wrote an account of them, "'twas nothing but the account of his miserable feelings." Nor was Mundungus, another character of Sterne's, much less objectionable, for all his "immense fortune," to Irving; for did not Mundungus go a-touring "without one generous connection or pleasurable anecdote to tell of, but he travelled straight on looking neither to his right hand nor his left, lest Love or Pity should seduce him out of his road"?

At the Convent of St. Martino, near Naples, when Irving gets into a characteristically Sterne-like talk with the old Friar in charge of it, suggesting to the good-humoured Carthusian that the portraits of lovely Saints "are but ill calculated to repress the wandering desires of the good Fathers who have taken the vows of eternal chastity," he writes that "Sterne would have gloried in describing" the venerable man as he enthusiastically explained the more refined and spiritual appeal of all these charming pictures of youthful beauty. And when, in visiting the Barberini Palace at Rome, Irving especially admired the Magdalene of Guido Reni (the one picture that comes in for any extensive comment, proving Irving more the sentimentalist than the critic of art), he writes: "The countenance more gentle—the eyes cast up to heaven with an expression of languour —of grief—of devotion, rapture, etc. that gives an indescribable interest in it—as Stern[e] observes an expression the very reverse of 'fat contented ignorance looking downward on the earth.' " [1]

Irving, it must be remembered, was at that time hardly more than a boy. If on the way from Bordeaux to Italy, or on the way back from Rome to Paris, he had fallen in with fellow travellers of a serious turn of mind, intent on the acquisition of knowledge, or (with the temperament and ways to win Irving's affection) especially versed in art or in literature, it is entirely probable that Irving's first journey to Europe would have taken on an aspect more in accord with the hopes of his elder brothers when they sent him abroad. But it so happened that during the first stages in France his favourite companion was a Dr. Henry, originally of Lancaster in Pennsylvania, a great gallant and a most amusing "little man of the world." Irving describes him as a droll fellow who, in five minutes, could win his way into friendship with anyone. He had had a wide range of experi-

---

[1] *Some time after completing the present chapter, its author was gratified to discover that Walter Scott had observed in "Knickerbocker's History" indications of Sterne's influence on Irving.*

ence, having been (or having pretended to have been) on familiar footing with the great, as well as in happy intimacy with the humble. "Ministers, Consuls, etc. were Tom, Dick and Harry—intimate acquaintances. The Abby Winkleman had given him a breastpin, Lavater had made him a present of a Snuff Box and several authors had sent him their works to read and criticize." Fond of quizzing, of flirting, of passing himself off as a wine merchant when he was with a farmer, as a tanner when he talked to a shoe maker, as an army officer, or a German professor or as an American diplomat "travelling with dispatches to Commodore Preble," Dr. Henry, with four or five languages to aid him, involved Irving in all manner of amusing adventures, sometimes introducing the young boy as an English prisoner, or again as a young Mameluke who, the doctor as his interpreter would assure the landlady, must have a large chair so that he might "sit cross-legged after the manner of his country."

With such a companion Irving readily became most absorbed in the pleasurably human phase of travelling. He found more entertainment in seeing a girl throw Dr. Henry's wig into the Canal of Languedoc, when that five-foot-four gallant was somewhat too attentive to the protesting young peasant, than in the study of any monument of architecture or phase of historical event. "I have come laughing all the way from London to Paris," said Laurence Sterne to an influential nobleman to whom he applied for a passport to Italy, "and I do not think Monsieur le Duc de Choiseul is such an enemy of mirth, as to send me back crying for my pains." Laughing most of the way Irving went from France to Italy where, on March 11th, 1805, he was introduced at Naples to "a very agreeable young fellow, Mr. Cabell of Virginia." It was this meeting with Cabell, more than any other one circumstance, more even than the prior meeting with Dr. Henry, that was to make Irving's tour abroad so much of a pleasure-seeking voyage, so little a travel of education.

Joseph Carrington Cabell was Irving's senior by five or six years. Born in 1778, of a family distinguished in the annals of its State (and now more than ever distinguished by Mr. James

17728

33

Branch Cabell), he had received his Degree of Bachelor of Arts from William and Mary, and had been educated for the law— like Irving—into whose practice—again like Irving—he never entered. In 1802 he set out on the European tour, even then rather the thing to do for young men of our wealthier families, and stayed abroad until his return in 1806. His marriage, the next year, to Mary Carter was the initial step in a career of importance. The record of his life shows him as the collaborator with Thomas Jefferson in the founding of the University of Virginia, whereof he was to become the Rector. For over a quarter of a century, from 1808 to 1835, he was a member of the State Legislature; he was offered diplomatic positions, candidacy for Congress, and is said to have declined an appointment in the Cabinet of President Monroe. But however serious and substantial a figure Cabell presented in later life, he was in his bachelor days in Europe so pleasure-loving a youth that he persuaded Irving to cut short his stay in Italy in order to enter, with as little delay as possible, upon the gaieties of Paris.

On March 24th the young New Yorker had set off with the young Virginian from Naples to Rome, where they arrived three days later, taking rooms in the house of a Frenchman, Marguerita by name. Although there they did some sight-seeing together, Irving's most valuable companion at Rome was not Cabell, but another young Southerner, Washington Allston of Carolina, to whom Cabell introduced him. "He is a young gentleman of much taste and a good education. He has adopted the profession of a Painter through inclination and intends to remain in Rome two years to improve himself in the art," wrote Irving on meeting Allston. So much taken was Irving by the work he saw going on in Allston's studio, and by their conversations on visits to art galleries, that for a brief while he seriously considered entering upon art as a profession. The original drawings that embellish later diaries, notably the journal of the tour in Wales in 1815, show a pleasant talent for sketching; inferior, it is true, to that of Victor Hugo and of Thackeray, but superior to the talent shown in the drawings of other famous

34

writers of fiction, such as Dickens and Stevenson and Kipling. The faculty of seizing on the picturesque that is so manifest in his written pages might well have brought Irving a modicum of distinction as an artist, but he could hardly have achieved more than this.   At any rate, Washington Allston stirred his ambitions at a time when he anticipated with reluctance the drudgery of a legal career, his European journeys ended; and Allston, whose nobility of mind Irving so eloquently praised in a tribute written after the death of that painter and poet, was, as far as we can see, the one fine influence under whose sway young Irving came during his first travels in Europe.   Coleridge, who might well have stirred him intellectually, Irving did not meet at Rome, although the biographer of Allston assumes that they were friends.

Irving did not entirely neglect the larger opportunities of Rome for those social pleasures in many of which Cabell participated.   There were visits to the Farnese Palace, to the Museum of the Vatican, to St. Peter's, to the studio of Canova (where Irving saw that sculptor engaged on portraits of various members of the Bonaparte family).   He attends "Conversaziones" in the homes of the nobility and of diplomats where, not caring for whist or faro (which were more in evidence than conversation itself), he is bored at not meeting any especially attractive women.   Rome does not seem to impress him, and save for the hours with Allston young Irving apparently derives little inspiration from the Eternal City.   He contrasts the Rome about him with the great city of ancient times and (one of his few political observations) refers deprecatingly to the Government "whose chief has to undertake a long and degrading journey to gratify the pride and ostentation of a distant Tyrant."   (The Pope, one recalls, had gone to Paris to crown Napoleon as Emperor of the French, only to see, at the last moment, the imperious Corsican himself place the crown on his own brow.) Rome, in short, meant so little to Irving, and left him so little in a mood for further visits to Italian cities, that when Cabell suggested their joint departure for Paris, Irving gave ready assent. He left Italy without going to see either Florence or Venice, a dereliction for which Brother William never quite forgave him, writing, indeed, in his letter of censure that he considered Irving's meeting with Cabell a most unfortunate happening.

I do not at all agree with Brother William. On the contrary, Dr. Henry and Cabell, whatever levity or minor dissipations their acquaintanceship involved, were, in the long run, very valuable companions for the boy who, with a tendency towards consumption, a tendency towards neuroticism, was now (after a youth somewhat clouded by a narrow-minded father) for the first time seeing the world. The manner in which he entered into the life about him was, indeed, not the best training for an incipient lawyer, but he developed those traits of humour and merriness that, after his return to America, were to blossom forth so richly in *Salmagundi* and in "Knickerbocker's History of New York." Carefree and happy he grew stronger in health, and if he did not see the Doges' Palace, and failed to attend lectures at the Sorbonne (save for a few on Botany) he came into warm contact with life on its joyous side, and into fuller sympathy with humanity itself.

Cabell and Irving left Rome early in May, 1805. At the little town of Iornina, in Switzerland, they engaged with the landlady and her two daughters in the kind of conversation that would have delighted Laurence Sterne, Cabell teasing the mother about some swelling she had, and Irving, as he mounted his horse at the hour of departure, calling back to the daughter Marianne, who hoped that he would some day return: "Alors je vous trouverais marriee avec une grande goiture." A more serious conversation took place at Bâsle, where the two young fellows sought to dissipate, in some measure, that crass ignorance concerning America which, in the first decade of the nineteenth century, was so prevalent in Europe. Many Swiss emigrants were then on the way to the United States, but their friends at home, perhaps at the instance of the Government, opposed their emigration. "Why!" said Cabell to one of these objectors, "have not several Swiss written back from America favourable accounts of their situation?"—"Ah," replied he, "that's nothing—When they write bad—Government in America open the letters and stop them so that we may not hear anything disadvantageous of the country."—"What!" said Cabell. "Do you think our Government is like your suspicious detestable Governments in Europe? Why should Government trouble whether the Swiss emigrate to America or no?" The answer to this was: "We know very well that you have wars with the Indians and you want people to assist you in carrying them on."

The next day, at Bellefort, Irving and Cabell were enlightening a merchant from Lyons concerning the United States. "He was very inquisitive about our manners," writes Irving in his journal, "and of course about our women. We assured him that they did not come short of the European ladies in respect to personal charms—and that they were remarkable for their affectionate fidelity to their husbands. This last eulogium produced a true Frenchman's remark—'Mon Dieu,' said he, 'c'est un pays malheureux pour les garcons.' 'Certainement,' said Cabell, 'il faut ce marrier la.' "

The ignorance of Europe concerning America was really astounding. When Irving set forth on his travels our republic, had, like himself, barely, since the Treaty of Paris, attained its majority. Napoleon absorbed the interest of the Continent, and no European Government, or, for that matter, no European people paid much attention to the twenty-one-year-old member of the family of nations. "I was asked the other day at dinner by a well-dressed Frenchman whether my Province (for he took the U. S. to be a mere Province) was not a great wine country and whether it was not in the neighbourhood of *Turkey* or somewhere thereabout!" At another time Irving records that Americans have a name for drunkenness and public disturbance. "Pho—it's only some drunken American or other," was a comment he overheard, at some street ruction, drunkenness being considered in an American "merely as a custom of his country." Still another time he was accosted by a French officer. "Vous êtes Englais, Monsieur?" asked the officer. "Pardonnez moi," replied Irving, "je suis des Etats Unis d'Amerique,"—"Et bien

37

—c'est la meme chose." Another Frenchman thinks that when America becomes stronger the Americans intend to drive all the Europeans out of their country. A merchant from Frankfort, while interested in our customs, knows little of the United States. At Lure a man asks Irving whether they are near Asia. On being told that they are not, " 'Alors,' said he, 'ils sont tout pres de l'Afrique.' 'Non, pardon monsieur, point du tout'—'Diable Comme je me trompe—ils sont dans la voisinage d'Europe'—I again informed him he was mistaken—'F—' replied he, 'est il possible—Ou sont ils donc Monsieur?' " And so it goes on, vast numbers of persons believing that whoever goes to America "runs the narrowest risks of his life there from the *yellow fever* or the savages." And everywhere Irving, and Cabell with him when they were together, satisfy the curiosity and dispel the ignorance of those they meet. A Geneva merchant, a Protestant Minister, an engraver of Bâsle, a gentleman of Lucerne, the nobility of Italy, the peasants of France, these and many more came into their first real knowledge of America, imparted to them with that charm, that courtesy, that gayness and geniality, and always that well-balanced patriotism, which made them friendly not only to their instructor but also to the country which so graciously he represented. As we go on with our study of the life of Washington Irving Esquire we shall, if I am not much at fault, reach the conclusion that no other American has won more friends than did he for his country, this first journey to Europe being the initial step in his imponderable yet magnificent service as our ambassador at large.

With the arrival of Irving and Cabell at Paris on the 24th of May, 1805 the journal ends for the time being, not to be resumed until his departure, some four months later, from that absorbing city. There are, however, a few observations drawn from its preceding pages to engage our attention. During his earliest weeks in Europe where Irving refers to his "sometimes being assailed by homesickness," he writes, "this however I hope will wear away in time as I become more 'a citizen of the world!' " The final phrase is the first indirect reference to

Oliver Goldsmith, whose Life was later to be Irving's finest achievement in the field of biography and whose character bore many resemblances to Irving's own. By Goldsmith and Addison Irving's style was strongly influenced, and that, while yet a boy, he was familiar with Goldsmith's "Citizen of the World," a series of letters of travel supposedly written by a Chinese philosopher, is a new fact all the more interesting in that this book had a share with Sterne's "Sentimental Journey" in affecting the mood, if not also the style, of Irving's own records of travel. The writings of Thomas Moore, with whom Irving some twenty years later was to become on such intimate terms, were also familiar to Irving in these early days, and at Troyes we find him observing that the incessant cracking of whips of the postillions on entering the town is ascribed by Moore to that "love of racket which every Frenchman sucks in with his mother's milk." "Humorously and perhaps justly, did Moore make this explanation," writes Irving; then adding: "The French certainly appear to enjoy themselves most when in the midst of noise clatter and hubbub." But Irving, with his keen observation of life in the streets of French cities and towns—the fruit women—peddlers—shoe blacks—tumblers—players of musical instruments—ingenious beggars—has a keen eye for all the more beguiling traits, the excellence of French taste coming in for his especial notice. So too with French thrift; and "No nation," he writes, "seems to enjoy their hours of recreation better than the French." Indeed, the only direct criticism, of a general nature, that the pages of his journal disclose, relates to the immodesty, according to his "old fashioned American ideas of propriety" of the French stage. At Marseilles he observes that the stage "should be employed by 'holding the mirror up to nature' to inform the understanding and improve the heart" and should not be "degraded by performances devoted to sensuality and libertinism."

Of that Irving who was really our first author to bring out the lyric and romantic sentiment in American scenery, our first author caught, as far as literature is concerned, by the great appeal of the beauty of our streams and forests, there is, in these early journals, prophetic evidence. But while his descriptions of such extraordinary objects as Vesuvius, where he and Cabell were almost overcome by the poisonous vapours, and of the Ear of Dionysius at Syracuse (that cave to whose rocky chamber the Tyrant resorted in the hope of overhearing secret conversations made audible by its strange acoustics), show the fluent pen, it is rather to the shores of Lake Maggiore, or to the open country near Belfort that we must go for passages whose emotional content, whose melody, whose simplicity of style best suggest the author of later years. "The repose of the scenery only interrupted by the melody of innumerable little birds the nightingale, robin, etc. And the distant song of the peasant of the innocent mirth of the peasant children sporting on the hills." Or again—and long before Shelley wrote his famous "Ode"—"The country resounded with the notes of the sky lark and we saw great numbers of those birds mounting up in the air and pouring out a strain of the richest melody." And yet again, resembling a dramatic etching: "Our march however was unmolested" (by banditti) "except now and then a shepherd's dog who disturbed by the noise of our bells and the bawling of the muleteers sallied out with open mouth in defence of his master's property." It is in such pictures of the life of nature, and of animal life, that the young boy gives promise of the later stylist.

Irving's faculty of observation led him to note down such an obvious, yet interesting, fact as the presence of a public promenade in almost all French towns (though he intimates his own preference for "a solitary ramble through silent groves or peaceful vales") but he was equally attentive to less apparent phases of the scenery and activities about him as where he observes that the French peasantry dwell in villages and, to plough, to sow or to reap, visit their fields at regular seasons in contrast to "the American farmers whose pride and delight is to be continually watching the progress of their crops." Yet most of all is he, even at so early an age, happy in the pictures he evokes

of individuals. Dr. Henry is as well drawn as Diedrich Knickerbocker himself. Equally satisfying and humorous is the portrait, when Irving was quarantined at Messina, of the ship's
captain who has "a great attachment to Methodism and a violent
affection for Lunar observations. He has also an invisible propensity to familiarize names and Jack's and Jill's everybody he
speaks of. Our conversation therefore is whimsical enough and
we alternately discuss the New Testament and the Nautical Almanac and talk indiscriminately of *Kit* Columbus and *Jack* Wes-
ley, etc." Then too, how appealing is a passage concerning the
old German gentleman who played on the pianoforte tunes that
he had himself composed, and who was so pleased by Irving's
praise of them, that he called the next morning with variations of
"Yankee Doodle" and "Hail Columbia," and "a little German
air of great sweetness." "He begged me to accept them as a
testimony of regard and finding I played on the flute he told
me he would bring me one or two more pieces adapted for that
instrument." Here, we have probably the first instance of a
German composer offering to an American a European version
of our national songs, a gift in consonance with Cabell's comment, on receiving a letter from Irving some years later in
America, that the writer was "still the same Washington Irving
whose name resounded so long in the valley of Ticino." As
I have said before, as I shall have occasion to say again, wherever he went, he made friends.

When Irving and Cabell arrived at Paris the journals ceased;
and only one home letter, to his brother Peter, appears in the
Life, Pierre remarking that Irving "would seem to have remitted his usual punctuality to the family." During the first
few weeks he jotted down some brief notes recording engagements with tailors, boot-makers, shirt-makers, etc; walks in the
Tuileries; the purchase of flowers from a *fille de joie;* night
after night of theatre and opera-going and—an educational sop
to Cerberus—attendance at some lectures on Botany. In these
memoranda, as well as in the letter to Peter—but not written
until July 15th—he reveals as one of his favourite companions

41

at Paris, John Vanderlyn, the young American artist who had
been sent out by the young American Academy to collect casts;
and Vanderlyn's portrait of Irving, made in those days, was
presumably due to Irving's desire to aid his rather indigent
friend. But apart from these notes and a few letters to New
York, we meet with a silence eloquent of the good times he
was having in that "most fascinating city" which, as he writes
to Peter, "has attained complete possession of my head." And
though he assures his brother that "America has still the strong-
hold of my heart," he was, in no serious way but at a sufficiently
lively pace, letting his heart go in Paris. His purse, too, he
opened wide for a final gay dinner party.

Towards the end of September Irving left Paris for Brussels
in company with Thomas Massie of Virginia and John Gorham
of Boston. In his conversation at Peronne la Pucelle with an
old woman servant who took great pride in that town which had
withstood the sieges by the Austrians in the time of the Grand
Monarch and attacks during the days of the French Revolution,
Irving showed some of the influence of Paris in his teasing remark that from what could be seen "of the maiden town it was
too ugly and old to merit any great pains and we supposed the
besiegers were of the same opinion." As the journal of this
trip continues, with its brief notes that lead on from Brussels
to Mestricht and thence to Rotterdam, the main interest resides
in Irving's earliest observations concerning the Dutch character,
"each peasant whether at work or idle, with pipe in mouth."
Here we have his first quick sketches of that nation which, in
its American descendants, was to provide the treasury where-
from Irving drew the nuggets in "Knickerbocker's History."

Then came the voyage from Rotterdam to Gravesend, Irving
foregoing a visit to "the phlegmatic cities of Holland" because,
as he said, he feared detention (the European war creating
difficulties for travellers), and also, as he did not say, because
Paris had given him a taste for the excitement of large cities
which could not be satisfied by what Amsterdam might have
to offer. Especially had he been caught up with a passion for

the theatre, and during his days in London, as previously at Paris, he kept no journal, although notes in a memorandum book record a few days' visit to Oxford, Bath and Bristol. In London he revelled in the acting of Mrs. Siddons who, by turns "froze and melted" his heart. He saw the great actors Charles Kemble and George Frederick Cooke, and Kemble he met personally at the home of one of the Covent Garden actresses, Miss De Camp, who was later to become Kemble's wife. It was at a theatre that Irving heard the news of Nelson's victory and of Nelson's death; but beyond his enthusiasm for the stage, his attendance at theatres, his meetings with actors, very little has come to light concerning those months in London. Had not letters of introduction, which he was awaiting from New York, miscarried, a range of experience wider than that of the dramatic field would have been enjoyed by the young traveller. As it was, his real knowledge of English life, and the influence of his charm and of his talents in affecting the attitude of the English towards America, were not, in any appreciable way, to begin until ten years more had gone by.

A hitherto unstudied memorandum book adds interestingly to the meagre information concerning Irving's last months in Europe. It consists of a number of pages given over to notes taken down at one of the lectures on Botany that he attended in Paris; some sixteen pages of pencil drawings—studies of various types of men, some of them very spirited, and one of them a drawing of a man shaving himself, not impossibly a self-portrait; and a record of the plays which Irving saw during those lonely weeks in London when the theatre was his mainstay. "Othello," "Macbeth," "Romeo and Juliet," "Richard III," "King Henry IV" and "The Merchant of Venice" were the Shakespearean plays wherein he saw Mrs. Siddons, Cooke and Kemble. "Isabella," or, "The Fatal Marriage," "The Honeymoon," "Venice Preserved," "The War of the World," "The School for Friends," "Lovers' Vows," "The Country Gentleman," "The Siege of Belgrade," "The Haunted Tower," these were among the other plays showing how constantly Irving was in attendance at the theatre. He did not have overmuch money to spend (he had to borrow twelve shillings from Massie for his journey from Paris to London), and he kept a very careful account of his outlays. Sometimes he would limit himself to a sandwich in the morning, and a piece of pastry in the evening, which, with the mid-day dinner, made his food for the day cost him less than five shillings. Even so we find him giving a few shillings for charity; and there is an item, "gave a poor girl seventeen shillings," though whether this was altogether charity is not recorded. His seat on the coach from London to Oxford cost one shilling fivepence, and to Bath one shilling eightpence. At Bristol he attended a ball, obviously not alone, and the tickets came to ten shillings. On the last day of November, he attended, at a cost of fourteen shillings, his only public dinner in England, a Masonic affair. He gambled in a few lottery tickets, subscribed to a circulating library, and went to exhibitions of paintings. Living was not dear, and he paid a serving-maid twelve shillings sixpence for one month's services, and ten shillings to a man servant. For the "likeness of Miss D. C.," he paid two shillings sixpence, and minor articles of clothes, including Hessian boots, were purchased at moderate prices.

The little memorandum book, leather-backed and with blue paper sides, contains also a few puns, some of them perhaps of his own making. He suggests that Martial Music appeals to him because he is fond of General Music, and jots down that "Ireland will be the richest country in the world, for its capital is always doubling (Dublin)." Both in drawings and in notations the little book has many touches of humour, and certainly he had a jolly time on the voyage home after he had left Gravesend in the ship *Remittance,* on January 19th, 1806. Of his entries on ship-board, the following passages are characteristic: "Turned out put on Grigo mount companionway door is shut peeped over fine morning, smacking breeze. Second mate on deck in high glee singing a doleful ditty. Good morning, Mr. Williams—rolled his quid, ret^d my salutation and finished

his song.   Six o'clock pump ship pump sucks hold the reel glass
clear clear glass turn—stop—how many knots Mr. W.— 9 &
an half by G^d—pulled up his trousers, squirted out tobacco juice
looked pleas^d & whistled Barbara Allen.   Sea broke over our
quarter.   Had a salt salute over the head & shoulders.   Dodg^d
my head and laugh^d & said nothing.—He is a fool who can't
take a hint so descended into cabin.   Shaved, washed face &
hands & cleaned teeth poor Don Pedro mounted companion way
as he peeped out sea broke over & completely soused him from
head to foot.   So much the better—he will have to change his
clothes and be clean in spight of himself.   Tie on my cravat
put on cap & once more mount."

This entry is followed by a magnificent attempt at poetry
which, as unpublished verses by Irving are rare, shall be given in
their entirety.   The Eliza mentioned in the poem is doubtless
the young girl with the large bonnet of whom Irving makes a
sketch that has in it some of the charm of Kate Greenaway.

> Tho england's sons are kind
>   Their hearts burn warm & true
> Yet english hearts you'll find
>   Can beat in foreign bosoms too
>
> The good remittance freely rides
>   And woos the favouring gale
> That lightly curls the glassy tides
>   And fills the swelling sail.
>
> Sigh not Eliza tho you leave
>   England's shores behind
> For other shores may prove as fair
>   And other climes as kind.
>
> Fair virtue's plant is not confined
>   In english soil to keep
> Kind heaven convey'd its radiant seed
>   Across the atlantic deep

WASHINGTON IRVING ESQUIRE

> Then may you find a happy home
> Each stranger prove a friend
> Peace be your lot where'er you go
> & Joy your steps attend.

That the young Washington was attentive not alone to Eliza we gather from the following notes. Irving after having mounted the companion ladder finds some ladies on deck: "Wish them good morning, put my arm around their waists and hug them tight to keep them from falling. What it is to be cautious! Steward calls to breakfast. Great havoc among coffee ham & hot cakes. Breakfast table dull Admiral sick cousin John & the doctor in bed. Myself too busy to talk. After breakfast go to after cabin. Miss B. wished tune on flute—I play—little Guitar & admiral sings most hideously. Ladies cover their ears. Miss Bayley scolds—Eliza laughs, Miss B. requests a serious sentimental tune—Play her Yankee Doodle for half an hour till she is sufficiently satisfied with the concert. Hard work to kill time. Deck wet—cabin too warm. Go & sit in jolly boat over the stern & finish a volume of Virgil. Return into cabin—Nothing to do—Sit down & scribble this nonsense."

Chapter III

LOVE AFFAIRS

WHEN Irving returned from Europe he was vastly improved in health and in spirits, but he was more than ever unfitted for the routine of workaday life. The independence and irresponsibility of the two years of travel had done much to remove the depressing influence of his father the Deacon who was now seventy-five years of age, and whose death a year later was further to clear the way for that period of merry young manhood which preceded Irving's second departure for Europe in 1815.

There was only one great cloud whose shadow deeply darkened for a while Irving's life during these nine years, a cloud that never wholly departed from the horizon of his memories. But this shadow has been so sentimentally magnified that, in order to do away at once with an unnecessary myth, it is worth while to depart from the usual strictly chronological method in the consideration of the part that love of women played in Irving's life.

The devotion to his mother, to his sisters, to his nieces, offers little possibility for new comment. But his love affairs—that is to say, those episodes which concern the women who cared very much for Irving and the women who were loved by him—are in part only casually known, in part not known at all.

In 1806 Irving was admitted to the bar after that examination where Martin Wilkins, in reply to the comment of his fellow-examiner, Josiah Ogden Hoffman: "Martin, I think he knows a little law," had answered: "Make it stronger, Joe, *damned* little." The friendship of Hoffman, in whose office Irving had studied, probably accounts for Irving's passing. Although he took a minor part in the proceedings for the defence of Aaron Burr, Irving as a lawyer had hardly any more accomplishment to his credit than had that later barrister, Robert Louis Stevenson, who, like Irving, was temperamentally the wanderer and the man of letters, not the man of law.

Indeed, the main interest of Irving's brief career as law student and lawyer centres in its connection with the Hoffmans. Josiah Hoffman had a delightful and gifted family both by his first wife and by his second wife, who had been Miss Fenno, and who was so consistently and affectionately Irving's friend. Ann was the elder, Matilda the younger of her step-daughters. With the bright and witty Ann, Irving was on the most companionable of terms; with Matilda (Sarah Matilda, but Matilda her friends called her) he was in love.

One has but to look at the portrait of this young girl to feel her fineness, her reserve, her spirituality. To Irving, whose derelictions of youth so unduly affected his sensitive nature that in some of his early letters to his mother and sisters he considers himself a sinner, the high-minded young girl was, even while she lived, an angel of purity. When consumption claimed her as a victim in the springtime of the year 1809 (in her eighteenth year, the springtime of her life), Irving more than ever associated her delicate and gentle spirit with those influences which are not of earth. "Beautiful, and more beautiful, and more angelical to the very last," he wrote of her on that one occasion when he opened his heart concerning the hallowed passion of his youth—and then only to make his whole nature more clear to the woman he loved in later years. As he sat beside the bedside of the dying girl "the beauty of her mind," "the sweet, natural and affecting eloquence" of Matilda Hoffman showed through her delirium, and her death left Irving consecrated by an ideal love.

Nothing, however, could have been further from the intent of Washington Irving than the translation of this sacred romance of his young days into a misleading legend. In "The

48

Broken Heart," the pathetic story of the daughter of Curran, the famous Irish barrister, Irving had, in "The Sketch Book," avowed his belief that people could indeed die of broken hearts, but added that exclusive devotion to the memory of a lover departed, was to be found in women rather than in men. A man—and he was writing from personal experience—had a multiplicity of outer interests—practical success—fame—excitement, and so on—to mend, in some measure at least, the broken heart. The legend that Washington Irving remained a lifelong bachelor because of Matilda Hoffman's death half a century before his own, is due solely to the sentimental desire of his nephew and first biographer, Pierre M. Irving. In his attempt to perpetuate this gentle myth, Pierre M. Irving had recourse to comments, to suppressions, and to elisions whose nature is now apparent through a careful study of Irving's Dresden diaries.

It is true that in later editions of Irving's Life, his nephew found himself forced to include in the Appendix passages which had without his knowledge been contributed to the English edition by Flora Foster, the sister of the English girl whose hand Irving, at the age of forty, had sought in marriage. Even so, the biographer attempted to treat very lightly this episode, which he had previously scamped. In the Hon. David J. Hill's Life of Irving a few lines are given to the Fosters, but the name of Emily does not appear. In Mr. Charles Dudley Warner's Life, drawn, like Mr. Hill's, for the most part from the Pierre M. Irving volumes, Irving's romance with Emily Foster is passed over in briefest manner, although there is a phrase suggesting that Mr. Warner gave credence to the detailed statement which had been issued by Emily's sister. Mr. Henry W. Boynton, in a later Life of Irving, again recurs to the subject, more fully and more frankly than any of his predecessors; but Mr. Boynton concludes with the statement that the Emily Foster episode is the only mystery in Irving's life. It is no longer a mystery at all; yet how firm and enduring has been the myth is best proved by the statement which anyone may find in the latest edition of the British Encyclopædia, to the effect that Irving never married because of Matilda Hoffman.

Before analyzing Irving's note-books that dispel the mystery and reveal how it came to be created, let us approach another romance, altogether unrecorded. Here, we grant, we are somewhat in the sphere of surmise, and not, as in the case of Emily Foster, in the realm of indubitable fact; and here, too, we are concerned with an affection far less overpowering than that of Irving's love for either the American or the English girl. None the less, Washington's delightful relations with Mrs. William Renwick, the blue-eyed lassie to whom Robert Burns wrote more than one of his songs, are of particular interest in considering his susceptibility to feminine attraction.

William Renwick's father had come to New York in 1783, the year of Irving's birth, and commenced his mercantile life with the importation of manufactured goods from England. These he was compelled to job and, on occasions, to retail. The division in mercantile selling was not a hard and fast one in those days, the importers often finding difficulty in discovering customers sufficiently affluent to buy entire packages. The ladies of New York would frequently insist on being present at the opening of the cases, the proceedings having somewhat the character of an exhibition of Parisian millinery in our own times. A direct descendant of William Renwick well recollects the congratulations received by her father on the subsequent changes in the mode of transacting business, whereby it became possible for him to exclude women from the warehouses.

Liverpool was then the centre of the trade with America and William Renwick was a pioneer in creating in any considerable way the salt and coal business between Liverpool and New York. His interests led him to reside at Liverpool when he was less than twenty years old, and it was during a trip from Manchester to Glasgow that, in these early years, he met his future wife at the home of a Mrs. Carruthers of Dinwiddie Green. Jane Jeffrey was hardly sixteen, a beautiful girl, with especially lovely hands and arms, and with a sweet voice that readily broke into

50

MATILDA HOFFMAN

merry laughter.   Robert Burns, just about this time, had written of her:

"When first I saw my Jeanie's face
I couldna think what ail'd me,
My heart went fluttering, pit-a-pat,
My e'en had nearly fail'd me.
She's aye sae neat, sae trim and tight,
All grace does round her hover,
Ae look deprived me o' my heart,
And I became her lover.

She's aye, aye sae blithe and gay,
She's aye sae blithe and cheery,
She's aye sae bonnie blithe and gay
O gin I were her dearie."

Whether Burns, with his powerful attraction for women, would have been able, had not parental objection intervened, entirely to captivate young Jeanie's heart, one cannot say. Certainly she adored his genius and was entranced by his voice and his eyes.   On one occasion she allowed him to carry her in his arms, and often she would sit at his feet listening to his eloquence.   But equally certainly her mother, the wife of the Rev. Andrew Jeffrey of Lochmabon, disliked the unkemptness of the dissolute poet whose life was nearing its end, and would, with the peremptoriness of the Scotch housewife, send Robert Burns to have his cup of tea in the kitchen when his shoes were too unclean for entrance into the parlour.   At any rate Burns realized that Jeanie Jeffrey was not for him, and phrased that realization in these verses:

"But sair I doubt some happier swain
Has gained my Jeanie's favour,
If sae may every bliss be hers,
Though I can never have her.
But gang she east, or gang she west,
Twixt Nith and Tweed all over,
While men have eyes or ears or taste,
She'll always find a lover."

WASHINGTON IRVING ESQUIRE

There were many men to fulfil, in its finer sense, the prophecy of Robèrt Burns. In 1791 Jeanie married William Renwick, and in 1794 they came to New York. There, for over half a century, till her death in 1850, Jane Jeffrey retained many of the attractions, physical as well as mental and temperamental, that had made her so fascinating in girlhood. Mrs. Renwick of Warren Street was one of the most delightful personages in the life of the city. She became a widow in 1808, when she was thirty-four years old; and if the little miniature that is still in the possession of one of her great-grand-daughters belongs, as its white ruched cap and black velvet dress seem to indicate, to the early years of widowhood, the lovely contour of the face, the small bow-shaped mouth, the ringlets, the blue eyes, the intelligence and sparkle of expression, are all-sufficient explanation of the charm exercised by Mrs. Renwick over a large circle of admirers.

Among these the two young men that especially appealed to her were Washington Irving and his bosom friend Henry Brevoort. Even before, through the channels of the Renwick family, there had come to me confirmation of the surmise that both Brevoort and Irving were her suitors, the belief in their courtship had arisen with the reading of various letters, some of them privately printed, others still solely in manuscript, preserved by the descendants of Jane Renwick. During the two years following the death of Matilda Hoffman, Washington Irving was gradually recovering from the impact of that grievous blow. Often during his lifetime, especially in those fits of melancholia which were as much a part of his nature as the intermittent periods of gaiety, the old sorrow would assail him, and to the very end the relics of Matilda—her miniature, a lock of her hair, her prayer book—were his precious possessions. But by 1811 the buoyant effect of the success of "Knickerbocker's History," the sympathetic companionship of a group of gay and intelligent young fellows, the general liking in which he was held by women young and old, all contributed to a restoration of spirits which left him, save perhaps to his own inner eye, very much the same sort of merry young fellow who had so richly seized upon the many happy possibilities of social and literary life in New York after his horizon had been enlarged by his first travels in Europe and his liberties confirmed by the death of his father the Deacon.

Nine years younger than Jane Renwick, Washington Irving was also nine years older than her son James, who in 1807 at the age of fifteen graduated from Columbia College where from 1820 to 1853 he was a professor of Natural Philosophy. His intelligence and attractiveness were very decided; but even so, on reading the letters that Irving wrote to the lad in 1811 and 1812—one of these letters over five thousand words in length, and all of them containing either brightly teasing or especially cordial comments and messages relating to Jane Renwick—the thought can not help arising that the twenty-seven year old Washington Irving, (one of the most sought-after young fellows in social life of the city and already, and beyond doubt, its most distinguished man of letters) was writing to the eighteen year old boy at such length and with such warmth primarily because the eighteen year old boy was the son of the fascinating widow.

In 1811 Irving and Brevoort were sharing rooms in Broadway, near Bowling Green, very near Mrs. Renwick's house where both the young fellows were in frequent attendance. The belief still obtains in the Brevoort family that young Henry, even more than young Washington, wooed the delicious widow; and if either of these attractive boys had been five or ten years older Jane Jeffrey Renwick might very probably have married one of them. As it was, she contented herself with retaining their admiring friendship throughout her life, with many charming acts of cordiality, whereof her gift of a slip of ivy from Melrose, green with the sentiment of Walter Scott's home, and planted with her own hands at Sunnyside is now the huge vine that so enhances the charm of Irving's home on the banks of the Hudson.

Ten years went by before Irving again came, in any compelling manner, under the spell of a woman. His Dresden note books (which, after remaining hidden for over half a century, were recently, under the editorship of Professor William P. Trent and myself, printed for private circulation among the members of the Bibliophile Society), show how Irving's bachelorhood might have been brought to an end, despite the sweet and gracious memory of Matilda Hoffman.

Mrs. Foster, the daughter of the Earl of Carhampton, had brought her four children to Dresden, especially for the purpose of educating her two girls, Emily and Flora. There Irving was introduced to them, in December 1822. In the course of the intimacy that so rapidly developed, it is at first a bit difficult to decide whether the hours spent, not infrequently alone, in walks and talks and music and in Italian lessons with Mrs. Foster, are solely to be ascribed to the diplomatic procedure of vicarious courtship, or whether the lady herself was well-nigh as attractive to Irving as was Emily. The situation had elements of curious parallel to that, so many years ago in New York, when Irving was in love with Matilda and on terms of great friendship with the young girl's step-mother, Mrs. Hoffman.

There are three of these Dresden diaries, and what dances and dinners and all manner of entertainments are packed in their entries! In the merry life of the little capital of Saxony we meet an Irving vastly different from that of immediately preceding or subsequent years—a gay and rejuvenated Irving. The financial cares and the physical ailments from which he was never, for any great length of time, wholly free, were then only the lightest of shadows. He immediately became a great favourite at court, the formal yet intimate, gracious yet intellectual little court of a kingdom still in its teens. Frederick Augustus, the King of Saxony who prior to 1806 had borne the less impressive title of Elector, spoke flatteringly to Irving about his works; and the King's brothers, the Queen, the many Princes and Princesses, all treated him with kindliest interest. He was invited to larger affairs at court, to family dinners of the Saxon royalty, to concerts in the Queen's apartment where Carl Maria von Weber, already famous through his opera, "Der Freischütz," played his own music. He took part in royal boar hunts, a form of amusement to which Napoleon, the King of Saxony's one-time hero, had been likewise addicted. After one of these "chasses" on horseback, Irving saw how wild boars are caught in nets, a demonstration especially ordered for his delectation by the Queen. At every affair given by the foreign diplomats he was a welcome guest. But most at home, and most frequently, we find him in the palace where Mrs. Foster had her apartments.

Amateur theatricals, whereof various were given at Mrs. Foster's residence, with Irving as the prime spirit in getting them up, account in great measure for the rapidity with which he fell in love with Emily. That delightful comedy, "Three Weeks After Marriage," was not the only one of the plays in which Irving was either the avowed lover or the actual husband of the young girl. There were frequent rehearsals where histrionic love-making, on Irving's part at least, soon began to take on the character of serious courtship. In the early Dresden weeks Madame de Bergh, the wife of the Danish Minister, obviously a fascinating woman (whose past, however, rendered her unacceptable at Court functions) beguiled Irving's fancy. As the entries in the note-books continue, there are less and less frequent references to the Countess, while almost daily his meetings and his doings with Emily Foster and her mother are recorded. At breakfast or dinner, morning or evening (and frequently both) is Irving with them during the concluding weeks of March; and on the twenty-eighth—Good Friday —after passing the evening there, and hearing Emily read "Faust," he writes: "Early part of the day triste—Emily delightful."—Now, it so happens that this entry is almost indecipherable, and the reason therefor is one no less significant than that the words were rubbed out by Pierre M. Irving, who, however, recorded them on a flyleaf at the end of the diary. Here was a clue to Irving's feelings that his nephew and biographer, intent on perpetuating the tradition of Irving's exclusive devotion to his early romance, sought to suppress. So, too, in the

entry for March 31st is there deletion. On that day, after dining at the Fosters, Irving returns from an evening party, from
which, on scrutinizing the diary, we are able to make out he
goes "home very much   ." "Very much" *what?* Oh
Mr. Nephew and Biographer, we surmise that the adjective
you so provokingly rubbed out was "depressed," and that it
was during these last moments of March that Washington Irving
unsuccessfully asked Emily Foster to be his bride.

The entries for April bear much evidence corroborative.
"If she be not fair for me," thinks Irving of Emily, "I shall
remember that there are other fair women,"—although he has
not reached that stage where he concludes the couplet with:
"What care I how fair she be?" Accordingly we look for, and
immediately find, much more frequent mention of Madame de
Bergh. On the first, she plays an April Fool joke on him; on
April 3rd, (his birthday) she "admirably" takes part in the
picture of Dutch Courtship, in tableaux from a scene in "Knickerbocker's History of New York"; on the 8th, "Mad. de Bergh
played and sang for me"; on the 12th he is at her home; on the
15th he is her partner at a dinner at Baron Lowenstein's—
"Madame de Bergh looking very pretty." After leaving the
Baron's he returns later and stays there until Madame de Bergh
goes home; after which, Irving goes to the house of Colonel
Livius and "waltzed with the governess till near 12."—When
we recall that Colonel Livius dwelt with his mistress, whom
Irving generally calls "the little governess," we find in this
record of April 15, an evidence of restlessness which we might
understand even more thoroughly if his nephew had not rubbed
out several lines referring to Emily Foster in an earlier portion
of the entry for this day. Irving had continued his visits to
the Fosters throughout the first fortnight of April during which
his appearance at rehearsals of amateur theatricals was necessary. His walks and talks and Italian lessons with Emily's
mother went on; and there are many indications that Mrs. Foster
was eager to have him as a son-in-law. It may well be that
on this 15th of April, Irving again attempted his fortune, and

that after having become convinced of the futility of his quest, he sought the excitement of the dance at Col. Livius', after leaving Madame de Bergh. Two days later Irving writes in his diary: "Determine to quit Dresden soon."

His departure, indeed, did not take place until the following month when "Mrs. F.—— very anxious for me to change my travelling plans and accompany them to England." His friendly relationship with the Foster household was maintained and he wrote for Emily's birthday on May 20th the lovely verses beginning:

> "'Twas now the freshness of the year
> When fields were green and groves were gay,
> When airs were soft and skies were clear
> And all things bloomed in lovely May—
>
> Blest month, when Nature in her prime
> Bestows her fairest gifts on earth—
> This was the time, the genial time,
> She destined for her favourite's birth."

But not as a confident, or even hopeful, lover, did he offer them to Emily. He sent them to her mother, with these words: "If you think them in any way worthy of the subject, and that they would give her any pleasure, slip them into her scrapbook; if not, slip them into the stove, that convenient altar, and sacrifice them as a burnt-offering to appease the Muses. I have no confidence in my rhymes."

Mrs. Foster did her best to persuade her daughter into marriage with the distinguished and charming American, but when Emily thanked Irving for his lines, it was as a friend; and that was all. Yet he persisted in the hope to win her, and it was years before Irving entirely gave up that hope.

With the New York girl who died during their betrothal, with the Scotch-born woman who was too old for him, and the English girl who was too young, there is completed the list of the women who were desired in marriage by Washington Irving.

Much more difficult it is to determine who and how many were those who were disappointed at Irving's failure fully to return the affection they felt for him. Madame de Bergh we may dismiss as merely a partner in a casual flirtation. Not so lightly can we pass by Mary Fairlie, Mary Shelley and Antoinette Bolvillier.

In the period of Irving's early manhood there was in New York no more fascinating girl than the daughter of Major Fairlie, himself of so engaging and contagious a wit that even George Washington would break into uproarious laughter at the keen sallies of this one of his favourite officers. Mary was the scintillating leader among the belles of her day, and so generally liked that no envy was felt when Washington Irving portrayed her with enthusiasm in the pages of *Salmagundi* where she fittingly appears as "Sophie Sparkle." Her reputation preceded her when she went visiting in Boston or in Philadelphia, and in the Pennsylvania city the one girl who seems to have been her equal in charm and her superior in intellectuality was her friend Rebecca Gratz, the young Jewess whose character and personality were described by Irving to Walter Scott and who became the prototype of the Rebecca in "Ivanhoe." The letters that passed between Mary Fairlie and Washington Irving in the year 1807, just before Irving fell in love with Matilda Hoffman who was then only fifteen, are the gayest kind of epistles, yet none that Irving wrote indicates that he was in love with the girl whose general fascination he was only too ready to admit. But in her letters to him there may be detected, however deftly covered by the light veil of wit and camaraderie, the deeper note. Lightly she writes to him (on March 13th, 1807 when Irving was in Philadelphia and Mary in New York): "I have just received your letter, that is just before dinner, which important meal I have dispatched with such expidition as my appetite will allow, and now hasten to express to you the joy, the extatic felicity which the great favour has occasioned. Permit me before I proceed any further to offer my congratulations to you and Maria Cranford on your *pleasant journey*. I am sure that your great minds rise superior to the inconveniences that common mortals feel from bad roads, dirty stages, inclement weather, and inhospitable inns; I am sure that these 'miseries of human life,' you think quite beneath your consideration, and that riding in the winter to philosophic souls, is precisely the same thing as in the most delightful season, so without any risk, I may congratulate you on your pleasant journey." Lightly, in this unpublished letter found among the papers of Washington Irving after his death, Mary goes on to write of a "Conversatione" where "Signore Clementi Moore" (who is remembered by posterity as the author of the poem beginning "'Twas the night before Christmas and all through the house") was the "hero of the evening." Yet as she goes on to tell of a brilliant assembly to which she did not go because "solitude offered charm more congenial to my soul," and, however whimsically, suggests to Irving that she has "grown over romantic of late," we begin to see the truth beneath its gay and jesting guise. After all manner of news of friends, Mary approaches the conclusion with "If you write a very long letter I may be again induced to follow your example. If you do not I shall consider it as a hint, that you do not wish to be troubled by me. All our family send their love to you. And Mama particularly requests that you take care of your health." Then, after she has signed herself as "Your Friend, M. Fairlie," Mary adds as a postscript: "Don't you admire this pretty paper—I like it so much that I have been trying, in vain, to leave it, these ten minutes, but my pen today has the same propensity that my tongue has, when talking to you, I know not when to have done."

A few days later, on March 17th, Irving sent a long letter in reply to Mary's, and in it found occasion to say: "You need not be under any apprehensions of my forgetting New York while you are in it." Mary allowed no time to pass before writing again to him, and on March 19th asked him to make an attempt to return to New York in time for the next Assembly, the last of the season, which was to be held the following week.

When, shortly thereafter, she is in Boston, and Irving again in New York, she again asks him to write to her, and the sprightly correspondence goes on at such a rate that the interchange sometimes takes place by the very next mail; but while in some of these missives Irving signs himself as "Truly and affectionately your friend," the impression remains that the affection was stronger on the side of the girl than of the young fellow. Irving's devotion to Matilda Hoffman was soon to become known in the social circles which he and Mary Fairlie frequented, and subsequently the "fascinating Fairlie," as Irving called her, became the wife of the noted tragedian, Thomas A. Cooper.

To my mind the most amusing of Irving anecdotes recorded by his nephew is one associated with Cooper. The two were friends, and Cooper was acting at Richmond when Irving was also there, in June 1807, attending, nominally as a lawyer, but actually as a socially occupied spectator, the trial of Aaron Burr. On some occasion Irving lent the actor a pair of his breeches. In them Cooper, a few days later at Baltimore, found a heart-shaped locket containing some strands of hair. He returned it to Irving with an amusing letter partly in rhyme, the verses closing with these witty lines:

> "Receive these inquiries, dear friend, in good part,
> And since you have locked the fair hair in your heart,
> Ne'er trust, of the girl who your fancy bewitches,
> Such an emblem of love in another man's breeches."

The story of this locket goes back to Irving's days in Genoa in 1804 where he had been captivated by the sight of the young Italian wife of a Frenchman. He had not met her, but had managed to pick up her handkerchief, at some social affair, and had kept it as a souvenir of the lovely Bianca. This was just before he left Genoa. At Catania he lost the handkerchief, much, it would seem, to his despair. He wrote to his friend, Hall Storm, of his misfortune; Storm, in turn, told Bianca, and she then sent to Irving the locket and the lock. What romance might have developed had Irving ever gone back to Genoa, one can only surmise; but that he carried it with him for years is indicative of the idealism of his sentimentality; and that he was carrying it at the very time when Mary Fairlie was sending him her warm and sparkling letters, is the best evidence that Irving's liking for the young American girl was not a matter of love.

Irving's friendship for her never ceased. Shortly after his return to America in 1832 he visited the actor's wife at her little cottage in Bristol, on the banks of the Delaware. "She was pale, and thinner than I had expected to find her, yet still retaining much of her former self." "Sophie Sparkle" had had many tribulations in the intervening years. Her husband's talents had been dimmed by excessive drinking, and he no longer aroused the enthusiasm of his audiences. The quarter of a century since Irving and Mary Fairlie had, for a few brief months, interchanged so many letters, had brought much grief to both of them, but that loyalty of friendship so characteristic of Irving, still held its pleasant savour for Mary Fairlie and himself.

The second Mary to come under the spell of Irving's charm was the daughter of William Godwin, the philosopher, and of Mary Wollstonecraft, a pioneer in the assertion of Woman's Rights. The widow of Percy Bysshe Shelley was twenty-eight years old, and Irving forty, when the two were brought together in 1824 by John Howard Payne. Payne himself was at the time deeply devoted to Mary Shelley, but losing hope as a suitor for her hand (or for her less formal favours) he seems to have resigned himself to the thought that Irving, to whom he was under obligations and with whom he then was collaborating in dramatic writing, might as well be successful where he had failed. In a mood wherein motives of friendship for Irving and Mary Shelley mingled with other less happy emotions, Payne wrote to Irving of his belief that Mary Shelley had sought him merely as a source of introduction to Irving. While this may be regarded as an over-statement, Mary had told Payne that Irving "had interested her more than anyone she had ever seen since she left Italy"; that he was "gentle and cordial"; and that "she

longed for friendship" with him.   Shelley had died, by drown-
ing, in 1822; Byron met death the next year, during his high-
hearted participation in the Greek struggle for liberty.   The two
wonderful poets with whom her life had been so closely allied
had thus gone down in tragedies of romantic atmosphere.
Mary Shelley, with her own romantic temperament that was to
find such startling expression in her novel of "Frankenstein,"
was drawn to Irving not only because of her loneliness and his
own charm as a man, but also by reason of the glamour of his
name in the field of romantic literature.   It is entirely conceiv-
able that Shelley's widow and Byron's friend would have been
willing to become the mistress (or even the wife) of Washington
Irving for whose friendship "she longed."   But Irving, in 1824,
was still caught up in his infatuation with Emily Foster.   The
situation was much like that which Heine describes in one of his
ironic lyrics: Payne was in love with Mary; she, it would seem,
with Irving; he with Emily; and Emily was later to marry a
fifth.

It is in consonance with the cosmopolitan temperament and
career of Irving that, after these episodes of romance in New
York, Dresden, Paris and London, with women American,
Scotch, and English, Spain should have been the scene of the
final episode, with a young French girl as his great admirer.   At
Madrid, in 1826 and 1827, where Irving was so industriously
engaged on his history of Columbus, the home where he was
most often, and very often, a guest was that of the Russian
Minister, D'Oubril.   Antoinette Bolvillier, Madame D'Oubril's
niece, was the most delightful member of the Russian Minister's
household, and with her Irving became on terms of really rare
friendship.   When he left Madrid in the early part of 1828 to
spend his remaining two years in Spain mainly at Seville and
Granada, Antoinette received his promise to write to her.   It
is a thousand pities that her side of the correspondence has never
come into print, but from Irving's letters it is apparent that he
was writing to a young girl who had for him not only a romantic
attachment but also a profound admiration.   No other letters

of his compare to these in their combination of beautiful revela-
tion of his own nature with beautiful description of nature in
general, so that both subjectively and objectively they constitute
a series strikingly illustrative of the man, and of the man of
letters. "With me it is in letter writing as in conversation," we
find Irving saying to her, "I must feel a particular interest in a
person to be able to acquit myself with any degree of attention
and animation in either; but there are those with whom it is a
real pleasure, both to converse and correspond"; and he assures
"my dear Mlle. Antoinette" that she belongs in this number.
He refers to her promise of "news of the gay world of Madrid,"
and comments "I shall be delighted to receive it from you, but
you need not go out of the walls of your own house to find subjects full of interest for me." Her statement that she has renounced bull fights forever, he adverts to with the reflection that
"I should be much mistaken in the opinion I have formed of you,
could you relish those barbarous spectacles. Depend upon it,"
he adds, "it is neither the better nor the braver parts of our
nature that are gratified by them. There appears to me a mixture of cowardice and ferocity in looking on in selfish security
and enjoying the perils and sufferings of others. The 'Divinity
that dwells within us' has nothing to do with pleasures of the
kind; they belong to our earthly, our gross and savage nature.
I have sunk considerably in my own estimation since I found I
could derive gratification from these sights; I should have been
grieved to find you as bad in this respect as myself."

Irving's Spanish diaries (as, for instance, in the entry on
April 24th, 1826, where he records having given Antoinette a
book), show Irving referring to her, for his own private eye,
merely as Antoinette. The letters, beginning with his addressing her as "my dear Mademoiselle Bolvillier," show, after her
first reply, the change to the use of her first name. Whether the
asterisks employed by Pierre M. Irving in various passages
where his uncle enters into scenes of moonlight take the place of
touches of sentiment whose suppression would be in accordance
with that editor's approach to all of Irving's affairs with women

(save the outstanding romance with Matilda Hoffman), one cannot say; but that Irving himself was in love with Antoinette there is no reason to believe. To her, however, he confides intimate thoughts such as are absent from his published correspondence with other women, save his mother and sisters. He tells her of the tranquillity of spirit that the country brings him; he wonders at having passed "so much of my life in scenes in which I take so little relish and to which I feel myself so little adapted. . . . By dint of passing our time in the distractions of a continual succession of society, we lose all intimacy with what ought to be our best and most cherished society, *ourselves*." He tells Antoinette how "a quiet saunter about a cathedral" affects him like a walk in one of his beloved American forests. "I cannot compare the scenes, but their sublime and solitary features produce the same dilatation of the heart and swelling of the spirit, the same aspiring and longing after something exalted and indefinite; something—I know not what—but something which I feel this world cannot give me." Irving is at his very noblest in these letters to Antoinette, and what their effect must have been on the young girl who withdrew from the most exciting pleasures of Madrid after his departure, and who, if we are not mistaken, ended her life in a convent, can readily be conjectured. Intelligent and high-spirited, Antoinette Bolvillier struck some of the finest chords in Irving's nature, and led him to write, from the sheer point of artistry, the most perfect of his letters. Entering again upon the fields of surmise, we venture the opinion that if, with his second great disappointment in love, Irving had not forever renounced the idea of marriage, this girl who was so sympathetic a companion in the Madrid days might have won his enduring affection.

Chapter IV

MERRY YOUTH AND FIRST FAME

IT seems, perhaps, a cruel thing to say, but I am convinced that if Matilda Hoffman had lived, the man of letters that the world of literature knows as Washington Irving would never have come into being. As the son-in-law of Josiah Hoffman, Irving would in all probability have had a sinecure as a junior partner in a distinguished law firm and later, perhaps through the influence of Hoffman, of Judge Van Ness and of other New Yorkers with voice at Washington, have obtained in early manhood the Secretaryship of Legation which he unsuccessfully sought during the administration of James Madison. There might, from time to time, have issued some piece of writing from his facile pen, but would there have been that prod of necessity which ultimately forced Irving into the career of an author? Not even the success of "Knickerbocker's History" could stir Irving from the happy, indolent life of a young man about town. It is difficult to say whether his aversion from work or his love for society was more marked in the days of his early manhood; but in any event he presents the unparalleled case of an author leaving his pen almost unemployed for a period of nine years immediately following the appearance of a phenomenally successful book.

His first piece of literary work after the early tour in Europe was his translation of "A Voyage to the Eastern Part of Terra Firma, or the Spanish Main in South America," from the French of F. Depons. This publication is, quite apart from the original work itself, of note as Irving's first adventure between book covers; and as a direct result of that boyhood interest in foreign travels so greatly increased by his own just completed journey. But I am not sure that the most noteworthy part of this work is not the one line on the title page where, instead of Washington Irving's name, appears: "Translated by an American Gentleman." Even if we accept his long list of *noms de plume* as indicative of his habitual shyness, there remains a curiously significant suggestion in his appearance for the first time on the title page of a book as merely "an American gentleman." It was as an American gentleman that Irving had spread knowledge of America, good-will towards America, in his early European travels, and again as an American gentleman that he was later to be of similar, but vastly increased, service the Continent over. The present volume has been called "Washington Irving, Esquire," and it is in the life of a great and lovable gentleman that we are far more interested than in the easily ascertainable achievement of the writer whose works have long been the subject of critical evaluation. I do not know whether attention has already been called to the fact that until Irving had passed the age of fifty no one of his books carried his own name on the title page. As Jonathan Oldstyle he contributed papers to the *Morning Chronicle* edited in 1805 by his brother Peter; as Anthony Evergreen, Gent. he was one of the gaily audacious three authors of *Salmagundi;* Diedrich Knickerbocker appeared as the author of the "History of New York"; in 1813 Irving was the anonymous editor of the *Analectic Magazine;* and so the record continues even up to the year 1829 when "Fray Antonio Agapida" (not only Irving's *nom de plume,* but a character reminiscent of Irving's own) is shown on the title page of "A Chronicle of the Conquest of Granada." Later we shall have, though not always, Irving's own name (perhaps at the solicitation of the publisher) as in the Life of Washington; but it is either the whimsical *nom de plume,* or that mere phrase including the word "gentleman," which was most to Irving's liking. We find it not only in the French translation, but again when, in 1810 he wrote a biographical sketch to accompany the American edition of "The Poetical Works of Thomas Campbell," the memoir being by "A Gentleman of New York." Most interesting of all is the appellation used in "The Sketch

Book" and in "Bracebridge Hall," those two volumes which, in the years 1819 to 1822, established Irving's world-wide fame, and which were, at the same time, his greatest single literary contributions to international relationships. Here we see him as "Geoffrey Crayon, Gent." The "Crayon" is the man of letters; the "Gent." is, however little Irving himself may have had it in mind, however modestly he would have disclaimed the connotation, symbolic of those qualities in his nature which made him a citizen to whom our country owes so great, and not sufficiently appreciated, a debt.

But let us not get into an analytical or thoughtful vein at just this moment. In lighter mood should be the approach to the life of Irving during those years when he was pre-eminently the sought-after gallant in New York, Philadelphia, Baltimore and Washington. The translation of the Spanish Main Travels may not unfairly be regarded in the light of requital for the generosity of his family in having sent him abroad. After William had reprimanded him for having failed to visit Florence and Venice, Washington's letters to his oldest brother came almost entirely, if not entirely, to an end, and the less censorious Peter was the recipient of the comparatively few epistles in the post-Italian period of Irving's journey. But however easily the boy's sensitiveness accounts for the silence, Washington never forgot favours, and his work of translation was a natural way for him to make evident to William and the others that foreign travel had quickened his interest in the direction they had in mind when their generosity sent him abroad.

Fortunately for Washington, William Irving had both literary talent and a decided sense of humour. He never long maintained the critical paternal attitude to his junior by seventeen years, and when William's brother-in-law, James K. Paulding, and Washington conceived the idea of starting a little journal that should "amuse, edify and castigate the town," William himself joined them in this literary lark. From that day on Washington Irving as a lawyer (he was then sharing an office in Wall Street with his brother John) becomes a shadowy figure; and with *Salmagundi,* flourishing for twenty issues, Irving's wide reputation as a writer begins.

However obvious may be the debt of its authors to Addison's *Spectator,* the little journal which set all the town talking had its own rare flavour of gay and audacious youth. "If we moralize, it shall be seldom," the editors announced; "and, on all occasions, we shall be more solicitous to make our readers laugh than cry; for we are laughing philosophers, and truly of the opinion that wisdom, true wisdom, is a plump, jolly dame, who sits in her arm-chair, laughs right merrily at the farce of life —and takes the world as it goes." So, after having cleverly stated that "the ladies of New York are the fairest, the finest, the most accomplished, the most ineffable beings that walk, creep, crawl, swim, fly, float, or vegetate in any or all of the four elements" they proceed to have fun with them, satirizing the ways of the fashionable world, gently as far as the women are concerned, a little more severely, the men. Individuals are portrayed under a thin disguise, thus giving an added tang to these papers where "parents shall be taught how to govern their children, girls how to get husbands, and old maids how to do without them." Actors and critics come in for a little flick of the whip; notes on the latest mode in dress have daring remarks concerning flesh-coloured stockings, *"nudity* being all the rage"; "open war" is declared against "folly and stupidity." There are amusing verses; descriptions of dances; letters from "Mustapha Rub-a-dub Khan," giving his impressions of Western civilization, as where he writes "The barbarous nations of antiquity immolated human victims to the memory of their lamented dead, but the enlightened Americans offer up whole hecatombs of geese and calves, and oceans of wine, in honour of the illustrious living; and the patriot has the felicity of hearing from every quarter, the vast exploits in gluttony and revelling that have been celebrated to the glory of his name." And so the papers proceed with all kinds of subjects, but ever in the light vein.

The little New York of those days, with its one social set, instead of scores as now, and with that set gladly admitting men of letters and men of wit, naturally gave welcome to so amusing a publication. Before long its disguised authors became known, and Irving, who had had some local fame because of his earlier papers humorously written on such subjects as the theatre, marriage and divorce in the columns of the *Morning Chronicle,* was in greater favour than ever. He shared, it must be admitted, in the levities he satirized, danced a great deal, dressed in fashion, and became intoxicated on the proper occasions. It was a period of sentiment, of persiflage, and of much social drinking. Especially in evidence was the group of young fellows who, largely under Irving's leadership in the way of pranks, often met at "Cockloft Hall," Gouverneur Kemble's home in the highlands of New Jersey. Henry Ogden, Peter and Ebenezer Irving, James K. Paulding, Richard McCall, David Porter and Henry Brevoort were the others in this coterie of merry youths. All had nicknames, and collectively they were known as "The Lads of Kilkenny," "The Ancient Club of New York," "The Nine Worthies," and "The Ancient and Honourable Order." They had high old times in the "Bachelors' Hall," and "Who would have thought that we should have lived to be two such respectable old gentlemen?" Washington Irving asked Gouverneur Kemble many years later.

The present Mr. Gouverneur Kemble tells me that his great-grand-uncle continued his early hospitality until the end of his life, and that a dinner would take place every Saturday night at Kemble's home on the Hudson. On one occasion, Paulding, somewhat affected by the good wines he had imbibed, sought to find his way to a neighbouring house where he was staying over-night. The path led through some woods, and the next day Paulding spoke with feeling of the "interminable forests of America." Of Henry Ogden it is told how one evening he was a bit discomfited when his unsteady steps caused him to fall through a grating, but was much comforted when various of his companions followed him into the vault below.

In New York two favourite places of meeting of the "Lads of Kilkenny" were Dyde's Public House in Park Row and a less expensive tavern at the corner of Nassau and John Streets. But riotous living was not the main interest of this little group. On the contrary, it would be hard to find more wit, talent, and ability than were included in these nine young men. Apart from his brothers, the most important of them in connection with Irving's life was Henry Brevoort, and in the pages of the extensive correspondence between Brevoort and Irving many intimate revelations of Irving's nature may be found.

During the first few years after Irving's return from Europe he lived at the family home in William Street where his father died in 1807 without, it must be admitted, any great regret on Irving's part. Irving was very fond of his mother, but she was sufficiently well off, and she had others of her children in the homestead. The friendship with Brevoort, and his many interests in common with him, decided Irving, early in 1811, to share bachelor quarters in a house on Broadway, not far from Bowling Green. The intervening years had seen Irving develop from irresponsible youth into famous young manhood, with "Knickerbocker's History" as the great achievement, and Matilda Hoffman's death as the sobering influence over spirits that could not, even so, become permanently depressed. He had —possibly in the hope of some office of legal character—taken a slight hand in matters political, as when, in the election of 1807, he "talked handbill fashion with the demagogues and shook hands with the mob—whom my heart abhorreth." In the first day of his campaigning he "merely hunted for whim, character, and absurdity according to my usual custom; the second day being rainy, I sat in the bar room at the Seventh Ward, and read a volume of "Galatea." But the third day— as he writes to Mary Fairlie—"My patriotism all at once blazed forth, and I determined to save my country, and truly this saving one's country is a nauseous piece of business, and if patriotism is such a virtue—prithee, no more of it." The dirty places he had to visit and the smell of bad tobacco and bad beer were not pleasing to our young man of fashion, who always disliked politics anyhow. He had, in July, 1807, attended

70

with equal ineffectualness Aaron Burr's trial at Richmond where again we may think of him as hunting for whim and character. The crafty Burr had Irving in his array of lawyers in the hope —which Irving would not fulfil—that the well-liked young author would write in his favour in the public press. After that Irving visited Judge Van Ness at Washington where he was over-pursued by the attentions of young women who wished him to go riding at daybreak, walking at moonlight, and invited him to "red hot strolls in the middle of the day" when the thermometer was "98½ in the shade." He had, in 1808, made a trip to Montreal on matters of business, and had come down the Hudson on Robert Fulton's steamboat. This year marked the beginning of "Knickerbocker's History," first planned as a skit on a kind of guide book entitled "The Picture of New York," by Dr. Samuel Mitchill. But soon it changed from a brief imitative burlesque into a work which called for considerable original research before Irving could let his fancy and humour transfuse his accumulation of historical data. Despite its caricature in characterization Irving's history presents much accurate information, and is his first of varied achievements in the field of history. It is only fair to our indolent young gallant to say that in 1808 he really did quite a little hard work in the course of its composition.

We find Irving writing, in 1808, to Henry Brevoort of Mary Fairlie, of Louisa and Maria Moore, and of Ann Hoffman, "fair and beautiful as ever and full of fascination," but Matilda is not mentioned. The inference is that towards the younger sister Irving's affection must have taken a swift turn, so that, despite the bevy of delightful girls nearer his own age, he swiftly became enamoured of the sweet Matilda as she passed from childhood into maidenhood. Then, when she crossed the ultimate threshold, Irving, overwhelmed in heart yet active in mind, gathered up his manuscript and left the gay life of New York for the quiet home at Kinderhook of his friend Judge Van Ness. From there he went to live, in August and September, with the Hoffmans at their place near Hellgate, frequently coming into town on Henry Brevoort's boat, *The Tinker*. In November he went to Philadelphia to supervise the publication of "Knickerbocker's History" which was issued from that city with the purpose of making less easy of discovery its authorship by a New Yorker. Assiduously and bravely Irving proceeded with his work, and 1809 remains the one year of his youth wherein, save for the few months preceding Matilda Hoffman's death, the social activities of our city went on without him.

The success of his book did much to rouse Irving from his unhappiness. As early as February 1810 we find him fêted in the social world at Albany. What, and how many, were the dark hours, the moods of reaction, of that period, who can say? No doubt they were many and intense; but by 1811 Irving was again, to all appearances, the merry and admired young fellow.

Washington had been given by his brothers Peter and Ebenezer a one-fifth interest in their hardware firm, with their offer to make his share a third in the event of his marriage. It was one of those generous arrangements characteristic of his kin in their relations with the talented youngest boy in the family to whom all were, with such pride, so attached. There was much importing from England, especially in the line of hardware. Washington was the "Co." of P. & E. Irving and Co., but as company his brothers were well aware that his talent lay in the social, and not in the mercantile, sphere. They desired to provide him with an income that should enable him to be independent and follow his natural bent as a writer and at the same time maintain the delightful position he had won in society. Still, not to let their benefaction be too obvious (and perhaps believing that Washington's social charm might be of service to them), his brother sent him, in the winter of 1811, to the Capital to observe those Congressional measures which were having so direct an effect on the mercantile life of America ever since the Non-Intercourse Act of 1809 had first prohibited the bringing in of goods from Great Britain. This Act, followed by a similar prohibitive enactment in 1811, did not lead, as James

Madison had hoped it would lead, to the observance of American rights on the high seas; and after Macon's Bill gave Napoleon Bonaparte his opportunity to embroil England with the United States, the War of 1812 became inevitable.

There is no evidence that Irving accomplished anything of commercial benefit to his firm during his months at Washington; but he certainly derived advantage from meeting all manner of people, his interest in individuals outrunning all the limitations of partisanship. He went by stagecoach, the hardships of the journey (including a night in a log house) being lessened first of all by his determination "to be pleased with everything, or if not pleased, to be amused." It took three days to reach Baltimore, where two additional days were passed in the "very agreeable society" of that little city where he met Tezier, the Frenchman who had translated "Knickerbocker's History," a work which Irving opines the Parisians "will understand and relish about as much as they would a Scotch haggis and a singed sheeps-head." It was dusk when he arrived at Washington, but, resolved to attend Mrs. Madison's levée that night, he managed, after a conference with his landlord, to meet a gentleman who offered to introduce him to the master and mistress of the President's House, as the White House was then called. Thus, after he had had just about enough time to wash, get shaved, and put on his pease blossoms and silk stockings, he found himself amid "the blazing splendour of Mrs. Madison's drawing room" where, in ten minutes, he was "hand and glove with half the people in the assemblage." Mrs. Madison he describes in his letter to Henry Brevoort as "a fine, portly, buxom dame—who has a smile and pleasant word for everybody—but as to Jemmy Madison— Ah! Poor Jemmy, he is but a withered little applejohn."

The day after his arrival John Van Ness insisted on Irving's becoming a member of his household, and as Mrs. Van Ness was pretty and "quite gay" and had as her guests "two pretty girls likewise"—one of them a Miss Smith from Long Island, the daughter of a Congressman, and a delightful belle,—Irving

73

is "in clover." Similarly in clover was he in the President's household, Mrs. Madison taking a great fancy to young Irving; while her sisters, Mrs. Cutts and Mrs. Washington, appealed to him like "The Two Merry Wives of Windsor." The President himself was, excepting for the post-prandial hour, too taken up with the affairs of state, and temperamentally too serious, to be much of a social asset, but there has been no Lady of the White House who over so long a period, and in so simple and gracious a fashion, was more of a favourite than Dolly Madison. As the wife of the Secretary of State she had, from 1801 to 1808, presided over many of the functions when the widower, Thomas Jefferson, was in office. When she became the mistress of the White House, in her thirty-seventh year, she dispensed hospitality with true Virginian liberality, and her cheerfulness, her gaiety, her kindness won her friends even among the political opponents of her husband. She rouged; she took snuff; she always wore a most conspicuous turban; and she was not in the least intellectual; but her simple dignity and the sunny quality of her nature made her probably the best-liked person in the United States. Naturally to such a woman the genial young New Yorker in the first flush of his fame was a welcome addition in the circle of the President's household, and we find Washington Irving at the more intimate parties as well as at the larger assemblies.

Although Irving enjoyed, as he writes to his friend Brevoort, "a constant round of banquetting, revelling and dancing," he did not miss the opportunities offered by the city of Washington in other directions, directions that were to affect him as an author and as a consistent adherent to an early formulated philosophy of life. He made it his business to associate with men of opposed political bias, and in both parties he found "worthy and intelligent men—with honest hearts, enlightened minds, generous feelings and bitter prejudices." He thus became more than ever free from party bigotry, developing that "good-natured habit of thinking, which I think every man that values his own comfort and utility should strive to cultivate." Through all the political controversies of later years Irving pursued his quiet way as a generously-minded American interested far more in the goodness of men than in the superiority of parties. It was, I think, the *Edinburgh Review* that, after Irving's death, was the first to point out how, in all his writings (even under the stress of attack), there was never a caustic fling, a mean or bitter word.

Let us follow Irving during one of his Washington weeks to observe the variety of his enjoyments. On Monday he dines with a group of officers at the barracks, and afterwards goes to a ball given at the home of his host, General Van Ness. On Tuesday he is with "several merry Federalists," and with Congressmen Knickerbocker whose patronym led to a jolly friendship with the author of the "History." On Wednesday General Turreau, reputed to be "a perfect sanguinary ferocious bloodhound," but found by Irving to be "an exceeding pleasant jocose companion," invites him to a gay dinner of Frenchmen and Democrats, after which the party go to a brilliant levée at Mrs. Madison's. Thursday he dines at Latrobe's, and, on Friday, with the Secretary of the Navy, going thence to a ball given by the Mayor of Washington. And so it went on until March when Congress closed its sessions, and, with the departure of the law-makers, their families, friends, and followers, Washington became a comparatively deserted city which Irving was glad to leave. But our young lawyer (who didn't practise law); our young hardware merchant (whose Washington letters to his partners were of so little business importance that for a considerable time they remained unanswered); our young author who was too delightfully the man of society to do any writing, did not go straight back to New York. For a second time he stopped off at Baltimore for some days and nights of "stout carousal," followed by such "sickness, sorrow and repentance" that he "hurried off from that sensual city." At Philadelphia we find him having more good times, both in March and in April. Ann Hoffman, Matilda's sister, was visiting Philadelphia those weeks and was Irving's best friend there among the younger girls, although he comments on the charm of "that little assemblage of smiles and fascinations, Mary Jackson." Yet his chief pastime at Philadelphia was the theatre and his enthusiasm was especially aroused by Cooke's great acting in "Macbeth."

Altogether the Washington, Baltimore, Philadelphia weeks were the highwater mark of Irving's social triumphs during his younger days in America. Quite apart from his own attractiveness to young and old, to Federalists and Democrats, to French diplomats and American Congressmen, to persons who liked to think and to persons who preferred to drink, when Washington Irving went to a dinner or a levée, the name that was announced (if they *did* announce names?) was familiar as that of the one American man of letters whose writings afforded jolly enjoyment not alone in the larger cities, but in such remote villages as Mackinac, where his "History of New York" went the rounds "from the Commandant to the smallest Indian trader."

But, as the old song tells us, life is not all beer and skittles, and the month of May largely passed by, at least as far as daytime was concerned, in incongruous tasks amidst hardware and cutlery, after the Irving brothers had moved their place of business. Washington was making a real effort to play his part in the commercial routine, though he confides to Brevoort that he would rather starve than permanently follow such a career, even were it to bring him the wealth of John Jacob Astor himself —and this, incidentally, is the first mention in Irving's letters of the famous merchant at whose request "Astoria" was written and who, in turn, allowed Irving to influence him in the foundation of the Astor Library. Yet it was not only the responsibility of business that led Irving to refrain from over much social activity in the spring and summer of 1811. He had been so lionized, and had indulged in such a variety of social entertainment during the preceding months, that he was for the time being weary of dissipation. His duties, however unimportant, in the hardware business, added to his general restlessness, and made him all the more desirous, sometimes of again taking up his pen, and, at other times, of lazy dreaming amid the beauties of nature. The letters that reached him from Henry Brevoort, then among the towns and forests of Lake Michigan and Lake Huron, brought him not only recountals concerning the Indians and the traders among whom Brevoort, as the young associate of Astor, the fur magnate, was residing, but also alluring descriptions of the magnificent woods and waters of our land. They served to accentuate Irving's dissatisfaction with the usual round of city tasks and pleasures, intensifying his longing for that recreation and re-creation which the quiet grandeur of natural scenery ever afforded him.

Irving was now living in the rooms which he shared with Brevoort at Mrs. Ryckman's, near Bowling Green. Brevoort had already begun to form a library ultimately, with the additions made by his son Carson, to develop into a collection of some ten thousand volumes, including such rarities as Smith's "Virginia"; "The Warres of New England"; "The Simple Cobbler of Aggawam" (these three presented to Brevoort by Walter Scott); a letter book of John Paul Jones when he was commanding the Bon Homme Richard and the Alliance; and a diary kept by George Washington when, in 1789 and 1790, New York was the Capital of the United States. At the outset Brevoort's library had in it the works of the foremost English and French writers, history and philosophy being represented as well as fiction, poetry and the drama. Both in 1811, when his room-mate was for several months among the fur hunters, and during the years 1812 and 1813, when Brevoort was in Europe, Irving often had happy recourse to the bookshelves of his friend whose purse was much more ample than his own; and it was thus that he greatly enriched his knowledge of continental thought and belles lettres, developing his natural taste for literature, and making amends for his general neglect of education in the earlier days of youth.

It was a period where we find Irving first showing in marked degree his vacillation between moods strongly contrasted.

77

Pleasure at times seems to him "but a transient stimulus" leaving the mind "more enfeebled than before" and he calls on Heaven to shield him from those "ennervating triflings, those syren blandishments," in which he has so often indulged and which lead to such "painful and humiliating struggles." At other times he gets "very much convived by wine and wassal" and ends up the evening with his merry companions, among them James K. Paulding, serenading some young woman. In his restlessness he contemplates marriage but seems to consider himself not wealthy enough to afford it. To Brevoort, at Paris in 1812, he writes of the stimulation of travel. "I always kept it in view as a kind of succedaneum for matrimony, and promise myself, in case I am not fortunate enough to get happily married, to console myself by ranging a little about the world."

The War of 1812 involved Irving further in those business responsibilities which were later to become so harassing, and in the autumn of that year he went to Washington for six weeks as a member of a Committee of New York merchants seeking to have their bonds remitted. He had spent a part of the summer as a lodger with a French family opposite Hellgate where he had settled himself "to read, and, if it please Heaven and the Muse, to write." Whatever Heaven and the Muse may have had in mind one cannot say, but Irving failed to accomplish anything worth while, perhaps because the attractive households of the Rhinelanders and the Gracies were so near by. From time to time he would ride into town, to visit Mrs. Renwick or to look in upon old Henry Brevoort whose farm, where Grace Church now stands, had as its most exciting resident a bear, "the wonder of the neighbouring swains."

The merriness of the summer parties of which Irving was so gay a member is delightfully shown in the letters which Margaret Brevoort (later the wife of James Renwick) wrote to her absent brother Henry. From some of these we shall pause to quote, without correcting the spelling of the bright little girl whose missives are such delicious documents relating to early New York society. "Yesterday," she writes from the

Bowery, on June 19, 1812, "I had the pleasure of meeting Mrs. Renwick, I have been staying with her a long time, and only returned two days ago; she insists uppon my giveing you a description of all the pleasant parties we have been at lately, in the country at Mr. Rhinelanders, I cannot exactly tell you in what the pleasures of the afternoon chiefly consisted, whether it was throwing one another down a steep hill or wet grass (a diversion which they seemed highly delighted with), or despoiling poor Mr. Rhinelanders Green house plants of all their beauties, and pelting each other with flowers? it is difficult for to determin, they seemed so equally pleased with each of these most refined amusements, 'thinks I to myself' I had better describe them both, and then he can judge for himself, I knew you would equally approve of them. The gayety of this scene was not a little hightened, by the good natured appearance of the red nose and jolly face of the Laird of the sugarhouse, constantly telling us to make ourselves as happy as we could, to which as you may suppose, we gave ready assent, and dutiful obediance. Now my dear Brother I must tell you of our yesterdays party, at Wards Island. You will laugh and shake in such a manner, if you can make out to understand my blundering description, this party, you must know, was given by old judge Benson, he particularly invited a number of ladies and Gentleman, my *consequencial* self included, to tea there, of course we all went highly delighted, and determined, to enjoy ourselves as much as possible, and so we did, Isabella and myself did not behave exactly as the rest did, for the sage Mr. Irving was of our party, and we considered ourselve in some measure, as in the presence of a grand Inquisitor, you know he detests all kinds of romping, as well as your literary self. he is the meekest man, I ever knew, he is the very counterpart of Moses *himself*—he thinks no more of *himself,* than the grand sultan of the East thinks of *himself.* My dear Brother I am only in *fun.* bless me!"

Further on in the same letter Margaret tells her brother Henry of the marriage of Mary Fairlie to Cooper the actor, although she does not give him details of the ceremony, which was unattended by the bride's parents (objectors to the match), and witnessed by only a few friends who, even as Irving himself, felt that no great happiness was to follow the fortunes of this ill-mated pair. Here too Margaret writes in her characteristically amusing manner of James Madison's vacillation in regard to war with England: "I had almost in my mania for babling forgotten to tell you that Aunt Dean was with us. All your friends are well, Mary Fairly is Married to Mr. Cooper and they are gone to spend their Summer, in the delightful cool climate of Carolina. The Governor says he intends calling all his officers in and shall shortly send a dispatch for the absent *Colonel*. They say war is seriously threatning us, but it dont trouble me much, for as sure as we hear of war one day, we are certain of hearing of peace the next. Our President fits are at present exactly similar to the ague and fever, I heartily wish I could administer a good dose of bark, to bring him to his own mind."

In another June letter of Margaret's (but this time in 1813, when her brother Henry was in Europe) there is a delectable reference to old Henry Brevoort, that great old fellow who wouldn't allow the City Fathers to cut a street in front of his dwelling, so that even to our own day the only missing street in New York is the one that should exist between Broadway and Fourth Avenue at Eleventh Street: "You say I must tell you how our dear Father looks what he says you will find but little alteration at your return he stoops a little more, and his hair is a little whiter, his nose is almost well and he is in perfect health, and quite happy, save now and then, a cloud of care passes over his face, when he thinks of the fate of his country he says things dont go on as they should something is wrong at the head, and he fears we are in a bad way, he dont understand these newfangled doings, our government is made up of upstarts, whose heads are as empty as calabashes, people dont do as they used to in old times & & &."

This same letter is rich in its references not only to Irving himself, but also to the Kembles, the Renwicks and the Hoffmans and to others in the social circle where Irving was most intimate. "Dear Mrs. Renwick, what shall I say of her; she is every thing that's good and amiable, my letters are never half red or enjoyed until she reads them with me she almost jumps for joy whenever we get one from you & really seems to feel the same satisfaction that an affectionate mother would who was blessed with such a son; When Uncle E. gets one he gives some part of it to Mr. Irving from him it goes to Mrs. Renwick from her to me and then to the owner mine go the rounds as regularly. I was at Mrs. R, when I received your last to Father & Mother, I absolutely could scarcely get sight of it there was such fighting, & boxing (I would have given any thing had you been behind the curtain), there was Mr. Irving flourishing about with his cane banging Isabella and myself as if we had been two little sticks and not Miss R and Miss B while we are fighting who shall read first Mrs. R finds some snug corner where she sits and reads the whole letter without the least interruption. . . Mr. Irving has grown quite a beauty, I told him so the other day at our house thinking it would have a tendency to make him very civil but I was mistaken, he's not a bit better than before. his face is not clouded with care as formerly he says he would be perfectly happy if his wife was here; who do you think that is? a wandering *Poet,* who was formerly seen in America, but he has taken his departure to a more congenial clime, in order to perfect himself in his profession; there's great suspicions entertained of him here, we actually heard he was to be married to some *great* scotch lass, this report has made the afore said husband extremely uneasy, and I really heard his mother say she would turn the vagrant out of doors if he offered to bring any of his high cheek bones here,—so if you should chance to meet with him in your travels, do for humanity's sake give the poor fellow a gentle hint respecting home affairs."

Irving's letters of this period to his "wife" are almost as gossipy, and in their own way as amusing as Margaret's. He writes of convivial parties, and midnight serenades. He loves to discuss the girl friends of Brevoort and himself. One of them is "like an ortolan, too rare and costly a dainty for a poor man to afford, but were I a nabob, 'fore George, ortolans should be my only food." Another "cannot enjoy her own chastity but seems unwilling to let anybody else do it"; and the doings of the beaux, as well as the belles, of old New York—especially in the letter of July 8th, 1812—are the subject of his sprightly pen.

In August, accompanied by James Renwick, Irving went up to Gouverneur Kemble's home in the Highlands, and then for a week was a guest of John R. Livingston where he made several delightful excursions in the company of attractive women. He was again, for the time being, a young man of elegant leisure— a happy rogue, as he calls himself, up to the ears in "an ocean of peacocks feathers"—or rather like a "strawberry smothered in cream." Obviously his brothers, hard at work in New York, did not make many demands on him, and the subsequent visit to Washington, where Irving was successful in regard to the petition of the merchants, closed a summer of pleasant social doings.

The next year, and a portion of 1814, he was the anonymous editor of the *Analectic Magazine*. Editing itself proved irksome work, and he derived no enjoyment from reviewing writings of others, mainly because he was inherently averse to saying anything unfavourable. Where he could speak in terms of praise, as in the short biographies of Commodore Oliver Perry, Captain James Lawrence, and Irving's old friend and fellow-lodger, Captain David Porter, he was in vein; although these naval biographical papers contributed to the *Analectic Magazine* are of less significance than those on "Traits of Indian Character" and "Philip of Pokanoket" that were afterwards included in "The Sketch Book."

Irving's interest in the Indian nations, originally stimulated by his brother William's adventures, was increased by Brevoort's letters from the Great Lakes, missives whose finest note is found in the young fur merchant's indignation at the wrongs to which the Indian tribes were subjected by the American Government.

82

The Indians had previously been recognized as an independent people, with laws of their own, the relationship between them and the United States being entirely governed by treaties. Thus while cruel and often illegal acts had been committed against the Indians by the early settlers, and even the fair-minded Thomas Jefferson had so yielded to his countrymen's desire to acquire Indian lands as to condone deeds of questionable barter, there had been no clear infraction of the sovereignty of the Indian nations prior to those regulations concerning the admission of goods from England for their use and the preceding exaction of duties on European imports which had begun under Jefferson. Deprived of their usual supplies, the Indian nations on the Great Lakes and in the valley of Mississippi, protested in forcible speeches against what they called "this invasion of their natural rights." Several of these addresses of protest Brevoort forwarded to Irving, asking him to see to their newspaper publication. In eloquent terms Brevoort refers to the wrongs done to the Indians, contrasting the attitude of the British Government in its benefactions towards various tribes with that of our own Government. He quotes the words of an Indian chief who was answering a claim regarding a stolen horse. The chief asks: "What right have you to obtain your horse? Do you ask our liberty to come into our Forrests and kill our Deer, to bait your hooks and spread your nets in our rivers and lakes, to take our fish? You first set us the example of stealing and when we follow it, you have the effrontry to reprimand us and ask satisfaction." Then the chief goes on to say that, notwithstanding this, the stolen horse shall be returned, the theft having been the act of one of their foolish young men not always subject to control, "but we caution you to beware of the future . . . We caution you not to do as others of your nation have done—to purchase our lands for a trifle of some drunken worthless individuals of our tribe, and make us all responsible for their acts."

Irving at once shared Brevoort's generous attitude of mind towards those original Americans whose treatment on the part of the immigrant Americans remains a blot on our national escutcheon. It was not only characteristic of him to feel sympathy for the under dog, as is shown by his partial condonation of Aaron Burr when that former Vice-President of the United States was on trial, and his noble words concerning Napoleon Bonaparte when that commanding hero was at the mercy of the contemptible Prince Regent: Irving's sympathy for the Indians had in it also the positive quality of admiration for their virtues of courage and of silence. And to this should be added the glamour surrounding these dwellers of the great plains and the great forests, these guardians of great legends, these children of the sun and the rain, and of the immemorial stars. Thus in the early papers which he published in the magazine whereof he was the editor, and published once again in "The Sketch Book"; and, years later, in his "Tour on the Prairies" and in the separate papers written for the *Knickerbocker Magazine,* Irving showed some of the finest traits of his own nature in acting as the defender, interpreter, and to some extent the historian of the American Indians. The defamation of Indian character—that they were liars, drunkards, thieves, he portrayed in its true light as either an inexcusable method of particular attack, or as an argument of defence, unworthy in view of those actions of white men that had brought into being the conditions making inevitable the gradual degeneration of Indian character. Nowhere is Irving more fearless than in his writings concerning the Indians, and it is almost as much to be regretted that he did not become far more fully their historian as it is to be regretted that Henry D. Thoreau left unwritten that record of the Indian nations for which, in eleven manuscript volumes that still remain practically unknown, he collected the material. Henry Brevoort also thought of writing such a history, and so did Walter Scott. One fancies that Irving's would have been the most meditative; Scott's the most vivid; Thoreau's the most trenchantly noble, and certainly nearest akin to Indian character itself.

If Irving owed a considerable debt to Henry Brevoort for

having aroused this deep interest in the Indian nations, he owed him a still greater debt for the intellectually stimulating qualities of the letters Brevoort sent him from Europe in 1812 and 1813, and perhaps the largest debt of all for having introduced the writings of Irving to Walter Scott, thus laying the foundation for the friendship in later years between Scott and Irving. While attending lectures at the University of Edinburgh in 1812–1813, Brevoort became a welcome member of that group of men of letters and of scholars including Jeffrey, the editor of the *Edinburgh Review,* Mackenzie the philosopher, Wilson (better known as "Christopher North"), and Professor Playfair, the great teacher of natural philosophy. Later in London, Brevoort met Thomas Campbell, Sir James Mackintosh the historian, Madame D'Arblay, Mrs. Barbauld, Joanna Baillie. To all of these he advertised the excellence of "Knickerbocker's History," which especially aroused the admiration of Walter Scott. Then, too, Brevoort became on friendly terms with Charles Kemble, and of him, of Mrs. Siddons, of John Howard Payne and others in the world of the drama he sent Irving tidings, so that, all told, these thoroughly well-written letters of Irving's friend and room-mate brought him into touch with the brains and the genius of Great Britain. They whetted Irving's appetite for a second visit to Europe, and the letters of introduction that Brevoort later gave Irving were an important factor in the immediacy with which Irving himself was welcomed into the friendship of many notable authors.

But before the time arrived for Irving's entrance into the intellectual coterie of Great Britain both he and Brevoort were to take their parts in the conflict between that nation and ours. Irving felt deep regret when the War of 1812 became inevitable, and so did young Brevoort; but neither of the two friends was wanting in patriotism, and before the struggle terminated Irving became the Aide-de-Camp (with the title of Colonel) of Daniel D. Tompkins, while Brevoort received from the same Governor of the State of New York his commission as First Lieutenant in the artillery company known as the Iron Greys. It seems strange to picture the gentle pleasure-loving young author in the uniform of a Colonel, and to see him, in 1814, at Sackett's Harbor on Lake Champlain ordering out a considerable reinforcement of militia as protection against an expected attack of the British forces.   There is, however, no record of his sharing in any bloody encounter.   Irving's most heroic action would seem to have been in connection with services rendered to his chief when, on one occasion, Governor Tompkins, despite his imposing titles of "General and Commander in Chief of all the Militia, and Admiral of the Navy of the State of New York," fell off his horse.   In February, 1815 the American victory at New Orleans was soon followed by tidings of peace, and Irving, whose career as a magazine editor had terminated with the failure, the preceding month, of the *Analectic* was now through with his military duties.   The war had left him in no mood to resume his role of *flaneur* in his little social group; he lacked the energy to increase the fame brought him by "Knickerbocker's History"; nominally the hardware merchant, he was actually just a talented, charming, restless young fellow, wondering what to do next.

Chapter V

LIGHT AND SHADOW

IT was thus not so much as the man of business, the junior partner in a commercial firm, as the lover of travel, the still sufficiently indolent young man of pleasure, that Washington Irving sailed for Europe on the 25th of May, 1815. He had looked forward to accepting the invitation of his friend, Commodore Decatur, to go on a Mediterranean cruise on the frigate, the *Guerrière,* but after Irving's trunks had been taken on board, a slight complication seems to have arisen, due to changes in naval plans on account of Napoleon's escape from Elba, and Irving, with his characteristic sensibility, decided that he had better not avail himself of Decatur's offer. But he could not bring himself to the thought of foregoing a visit to Europe. Five days after the departure of the American fleet, he left his native shores for an absence that was to stretch into the undreamed-of period of seventeen years.

Not the Mediterranean, but England where his brother Peter was conducting at Liverpool the affairs of their firm, became his first objective. Washington was still the favoured younger brother, and while he intended to give a casual glance at the affairs of the business in whose profits he shared, new pleasures, intellectual rather than social, were the figures that he hoped to set down in the ledger of his travels. He felt the need of a freshening of the spirit.

There is no commonplace more trite than that which points out the vagaries of fortune in her seemingly irresponsible distribution of the ills and joys of life. We all are aware of those contrasts, drastic as light and shadow in a painting by Rembrandt, which show a genius turned maniac, a millionaire be-

87

come a pauper, a Napoleon at St. Helena. Yet how can a biographer, as he approaches the darkest chapter in Irving's life, escape from suggesting that here is, not the saddest in the record of American literary history, but the most unexpected of such contrasts? The boon companion of pleasure-loving young men, the popular, widely-read author, the family favourite, the welcome visitor in the chief cities of his land, this delightful fellow who really has never had to work at all, and who has gone his way loved by men and women, playing with little children, writing only when he feels in the mood, is now soon to be a downcast, almost penniless, commercial drudge in a foreign city. But before entering into scenes and circumstances so far removed from the punch-drinking days at Cockloft Hall and the brilliant levées at President Madison's, there still remains a brief interval of enjoyment wherein to accompany our hero.

After arriving in England early in July, Irving remained in Liverpool for a week with his brother Peter who was already suffering from that ill health which was to make him an invalid throughout life. The two brothers, despite a seven years' separation, had always remained very fond of one another, and the kindnesses which the elder had shown the younger in taking him into his firm and, previous to that, in encouraging him in his literary work, Irving was to repay in full measure. Indeed, the long years in Europe were due in great part to his desire of remaining a companion to the invalid, although the main, and hitherto unrecorded motive, was his passion for Emily Foster.

From Liverpool Washington proceeded to the home of his sister Sarah at Birmingham, where, in the summer months of 1815, there was as yet little thought of the hardships in which all the Irvings were later to be involved. The Baron and Baroness Van Tromp (as Washington with his whimsical love of nicknames dubbed the Van Warts) presided over a happy household whose chief brightness flowed from the children. Immediately they took their new uncle from America into their merry little hearts. "The boys are noble little fellows, very good humoured"; while Irving's little god-daughter, named after Matilda Hoffman, "is a sweet playful child" and baby Mary Ann a darling. Telling stories, playing games, teasing in that delightful manner whereof we have had a hint in Margaret Brevoort's letters, Washington immediately became much younger and happier in the company of his sister's children. Then too, and as immediately, he was delighted with England. The War of 1812 had only for the moment interfered with his affection and admiration for the land of Milton and Shakespeare. On the voyage over, Irving's warmest friends had been two British officers, Sir William Williams and Major Hancock, officers who were gentlemen enough to deprecate those British excesses in the city of Washington which had so aroused the indignation of all Americans. And then, too, it should be remembered that England resented the War of 1812 much more than did the United States. The English felt that at a time when they were defending the liberty of Europe against the tyranny of Napoleon, the aid indirectly given to Napoleon by the Americans (of the English race, the English tradition, and professed lovers of liberty) was, whatever may have been those Orders in Council temporarily interfering with the freedom of the seas, an injury not easily to be forgotten, especially as it had come when England needed all her resources to defeat the Corsican luster after world dominion.

Sarah Van Wart, or "Sallie," as Washington called her (her husband Henry being "Hal" to him), was the youngest of the Irving girls, and thus nearest in age to Irving himself. After his years of bachelor living with Henry Brevoort, he was now again renewing associations of the old home in William Street, without any of the restrictions there imposed by the stern and depressing influence of their father the Deacon. Even so, Irving was too greatly the wanderer to settle down, until much later in life, into the quietness of any domestic circle, however attractive. Before the month of July was up he set forth, with James Renwick as his companion, first to Kenilworth, Warwick and Stratford, and then on a fortnight's tour through Wales.

The two days spent in seeing the most famous of English castles and Shakespeare's town are not described in any Life of Irving, but, fortunately, from a very long letter to Jane Renwick (among a number printed for private distribution by her great-grand-daughter, Agnes Adams), there is obtainable an insight into the merry mood that animated Irving during the early part of his second visit to England. After preparing their maps and purchasing sketch-books as well as guide-books he and the Laird—this being his nickname for Professor James—set forth on their jaunt. At the inn at Stonebridge, some ten miles further on, the objects which most aroused the enthusiasm of Irving and Renwick were a cold duck bought for later consumption, and a coach dog that shared their luncheon "with a condescension and familiarity that delighted us." The name engraved on the dog's collar showed that he belonged to a Lady Curtis, and Irving twitted young Renwick concerning the aristocratic circles with which the dog, this "sprig of nobility," now associated them. In more serious vein he records thoughts of feudal grandeur aroused by the impressive ruins of Kenilworth, but lapses again into the lighter mood when, on the ride to Warwick, pretty country lasses "kiss their hands to us in the true style of ancient chivalry"; and he writes that if he had not providentially caught young James by the skirts of his coat "he would have either flown back to these alluring syrens—or have tumbled into the ditch." At the Warwick Arms, where the two travellers are given a very poor room, with no wax candles, and with a chair that breaks down when Irving sits on it, he teases Renwick on realizing that their humiliating reception is due to the "ill-starred fit of thriftiness" shown by the professor who had failed to give the customary sixpence to the post boy that had brought them to the house. Irving's fineness of mood in romantic surroundings is again called forth in picturesque language when they come to Warwick Castle itself; but it is still the merry fellow who notices that, as he and his companion are ascending the steep stairs leading to the Donjon Keep, Renwick is a little too intent on some ladies who are preceding them, and Irving comments with humour on his young friend's later observation that these ladies were Scotch—although not a word had been spoken by them to indicate their nationality!

The next day was given over to Stratford where Irving experienced "almost indescribable emotions" on visiting the room where Shakespeare was born and on seeing the place where his bones lie interred. Seventeen years later, shortly before the end of his so long deferred return to his native country, Irving again visited Warwick and Kenilworth and Stratford in the company of Martin Van Buren and his son; putting up in Stratford at the Red Horse where he again found the little landlady who had so pleased him on an intermediate visit and who figures in his description of Stratford-on-Avon, one of the most delightful of "The Sketch Book" papers. An engraving of Irving decorated her walls, and one of her proud possessions was a poker with which he had stirred the fire, and which was now engraved "Geoffrey Crayon's sceptre."—But we are running ahead of our narrative, for "Geoffrey Crayon" was not to come into being until adversity had ended the career of the hardware merchant and had forced Irving into the profession of authorship.

The journal that he kept of the tour in Wales is the one diary written by Irving during his first four years in Europe; or at least, I know of no other. There is a certain pathos to it, in the retrospect, not merely because it is the record of the only thoroughly joyous weeks of adventure in those years, but also because it so clearly reveals the talents and the receptivities which were, under the stress of necessity, so long to lie fallow.

In a post-chaise the two young Americans set forth from Birmingham, the weather "uncommonly beautiful." Six miles out they visited the Leasowes where the eighteenth century poet William Shenstone had lived; and then, another six miles further, the noble estate of Lord Lyttelton, in his day a great patron of literature. The old church at Kidderminster they passed, and thence to the Cathedral at Worcester where the old sexton told Irving stories concerning the tombs. The next evening, at Cheltenham, they saw Mrs. Edwin (the popular actress Eliza Rebecca Richards) take the part of Miss Mandeville in that once famous play, "The Will." From the tower of Gloucester Cathedral they saw the Severn winding through its hill-flanked valley; and here Irving's sense of humour was delighted by the queer stories and jokes of another old sexton, and his interest in history stimulated by the tombs of Edward II and of Robert, son of William the Conqueror. Through various picturesque villages with the note of old Gothic, they drove until the Roman antiquities at Bath met their view; and at Bath the evening went by in their witnessing a melodrama. At Bristol Irving and Renwick visited the room (in the church of St. Mary Radcliffe) where Chatterton claimed that he had found the papers of the fifteenth century priest and poet Thomas Rowley, those curious forgeries by Chatterton which were exposed by Thomas Gray after Horace Walpole had received them from the younger poet. Chepstow Castle, its walls covered with ivy, and Tintern Abbey (we all recall Wordsworth's poem) delight Irving who notes that the surrounding scenery is "similar to the glens in the Hudson Highlands." Monmouth Castle, where Henry V was born; Wilson Castle, opposite to the village of Ross, where lived John Curl, the philanthropist immortalized by Alexander Pope; Ludlow Castle where, on Michelmas Night, 1634, Milton's "Comus" was first presented as "A Mask"; Shrewsbury Castle—all capture Irving with their romance and their beauty, so that he has recourse not only to the pencil of the writer but also to the pencil of the artist, in a series of drawings that bring to mind his fugitive ambition when, in 1805 at Rome, he visited the studio of Washington Allston.

His constant interest in the female sex led to various notations, as where we find him observing at Ellesmere "a lovely girl about eighteen," "in cream coloured house opposite the

Conwy Castle

DRAWING BY IRVING OF CONWAY CASTLE IN WALES

principal street by which you entered" and immediately thereafter "a very pretty girl," the landlady's daughter at Wrexham. A little further on, at Llangollen, he describes Lady Eleanor Butler, "in her flimsy muslin pelisse" and is much interested in that eccentric recluse who appears in the pages of De Quincey. The peasantry at market day; the old harpers playing on their instruments; wild precipices along romantic roads; the owls and bats in the towers of Conway Castle; interesting individuals that he meets at dinner, and so contrasting in their manners as a Cornish miner and the Master of Rugby, are material for his eager pencil, which also wanders often into references to, or recountals of, old legends, such as that of Llewellyn who caused to be publicly hanged the paramour of his wife, notwithstanding the fact that she was the daughter of King John; or another story of Llewellyn who slew in error his greyhound Cilian, believing that the dog had killed his child. Scenes of humour enter these pages, whimsical situations where an entire family is busy "coaxing and banging some refractory hog that will go any way but forward," or where a cart horse refuses to carry the travellers further. Irving and Renwick were in gay and romantic spirits, ready for all kinds of fun, and the mood wherein the Welsh tour was undertaken is indicated in a letter which, two days before setting out, Irving wrote to Jane Renwick, and where he states that he may pass himself off "for a young American nobleman" travelling with his tutor.

Come to think of it, this is probably the most deliciously whimsical thought that Irving ever had. The present writer, if he may for a moment interject his own personality, knows from a youthful experience at Niagara Falls when, fur-capped and blond-bearded, he was a Swedish nobleman and his two young companions passed as English baronets, what fun and what privileges aristocratic titles can bring in the land of democracy; but to travel as "an American nobleman"—who, excepting Washington Irving, ever had so original an idea? He may have adapted it from those days in France when he was introduced to the landlady as a young Mameluke, the eccentric Dr. Henry being his supposed tutor and companion.   But Dr. Henry was the older man of the two, while here Irving schedules James Renwick, his junior by nine years, as the tutor, not only, it may be thought, because Renwick had, in 1812, at the age of twenty, temporarily filled the chair of Professor of Natural Philosophy at Columbia (a professorship which he was later to hold for thirty-three years) but also because the fun-loving Irving felt himself qualified to adopt the younger rôle.

The capacity for enjoyment, so delightfully shown in these records of his excursions with Renwick, remained largely undimmed during the rest of the year 1815.   Irving's letters to his brothers, and notably to Henry Brevoort, reveal him taking pleasure in the purchase of books—he sends a copy of Byron's "Hebrew Melodies" to Miss Bradish, the daughter of his old New York landlady; chuckling at a description of Algerian affairs by "that worthy tar, Jack Nicholson"; visiting the home of Thomas Campbell at Sydenham, where Mrs. Campbell related anecdotes of Scott who, recently caught up in the failure of the Ballantynes, is not yet positively known as the author of "Waverley"; witnessing the performances of Miss O'Neil, "the most soul-subduing actress I ever saw"; and taking a lively interest in the acts of the British Cabinet towards Napoleon who, "in spite of all his misdeeds is a noble fellow," one who will, in Irving's opinion, far outshine his opponents in the eyes of posterity.   At Liverpool he meets old friends—Peter Ogden, with whom he used to carouse at the home of Gouverneur Kemble, and Charles King, later President of Columbia College, who is described by Irving in terms that impel quotation, so remarkably are they applicable to Irving himself.   "He is exactly what an American should be abroad—frank, manly and unaffected in his habits and manners, liberal and independent in his opinions, generous and unprejudiced in his sentiments towards other nations, but most loyally attached to his own."   This encomium comes with all the more interest in a letter to Brevoort, as the preceding letter had recorded Irving's humorous impatience with other types of

94

Americans of whom he met so many in England, and of whom he wrote: "Nothing can surpass the dauntless independence of all form, ceremony, fashion or regulation of a downright, unsophisticated American. It would delight you to see some of them playing Indians when surrounded by the wonders and improvements of the Old World." Irving had much pride in Robert Fulton's invention and had been one of the first to travel on the Hudson by steamboat, but he could not think (or, at least thinking, would not say as so many of his compatriots did), that all other mechanical improvements were "eclipsed and annihilated by an American Steam Boat." He would not, for all that devotion to American scenery which is so important to consider in estimating his services as our first man of letters, agree to call the Welsh mountains "mole hills to the Alleghany."

But interest in statesmanship, in the drama, in meeting new friends, gradually grew less when the winter months of 1816 brought increasing hardships to the Irving firm. By March things had come to a pass where the bills could not have been met had not young Renwick opened up credit for Peter and Washington. Peter was too ill to get to the office, and Irving had to hold the fort alone, inexperienced, harassed, his mercurial spirits fast approaching the freezing mark of despondency.

To only one person, Henry Brevoort, does he with frank fullness reveal the extent of his depression during those two years—1816 and 1817—when commercial misery held England so tightly in its grasp. Brevoort was his confidant, his refuge. Irving tells him how his heart is yearning towards New York, and the happy circle of friendships whereof he was so welcome a segment; he tells him of his reluctance to form new acquaintants; of his loneliness; of "times so hard that they sicken my very soul." He advises Brevoort to get married, and confesses that he himself has long hankered after marriage, for without it "you are like a bark without an anchor, that drifts about at the mercy of every vagrant breeze." Month by month his depression continues, increases. He writes: "It is not long since I felt myself quite sure of fortune's smiles, and began to entertain what I thought very sober and rational schemes for my future comfort and establishment. At present, I feel so tempest tossed and weather beaten that I shall be content to be quits with everything for a very moderate portion." If, "now and then a little gleam of sunshine" lightens his "painful miserable kind of life" it is "always sure to be followed by redoubled gloom"; but he adds in another letter "Do not imagine I suffer myself to be broken down and unmanned by complicated evils. I have made up my mind to them and indeed grown familiar with them by dismal anticipation. . . . The heart is competent to digest its own sorrows." Homesick and depressed though Irving often is during these early years in England he remains "solemnly convinced that there is a wise and good Providence that over-rules our destinies and directs everything for the best."

It could not have been easy in those days in England to have faith in a kind Providence. Men were working for a few pennies a day—a twelve hours' day at that. People were dying of hunger, and the appeals of a desperate population were met by a government whose main resource was coercion. The terrific cost to England of the Napoleonic wars, with its consequence of huge taxation; the failure of crops; the unemployment among men who had been in the army and the navy; the cessation of munition industries, all led to a chaos of misery bringing in its train unhappy seditions that the monopolists who controlled the government, and even the less interested statesmen frightened by the spectre of the French Revolution, sought to check by ruthless methods. The sensitive Irving was thus caught up in a crisis of national despair, and of personal hardships. As, harassed, he walks the quays of King's Dock and Queen's Dock in the shipping town of Liverpool, it is a far cry from the days of boyhood dreams on the docks of the Hudson, and the happy times of fêted youth.

In May, 1817, Henry Van Wart went into bankruptcy, and Irving could even then see the handwriting on the wall as far as his own firm was concerned. Brevoort was urging him to return to America, and Irving was indeed longing for home. "Nothing but my wish to be with Peter and relieve the loneliness of his life would induce me to remain an hour in this place," he had, at Liverpool, on March 24th, written to Brevoort. Loyalty was one of the main tenets in Irving's creed; and when, a month or two later, his mother died, the termination of the "one strong inducement that was continually tugging at my heart," made him all the more resolved to remain at his desperate task in England. Nor was he willing to be a drag on his comparatively few affluent friends at home; nor willing to witness the hardships of other friends without being able to aid them. "If I must scuffle with poverty let me do it out of sight."

With the proceedings in bankruptcy of the Irving firm in the early months of 1818 the business cares by which Washington had been "bowed down in spirit" for over two years came to an end. Brought up in a simple, economical household, Irving could the more easily become accustomed to the idea of poverty, and he now worried far more on behalf of his brothers than because of himself. Peter is a bachelor, and it is the situation of Ebenezer and his family that gives him most anxious thought. So he writes to Brevoort asking him to come to the aid of Ebenezer whose failure was due to uncontrollable circumstances and not to any lack of capacity, honesty, and indefatigability. A noble letter, the letter of a large-hearted gentleman, closing with the phrase: "I hope to find future good springing out of these present adversities."

Though few and far between there had, as Irving wrote, been little gleams of sunshine during this dark period. At Buxton, a watering-place where Irving went to spend a few days with the invalid Peter towards the end of 1816, he found amusement in the curious characters at the hotel. In his description of them there is seen his old ability at individual picturization. For instance, the old fellow who "had but one serviceable joint in his body which is at the bottom of the backbone, and that creaked and grated whenever he bent. He could not raise his feet from the ground, but skated along the drawing room carpet whenever he wished to ring the bell." Brevoort had written an account to Irving of an old New York lady with very brief nether garments, and from the hotel at Buxton Irving replies that "this fashion of short skirts must have been invented by the French ladies as a complete trick upon John Bull's women folk," for it had been introduced when, after Napoleon's downfall, the English were going in great numbers to Paris where the women have pretty feet and ankles while "the English are remarkable for the contrary."

At Birmingham, in January, 1817, Irving and his sister Sarah still have some happy hours with her "uncommonly fine children," and there is "a grand game of romps in the evening, between dinner and tea time," in the course of which the little girls dance while the American uncle plays the flute. The children consider him "the divinest musician in the world." Yet what pathos there is in Irving's mention of the flute, for he took lessons in this instrument as a distraction in hours "when I could not read and dared not think"; and though he humorously writes that he now begins "to know one end of the instrument from the other," the thought of Irving driven to this resource is one of strange appeal. Not even London, where in July, 1817 he spent three weeks, meeting Murray the bookseller, and finding a sympathetic acquaintance in Isaac D'Israeli, "a cheerful, social old gentleman, full of talk and anecdote," could distract him much, and the only two events of that year which temporarily raised his spirits were an excursion on the banks of the Dove, and a visit to Scotland, with W. C. Preston, later Senator from South Carolina. The former of these outings, when Washington and Peter were in the company of Sir Thomas and Lady Williams, Sir Francis Ford and the Misses Bathurst ("three lovely girls"), was much like those which Washington so revelled in when a gay party would go picnicing in the Hudson Highlands. "The path through the dale was urged and beset with petty hazard." There resulted those

98

"relative situations which endear the sexes. I had woman, lovely woman! clinging to me for assistance and protection." For a few brief hours the impoverished young merchant is again "in Elysium," and as the whole merry party takes refuge from a rain storm and has dinner in St. Mary's Cave, the singing, the country dance by the girl who carried the provisions, the ballads and anecdotes, drive away all dreary thought.

But the outstanding days of recreation were those in Scotland. Perhaps as an inheritance from his father who in youth had followed the sea, Irving was always in high spirits on shipboard. As he sailed, on the way to Edinburgh, close by the ruins of Bamborough Castle and the Holy Isle which Scott made the scene of the trial of Constance de Beverly, Irving's feelings were joyfully excited. At Edinburgh he met not alone that Mr. Jeffrey who, as Jane Renwick's brother, was especially glad to see him, but also met again (they had become acquainted in America) the great Mr. Jeffrey, Francis Jeffrey, whose caustic pen in the pages of the *Edinburgh Review* often determined the fame of men of letters. An "amiable and pleasant man in his own house," Irving thinks him, and is pleased with various of the important people of Edinburgh whom he meets there. But the great event was to come a few days later when Irving visited Scott at Abbotsford where he was welcomed with "the genial hospitality of the olden-times" and where he felt as if he were "at the social board of an old friend." This visit to Abbotsford is described in one of the loveliest of Irving's papers in "The Crayon Miscellany." The rambles around the country with Scott and his dogs; the melodies (reminiscent of Lizzie in William Street) sung by the daughters of the household; the anecdotes of Walter Scott the sheriff who so humanly administered the laws of his office; the little cabinet of curiosities with its blood-stained manuscript songs (picked up on the field of Waterloo), of, as Scott said, very possibly some gay young officer who had cherished them as a keepsake from some lady-love in Paris; the whimsical legends recounted by his host, all served to render these few days ever memorable for Irving. There and then was founded that friendship between the two men which reflects such honour on both. "I came prepared to admire him," Irving wrote to Brevoort, "but he completely won my heart and made me love him"; while Scott shortly thereafter wrote to his friend John Richardson: "When you see Tom Campbell, tell him with my best love, that I have to thank him for making me known to Mr. Washington Irving, who is one of the best and pleasantest acquaintances I have met this many a day." So immediately taken was Scott by Irving that, in introducing him to Hector MacDonald Buchanan, the Laird of Ross Priory, Scott, the Laird of Abbotsford, calls Irving his particular friend. "A particular friend of mine Mr. Washington Irving from New York makes a tour of the Highlands with Mr. Preston a friend of his," we find Scott writing in a letter which has never before found its way into print, "and if he should find you at Ross may I beg for them the hospitality of the Priory, and in turn you may draw on me in favor of any of your friends coming our way and put this trouble in accompt between our two liens Loch Lomond Crer to Melrose Abbey."

During these days in Scotland, with his journey to Edinburgh "by chaise, by coach, by gig, by boat, and in a cart," Irving's only serious difficulty seems to have been to persuade his companion, the twenty-three year old South Carolinian, to get up early in the morning—and if Washington Irving considered a companion indolent he must have been indolent indeed. But when one recalls the later career of William C. Preston, that statesman and orator is readily forgiven for whatever laziness he may have evinced during the holidays of his youth; and especially the world of letters should be grateful to him for his services in the initial stages of international copyright, a subject in which he was perhaps the first to interest Irving. Twenty years later, in 1837, Irving writes to him—in another letter hitherto remaining unpublished, and sent in reply to Preston's request for his opinion on the topic: "I am in favor of the extension of our Law of Copyright to all countries that allow our authors the same right. It is proper to enquire whether this will apply

My dear Hector

 A particular friend of mine Mr Washington Irving from Newyork makes a tour of the Highlands with Mr Preston a friend of his — if he should find you at Ross may I beg for them the hospitality of the Priory & in return you may draw on me in favour of any of your friends coming our way & put this trouble an accompt between our two deus Lochdemend Crer to Melrose Abbey. I hope you intend to come here yourself when on duty: you can easily start for a day or two as Brother David will be a fixture Kind Love to Mrs Buchanan & the nephews & nieces

   Affectionately yours
    Walter

Abbotsford
1st Sept

WALTER SCOTT'S LETTER OF INTRODUCTION
FOR IRVING

to France, whose English editions of our works are pirated without any benefit to the authors. As to England, I think the interest of both her authors and of American authors would be benefited by the extension to her of this law."

The enjoyable Scotch tour ended, Irving returned to Liverpool where he was at first made melancholy by the news of Brevoort's engagement to Miss Carson of South Carolina. "Marriage is the grave of Bachelor's intimacy, and after having lived and grown together for many years, so that our habits, thoughts and feelings were quite banded and intertwined, a separation of this kind is a serious matter." But the friendship between the two was to remain, Brevoort's services continuing at Irving's disposal, and Irving's affection steadfast. When, a quarter of a century later, he set forth as the American Minister to Spain, it was Brevoort's son Carson who accompanied him as attaché.

In America, during the summer months of 1817, William Irving, then a member of Congress, was trying to obtain government situations for both Washington and Peter, and had personal meetings with Henry Clay in this connection. He failed to get the Secretaryship of Legation at the Court of St. James for his youngest brother, but he did, the next year, succeed in having Decatur hold open for Washington the office of First Clerk in the Navy Department, with a salary that was to equal about twenty-four hundred dollars a year. Much to the disappointment of both William and Ebenezer, Washington declined the appointment. He had previously written to William: "In protracting my stay in Europe I certainly do not contemplate pleasure, for I look forward to a life of loneliness and of parsimonious and almost painful economy"; but both then, and later, he determinedly adhered to the desire to work out his own career, somewhere and somehow in the field of literature. His first plan was to become, as it were, a literary agent: his idea was to make arrangements in London for the American publication of English authors. But this came to nothing, and after the bankruptcy proceedings of his firm were concluded in March

1818 Irving gradually gathered up sufficient self-confidence to decide that his own talents as an author should furnish him his livelihood.

The diffidence and modesty of Washington Irving in matters of self-appraisal were traits that, however much they may have added to his winningness as a personality, however considerable an asset they were in his acceptability among persons of greatness and near greatness who found in this reticent young American an ever willing listener, were, in the main, elements of drawback as far as his career as a whole is concerned. Not only did his shyness and lack of self-confidence make it almost impossible for him to speak in public, but they placed him at a great disadvantage at the most precarious phase of his life. It is open to question whether he could have embarked successfully on the channel of letters had he not been the recipient of cordial encouragement from friends of importance whose judgment necessarily meant much to him. Even so, more than a year of non-accomplishment went by between two such letters as that of James Ogilvie, the eloquent lecturer and critic with whom Irving had become acquainted during his visit to the United States in 1809, and that of Washington Allston, written in July, 1818. "I am perfectly confident," wrote Ogilvie, "that even in two years you will look back on this seeming disaster as the most fortunate incident that has befallen you. Yet in the flower of youth, in possession of higher literary reputation than any of your countrymen have hitherto claimed, esteemed and beloved by all to whom you are intimately or even casually known, you want nothing but a stimulus strong enough to overcome that indolence which, in greater or less degree, besets every human being." A remarkable prophecy this; and, similarly, Allston—a man who was loved and revered by Irving ever since their early meeting at Rome—wrote: "Now that you are your own master again . . . pray do not turn your back upon your Muse for I have it on the testimony of thousands that she has not a greater favourite than yourself in all Parnassus. . . .

Your imagination has been so long fallow that I anticipate a most luxurious harvest when you again cultivate it."

Shortly after receiving this message of encouragement and of expectation from "the most delightful, the most lovable being" he ever knew, Irving went to London with some unfinished pieces of writing. The nightmare of commercial agony was over; he had rested a bit at Leamington, where he had accompanied his sister Sarah Van Wart whose husband had resumed business and was beginning to get along satisfactorily; and the artists, C. R. Leslie and Gilbert Stuart Newton, who were soon to become his best friends in England, compensated in some measure for Irving's unhappiness at the departure of Allston for America. Washington Irving was, in a word, beginning to get into better mood again. The struggle between his characteristic spirit of independence, and his equally characteristic tendency to underrate his own capacity was soon to terminate in the first international triumph of an American man of letters. After two months of hesitations and misgivings Irving settled down to the first serious attempt at literary work since his arrival in Europe, and so well did he get on that by the end of the following February he had finished the first number of "The Sketch Book," and had succeeding numbers in partial readiness.

In forwarding the manuscript to his brother Ebenezer, Washington wrote: "Should it not succeed—should my writings not acquire critical applause, I am content to throw up the pen and take to any commonplace employment." It is significant that success here connotes for Irving not monetary returns so much as the favourable judgment of those qualified to judge. But if success should crown his efforts "it would repay me," he adds, "for a world of care and privation to be placed among the established authors of my country, and to win the affections of my countrymen. . . . My greatest desire is to make myself worthy of the good will of my countrymen." This was indeed Irving's greatest desire, and if he was later to be misjudged for his protracted absence from his country, the blame must fall on the littleness of insight of his countrymen and not on the broadness of vision inherent in Irving's philosophy of what the life and the services of an artist should be.

Irving gave to America in this first number of "The Sketch Book" nothing less than the greatest of legendary figures in American literature, and, altogether, the most appealing character in the fiction of our nation. "Rip Van Winkle" so overshadows the others of these first papers of Geoffrey Crayon, Gent. that the appealing prospectus, the author's account of himself, "The Voyage," and the delightful paper on Roscoe (the English man of letters who, like Irving himself, so nobly rose above adversity), are, for all their charm, comparatively insignificant. Ebenezer Irving and Henry Brevoort between them, attended to the publication and to the correction of the proof sheets. Two thousand copies, at seventy-five cents, were issued simultaneously in New York, Philadelphia, in Boston and in Baltimore. The cities of America had not forgotten their old favourite, Diedrich Knickerbocker, and a great welcome awaited him from a public that immediately took Rip Van Winkle to its heart. Irving had felt intense diffidence about his reappearance in print; had feared that his mind had "lost much of its cheerfulness on account of the cares" he had gone through. When he sent his manuscript across the ocean he did not have the conviction that he had, with unerring instinct, struck the right note. ("I have preferred addressing myself to the feeling and fancy of the reader, more than to his judgment. I seek only to blow a flute of accompaniment in the national concert," he had written to Brevoort at the time, "and leave others to play the fiddle and French horn." He was fearful as to how his music would be received; and when success became apparent, he was almost overwhelmed.

The flute—that instrument which had brought him consolation in the black hours at Liverpool—well serves as the symbol of Irving's genius. It is the tender note—the call of the shepherd to the simple pleasures of life and nature—the voice of reminiscence and old glamour—the pastoral note, the romantic.

Through the flute blows the breath of olden days, and of gentleness which is of all times. It is neither moral nor immoral: the guileless young shepherdess danced to the flute, but so did Pan and his followers. Its music is clear and limpid, like Irving's style; and if old sensuous gods and old mystic legends lurk in the background of the flute, the simple human appeal is yet its predominating note.

As number after number was issued—first in the United States and then, shortly afterwards, in England—the enthusiasm aroused by "Rip Van Winkle," by that universal favourite "The Broken Heart," by the "Legend of Sleepy Hollow," grew greater and greater. If Scott was especially delighted with the legend of the Headless Horseman, William Godwin seemed to find most to praise in the essay on "Rural Life in England." "It is, I believe, all true," wrote Godwin; "and one wonders, while reading, that nobody ever said this before." Godwin's praise was the first in that great chorus which was, in 1819, to make Irving famous all over Europe; and the comment that Godwin made—Godwin, whose work on political justice was one of the epoch-making books of all times—is especially significant of what Irving began, in "The Sketch Book," to do for England, for English literature, and for the relationship between England and the United States.

"It is, I believe, all true," said Godwin of this paper of Irving's on English rural life; and it is, the world believes, all true, in reading Irving's paper entitled "John Bull." Of course the meticulous analyst is at perfect liberty to maintain that neither of these papers is "all true." The England that Irving saw and described is, whether in its country life, or in its international character, an England seen through the eyes of a poet and a gentleman, rather than a scholar and a gentleman. And although some might know and aver that his picturizings and characterizations were not in accord with the England of commerce, of wars of aggrandizement, still Irving painted better than they knew, probably better than he himself knew, and his pictures of English life and character have in them that essential verity which, uninterested in statistics, is justified by the reaction it evokes.

Thus, in "The Sketch Book," with its variety of legendary, sentimental, autobiographical, critical, and interpretive papers, Irving made the beginnings of American belles lettres, created a new form of art that might loosely be called the story-essay, and at the same time revealed to England, as no foreigner had ever done before, the soul of England.

The praise accorded "The Sketch Book" was, in more ways than one, unprecedented. There was even an enthusiastic critique by Gulian C. Verplanck who had attacked Irving for his caricatures of Dutch character in "Knickerbocker's History"; and another equally enthusiastic in the *New York Evening Post,* edited by William Coleman who had previously shown traces of ill-will towards Irving. Verplanck's oration wherein he had criticized the author of the "History of New York" had merely led Irving to send him, through Brevoort, his cordial greeting and the message: "Tell him I mean to grow wiser and better and older over it and to lay the castigation he has given me seriously to heart"; while after the unexpected tributes from Verplanck and Coleman he wrote: "Vanity could not bring the tears into my eyes as they have been brought by the kindness of my countrymen. I have felt cast down, blighted and broken spirited and these sudden rays of sunshine agitate even more than they revive me."

When, towards the end of 1819, John Miller published in London the first four numbers of "The Sketch Book," the modest man and the sincere artist who was their author was unwilling to have press copies presented to the critics, as not even to this extent would he seem to wish to gain their favour. The bankrupt American launched his little bark of literature without any attempt to have it sail before any winds save those of its own merit; and this at a time when he had reached the end of his tether, but yet had refused the remunerative office of editorship of an anti-Jacobin periodical that, through the intercession of Walter Scott, was his for the asking. Just as he was aware of his lack of fitness for the position at Washington which his brother William had hoped he would accept, so too he knew his inherent inabilities as the editor of a political journal. He wrote to Scott declining. "I have no command of my talents such as they are, and have to watch the varyings of my mind as I would a weather-cock." Whereupon Scott continued his interest in Irving in other directions, and after Miller had failed, was instrumental in obtaining Murray as Irving's publisher. It was Scott also who suggested to Lockhart, soon to become his son-in-law, to write that article in *Blackwood's Magazine,* whose favourable nature did so much for "The Sketch Book."

It must be remembered that not Irving's name, but that of Geoffrey Crayon, appeared on the title page of the various numbers. Not everyone knew who the real author was, and by some people Walter Scott himself was thought to be Geoffrey Crayon. Even as late as August, 1820, and after Jeffrey's article in the *Edinburgh Review* had crowned Irving's work with perhaps the highest critical honour of Great Britain, Lady Lyttleton, the daughter of Earl Spencer, and the supervisor of the education of Queen Victoria's young children, wrote to Richard Rush, the American Minister at the Court of St. James, to gain definite information concerning the authorship of "The Sketch Book." In his reply Irving said that "the doubts which her ladyship has heard on the subject seem to have arisen from the old notion that it is impossible for an *American to write decent English—* If I have indeed been fortunate enough to do anything, however trifling, to stagger this prejudice, I am too good a patriot to give up even the little ground I have gained." But in 1819, though his fame had been established in the inner literary circles, he was not yet so publicly known as to be lionized. That phase of the English days was to arrive after Lord and Lady Spencer had him as their guest at Wimbledon, where he first met Samuel Rogers, the banker-poet and the great patron of men of letters.

During the period in which the various numbers of "The

Sketch Book" were published in America and England, Irving's social life was mainly in the company of his brother Peter and the artists Leslie and Newton. Newton and Leslie Irving saw almost daily, and they had many delightful dinners together in the York Chop House in Wardour Street. Together they went to fairs in the suburbs, and made excursions, by stagecoach, to Richmond or Greenwich. Even after Irving was somewhat caught up in the pleasures of fashionable society, his friendship with Newton and Leslie did not abate. With the latter, in 1821, he journeyed to Birmingham, to the Derbyshire country, and to Oxford. We find him seated on a stone, or more precariously on some wooden fence, jotting down notes for such a story as that of "The Stout Gentleman," while Leslie is busied with his sketching. There is all manner of happy reminiscences of Irving in Leslie's journal, as where he notes that, at Stratford, Irving presented the caretaker with a large blankbook so that instead of defacing the walls of Shakespeare's house, visitors might write their names—as Scott was later to do—in this more appropriate place. Of the third of this gifted trio, Gilbert Stuart's nephew, young Newton, Leslie records anecdotes that are too amusing to forget. On one occasion a collector, showing Newton his paintings, and somewhat discomfited at Newton's apparent lack of enthusiasm, remarked: "At least you will allow that it is a *tolerable* collection." "True, sir,"answered Newton; "but would you eat a *tolerable* egg?" And with the same vein of curious humour this young American artist, who was so sadly to end his days in the cloud of insanity, had, after complaining that he often was in need of rags with which to clean his palette, met the query: "What do you do with your old shirts?" with the answer: "I wear them."

Irving's nervousness and occasional fits of depression still assailed him while he was at work on "The Sketch Book" whose irregular appearances were due to what he calls the "precariousness and inequality of my own fits of composition"; but he was getting more and more in the mood for meeting people, and at

Murray's, in the drawing room of the Countess of Besborough, and at the home of Isaac D'Israeli ("old D'Israeli is a staunch friend of mine") his circle of literary acquaintances was growing larger and larger. He frequently met such men as Southey, Campbell and Milman. Especially with Hallam, the historian, and Belzoni, the traveller, was he pleased, though even when among all these new friends he longed for the Highlands of the Hudson and "the little knot that was once assembled there." With his New York friends he kept in touch, and long letters passed between Irving and James K. Paulding, who had been his collaborator on *Salmagundi,* and who was now continuing that publication—rather to Irving's regret as he looked upon their early work as juvenile, too impertinent, too full of errors, and "had hoped for its oblivion." Yet when the American newspapers, in commenting on *Salmagundi* in its revived form, praised Irving at Paulding's expense, it was "excessively painful" to him and unjust, he thought, to Paulding. "I neither deserve the honour nor desire distinction of that kind, and those that make it do not understand our distinct and comparative merit."—Always the generous and modest gentleman.

Chapter VI

PARIS AND LONDON

"AND now, my dear fellow, I must take my leave, for it is midnight, and I am weary with packing trunks, and making other preparations for my departure. The next you will hear from me will be from France; and after passing five years in England among genuine John Bulls, it will be like entering into a new world to cross the channel."

The immediate success of "The Sketch Book" was financial as well as literary, and formed the bridge over which Irving, with Peter as his companion, crossed once more into the continent. What this meant to the restless man, imbued from early boyhood with a passion for wandering, is made apparent by his letters to his family and by the memorandum books wherein he records, if not with all the youthful zest of his early diaries, certainly with all the old keenness of observation, his experiences of travel.

The two brothers left London on the sixteenth or seventeenth of August. Winchester was, of course, replete with interesting associations for a man of Irving's temperament. In or near the great cathedral where reposed the bodies of Saxon Kings and Queens, where Henry IV had wedded Jean of Navarre, and Philip of Spain Mary of England, the coffins of famous church dignitaries—William of Wykeham, celebrated in the fourteenth century as Bishop of Winchester and Lord High Chancellor of England, Cardinal Beaufort, Bishop Gardner, the secretary of the great Wolsey, and confidential agent of Henry VIII—interwove memories of religious annals with those of royal events. Here, too, in seeing the burial place of St. Swithin, who held in the ninth century the episcopate of Winchester, Irving recalled the legend which to our own day persists; how, when the monks of the tenth century sought to transfer the body of the saint from the outer grounds to the vaults of the cathedral, for two-score days incessant rain prevented their task; so that even now, if the clouds burst on the 15th of July, there are those who prophesy St. Swithin's weather for forty days.   But equally, we fancy, was Irving interested in the grave of Izaac Walton who had, at the venerable age of ninety, laid his earthly rod aside in 1683, and gently fared forth to seek the treasure of celestial streams.

Always fascinated by ruins, Irving notes the shell of the palace begun after designs by Sir Christopher Wren, but, by reason of the death of Charles II, never brought to completion.   A great king (greater in the realm of men's imagination than any of the Tudors or Stuarts), spreads over Winchester the fragrance of his legendary deeds.   Irving gazed on the effigy of King Arthur, and made a pencil sketch of the famous relic—Arthur's Round Table—in the mediæval castle on Castle Hill.   This table, which had been presented to Henry VIII, is known to have existed as early as the days of Henry III and, with its place for Arthur and his twenty-four knights, was invested with all the glamour of Celtic tradition.   Irving in his drawing indicates the supposed places of two of Arthur's followers, Mordred the traitor, and the great Lancelot whom he quaintly calls "Sir L. Dulacke"—Lancelot, who had been found and guarded by the water-fairy, the Lady of the Lake.

From Winchester the brothers journeyed to Southampton, where Canute bade the sea stand still, and where the gateway of Sir Bevis suggests the prodigious feats of that hero—dragons overcome and giants slain—in the days of King Edgar.   Houn-slow and Bagshot Heath ("the latter with much of New Hamp-shire") passed on that same day, were for Irving still odorous with the smoke of early Roman and British camps, and with the gunpowder of daring highwaymen.

The next day (August 18th) the travellers embarked.   The Isle of Wight, Portsmouth, Spithead were left behind; and the following morning a pilot boat took the passengers from the packet and brought them to Havre.

The brief sentences wherewith Irving records the trip through Normandy are as much the quick sketches of a draughts-man as the jottings of an author; and we are again reminded of Irving's desire to follow art as a career. The red shawls of women; the light blue frocks and white metal buttons of officers; the card party playing by candle light; the great green alleys of an old chateau; the white seagull flying across green mountains; flowers and goldfish and monkeys and parrots; the sailors crying from the docks, and women clustering around the fountain in the public square—these are but a few of the themes to allure an artist.

Napoleon was still alive, a captured eagle, when Irving noted, at the little town of Quille Boeuf, a flag inscribed with "Vive le Roi et les Bourbons." Irving often had a kind word to say for "poor Bony," and he must have been delighted to meet in Normandy a dragoon—De Couvrer by name,—formerly an aide to General Ney—General Ney, who after Waterloo, was shot in the Luxembourg Gardens for having, during The Hundred Days, instead of following his King's orders to capture the escaped Emperor, gone over to his old master—a dereliction not destitute of noble appeal.

With earlier eras than the Napoleonic did Irving come into touch during this journey through Normandy unrecorded by biographers. The cathedrals of Rouen spoke to him in accents of beauty, and, among the old monasteries, the Abbey at Jumièges carried him back to a period antedating the time of William the Conqueror, when almost every great Norman nobleman became the founder of a monastery. The Château de Corset Rouge yielded him its tradition of the maiden who signalled with her red corset to her lover, a monk of St. George.

As far as Rouen the journey had been by steamboat—a matter of note for every biographer of Irving. This was the boat's second trip; steam navigation in Europe was then in its infancy. The proposal by the initiator of this enterprise on the Seine that

Irving and his brother take a share in the business venture met
with a compliance which, on Washington's part, was based on
his desire to find a suitable and remunerative occupation for
Peter.   But the project did not end in success, and the thousands
of dollars, drawn from his literary revenue, that Irving invested
in it were ultimately lost.

On August 26th, after having seen the ancient Benedictine
basilica at St. Denis where Henry IV, Louis XIV and so many
other Kings of France lay buried, the Irvings reached Paris.
Peter and Washington, who had shared lodgings in London,
settled themselves in rooms at 4 rue Mont Thabor, near the
Tuileries whose gardens Irving soon came to look upon as "a
park attached to his mansion."   Peter's anonymous novel, a
Venetian story entitled "Giovanni Sboggaro," and adapted from
the French, had been issued without success the previous year,
and all his hopes were now pinned to the steamboat scheme.
Although he agreed to having Washington take a half interest,
and provide five of the ten thousand dollars needed for the
investment, he refused, as always, to accept any loans from his
younger brother.   "A tenacious, and, as I think, a false and
squeamish delicacy," Irving calls it.   "Were I in his situation
and he had the fullest purse, I would share it without
hesitation."

During the eleven months before Irving left Paris the wor-
ries in connection with their navigation project considerably interfered with his doing much writing.   The sensitive fellow was
especially upset by the refusal of his brothers William and John
(so strongly did they oppose what seemed to them a foolish
speculation) to honour the drafts that he drew in order to make
good his subscription; and it was Henry Brevoort who again
came to his aid.   The separation from Leslie and Newton made
more of a break than Irving had anticipated.   "A grievous
thing, this life, and with all my vagrant habits I cannot get
accustomed to it."   All in all, had it not been for Thomas
Moore, these Paris days would have proved rather cheerless.

It is strange that Irving should have come into such affectionate terms with a man whose early actions had aroused his indignation and whose writings had been derided in the pages of *Salmagundi*. Moore, during his visit to the United States when Thomas Jefferson was President, had lampooned the head of the American Government, as well as many other things American, partially because Moore was not satisfied with his reception, but very largely because of an incident which has an unusual place in the history of diplomacy. Mrs. Langford relates the episode in the "Ladies of the White House." It seems that at a dinner given by the President when, according to custom, he should have escorted Mrs. Merry, the wife of the British Minister and a particular friend of Thomas Moore, into the dining room, he happened to be talking to Mrs. Madison at the moment dinner was announced. In his informal, democratic manner Jefferson walked to the table with Dolly Madison, the wife of his Secretary of State. Mrs. Merry was so vastly insulted that Madison thought it well to write to James Monroe (at the time the American Minister at the Court of St. James), so that Monroe might have all the facts in the event of a request of the British Government for an explanation. The affair was amusingly settled when, at a state dinner in London, precedence that should have been shown to Mrs. Monroe was, with Monroe's approval, granted to the wife of an English Under-Secretary; and of men of distinction only Thomas Moore was left as the angry critic of an incident involving three American Presidents.

To Washington Irving, Moore expressed his regret at the reaction into which his friendship with Mrs. Merry had led him, and his consequent expressions concerning American manners. Undoubtedly the charm of Irving's personality did much to cause Moore to reconsider his absurd point of view of earlier years; and this is but another example of Irving's functioning as a kind of private ambassador in dispelling foreign ignorance, or revising unfair estimates of his country and his countrymen. Irving, in turn, was swiftly won by the delightfulness of the Irish poet. A few days after meeting him for the first time at dinner at Meurice's, he and Moore visited (with Lord John Russell and an Irish gentleman, McKay by name, who was especially interested in inspecting French prisons) the dungeons under the Palace of Justice. The sentimental Irishman and the sentimental American were especially stirred when they reached the cell where Marie Antoinette had awaited the hour of the guillotine. "Never have I felt my heart melting with pity more," writes Irving, "than in beholding this last abode of wretchedness. What a place for a Queen, and such a Queen! One brought up so delicately, fostered, admired, adored."

Still a few days later and Irving is dining with Moore at his cottage on the Champs Elysées. The friendship advanced so rapidly that in the early months of 1821 hardly a day passed without their seeing one another, and through Moore Irving became acquainted with all the most interesting of the British contingent in Paris. "He is a charming, joyous fellow; full of frank, generous, manly feeling," Irving writes to Brevoort; and to this "joyous fellow" Irving owed not alone his happiest hours in Paris, but also valuable ideas in connection with "Brace-bridge Hall." In an entry of Moore's journal for March 19th —a day when Irving had come in to dine informally with Moore on a roast chicken—the Irishman notes that Irving (who wrote rapidly when he was in the mood), had finished about one hundred and thirty pages in the last ten days and had "followed up an idea which I suggested, and taken characters in his Christmas Essay, Master Simon, etc. for the purpose of making a slight thread of the story on which to string his remarks and sketches of human manners and feelings." Here we have the origin of "Bracebridge Hall."

Of Irving's friends in this Paris period John Howard Payne takes place next to Thomas Moore. The author of the world's best beloved song had tasted none of the sweets of home, had indeed dwelt precariously, ever more and more harried by poverty, after his arrival at England in 1813. Born in 1791, this gifted fellow-citizen of Irving had been much of a youthful prodigy in the fields both of literature and of drama. He was, in the first year of his teens, the anonymous editor of the *Thespian Mirror,* and, five years later, as young Norval in the play of "Douglas," he aroused the audience at the Park Theatre in New York to a pitch of enthusiasm that made him instantly famous. In Boston, in Philadelphia, in Baltimore his success was no less; and to England he was eagerly welcomed as "Master Payne, the American Roscius," the appellation of "the Young Roscius" having only a few years earlier been given to that other youthful prodigy, William Betty. The critics had gone back to the Roman days of the first century before the Christian era to find an actor with whom these two juvenile marvels might fittingly be compared. But after Payne's early appearance at Drury Lane, and with the necessity of competing with far greater dramatic talent than America could offer, Payne's vogue rather swiftly diminished. As he grew older and stouter the glamour of the youthful prodigy fell away from him, and he found it increasingly difficult to obtain engagements in leading rôles. Hamlet, Romeo, Jaffier in "Venice Preserved," Charles the Moor in "The Robber" were some of the parts that he played with fair capacity before he turned to the career of theatrical manager. His failure as the manager of Sadler's Wells Theatre led, in 1820, to his imprisonment for debt. The next year he is at Paris engaged in the task of finding and adapting French plays for the English stage.

It was thus a countryman down on his luck with whom the warm-hearted Irving gladly consorted in the spring and summer of 1821, all the more gladly as Payne had so long been acquainted with the Irving family, especially with Peter. Indeed, when Payne first came to Europe, Peter Irving and Sarah Van Wart were among the first friends with whom he dined, meeting at their table Henry Brevoort.

The first record of Washington Irving's association with Payne at Paris—at breakfast at the actor-manager's apartment —shows how immediately Payne intensified Irving's interest in affairs of the drama, an interest which later led to collaboration between the two Americans. As early as 1815 Payne had crossed over from London to Paris for the particular purpose of seeing Talma act. His admiration for the great Frenchman was unbounded, and through Talma, Payne received the distinguished privilege of the freedom of the Théâtre Nationale. One morning, breakfast over, Payne took Irving to call on Talma at his apartments in the Rue des Petites Augustines. With his usual shyness, accentuated by the prospect of meeting so renowned a personage, Irving persuaded Payne to go upstairs ahead of him, to be sure that Talma should not be approached too unceremoniously by a stranger. The great actor was changing his linen, but he asked Payne to bring Irving right up, and received him "in a very friendly, frank way." Talma's first remark, with the charming courtesy of France, was: "Why, he is quite a young man"; doubtless a pleasing observation to the thirty-eight year old visitor. Then came the usual question—in English, with which Talma was much at home—as to whether this was Irving's first visit to Paris; and to the reply that Irving had been there in 1805, "Ah! that was in the time of the Emperor," said Talma.

Napoleon had been not only Talma's friend, but his idol. Art as well as life had changed for the great actor with the rise and fall of the great conqueror on whose closing days at St. Helena the ineluctable curtain of death was so soon to descend. To Irving, after discussing with him the French version of "Hamlet" and other plays of Shakespeare, Talma explained why the French public after seeing "so many strong and vivid scenes of real life pass before their eyes" in the days of the Revolution, could no longer be satisfied "by mere declamation and fine language; they require character, incident, passion, life." He foretold the manner of drama that the nineteenth century so richly brought forth.

Not long after this interview Irving witnessed Talma's overwhelming effect in the rôle of Hamlet. In the version shown at Paris the ghost of the murdered king did not appear; "yet," Irving writes, "he hovers in idea about his son, and the powerful acting of Talma gives an idea of this portentous visitation far more awful and mysterious than could be presented by any spectral representation . . . The audience continually passed from intervals of breathless attention to bursts of ungovernable applause. I have seen a lady carried fainting from the boxes, overcome by the acting of Talma in the scene with his mother, where he fancies he sees the spectre of his father."

With Payne to draw him more and more into the realm of the theatre, with Lord and Lady Holland offering him frequent hospitality, with Thomas Moore making him "a gayer fellow than he could have wished," with Lord John Russell, Kenney, the author of "Raising the Wind," Luttrel, who wrote "Advice to Julia," and the young George Bancroft among his more gifted companions, and with the gracious women in the English and American sets the summer of 1821 went rather idly by. Irving worked now and then on the manuscripts that were later to constitute "Bracebridge Hall," until, towards the middle of July, drawn by the desire to arrange for their publication in England, and prompted by the kindly intention of being of some service to Payne in connection with a French play for the English stage, he left Paris. He had, the night before, been a guest at Lord Holland's where, after dinner, came Talma with the news of the death of Napoleon.

Again in London, the first day was made memorable by the coronation of the licentious weakling to whom Napoleon, after the disaster of Waterloo, had pleaded for mercy. With his chums, Leslie and Newton, Irving saw the State coach of the Prince Regent approach Westminster Abbey and, the coronation proceedings ended, saw George IV of England issue from that historic church. As the stand whereon he and his friends were seated was just outside of Westminster, Irving may have witnessed the unsuccessful attempt of the discarded Queen Caroline to gain entrance to the ceremonies. That he himself, having only the day before come over from France, was not within the Abbey could have been obviated but for his usual modesty; or at least so thought Walter Scott who, when Irving visited him the following day, said: "Hut mon, you should have told them who you were, and you would have got in anywhere."

The general liking in which Irving was held in England, and which soon was further enhanced by "Bracebridge Hall," the most delightful of books ever written by a foreigner concerning the country and the customs of England, was in contrast to increasing indications of American impatience at Irving's protracted absence from his native land. In a letter the preceding March to Henry Brevoort Irving had written: "You urge me to return to New York—and say many ask whether I mean to renounce my country. For this last question I have no reply to make—and yet I will make a reply. As far as my precarious and imperfect abilities enable me, I am endeavouring to serve my country. Whatever I have written has been written with the feelings and published as the writings of an American. Is that renouncing my country? How else can I serve my country— By coming home and begging an office of it; which I should not have the kind of talent or the business habits requisite to fill?—If I can do any good in this world it is with my pen. . . . In remaining therefore abroad, I do it with the idea that I can best exert my talents, for the present, where I am."

This reply, temporarily at least, satisfied Brevoort, but Irving was still subjected to criticism by persons who could not—or would not—understand the point of view of an artist who ever remained in the deepest way loyal to his country.

The company of Leslie and of Newton did much to raise Irving's spirits. It was with Leslie that towards the end of the summer he made the enjoyable excursion to Oxford, Stratford, Warwick and Kenilworth, taking his friend also to Birmingham where the artist and the author became such happy companions of the children in the Van Wart household. There were six of these little folks; and the picture that Irving gives of George, aged four, is too delectable to forego. "To balance his ball and marbles, he has the opposite pocket filled with a peg-top and a prodigious quantity of dry peas, so that he can only lie comfortably on his back or his belly." As to the little girls, Leslie had initiated them into the pleasures of drawing and they were "continually taking their dolls' likenesses."

Illness—Irving was intermittently assailed by eczema and trouble with his ankle in those years—kept him for some months at the home of his sister, and during this period his chief joy was in the company of his nephews and nieces. His chief sorrow was the death of his brother William who had been "a kind of father to them all."

The day after Christmas—Christmas, of course, he celebrated with his family—Irving returned to London where he sold "Bracebridge Hall" to Murray, the publisher, for a thousand pounds, and where, during the greater part of the next seven months, he was busy with correcting proof sheets, and with visiting doctors who did little for him. Thomas Moore had meanwhile returned from France, cleared of those debts that had necessitated his departure from England; and we find the two friends, during Moore's stay at London in April and May, breakfasting together at Holland House; walking together in the spring sunshine; calling together on Lady Blessington. Irving was now persona grata in all ranks of fashion and of talent, and he went "the rounds of routs, dinners, operas, balls, and blue-stocking coteries." He was the guest of Mrs. Siddons and heard that greatest of English tragediennes, now nearly seventy years old, reading the part of Constance, "the greatest dramatic treat I have had for a long time past." Samuel Rogers became his enthusiastic friend and attempted, to Irving's amusement, to be his social mentor, seeking to advise him what invitations to accept, what to decline. Thomas Hope, the author of "Anastasius," and one of the wealthiest and most unusual men in England, had him down for some days at his country place where Irving was delighted with the unpretentious manners of his host and of the wife of his host, "one of the loveliest women in the kingdom, and one of the reigning deities of fashion." And everywhere that Irving went he made friends not only for himself but for his country.

SAMUEL ROGERS

With the publication, in May, of "Bracebridge Hall," the old restlessness of the wanderer seems to take possession of him again. In June he writes to Brevoort that he hopes soon to leave "this scene of bustle and dissipation and go to a watering place on the Continent (Aix la Chapelle), where I hope thoroughly to re-instate my health"; and after that to "make a hasty tour, that I have been contemplating for several years past." This tour over, he intends to arrange his affairs "so as once more to see my native land which is daily becoming dearer and dearer to my imagination."

But the hasty tour that was to precede Irving's home-going proved only to be the precursor of a long series of wanderings broken into by sojourns in cities of Germany, France and Spain before, finally, in 1832, he was again to tread American soil. The years of family life in New York and the close association with his sister's home at Birmingham, were to fade further and further into the past, and it is indeed an often lonely and solitary man that, despite the warmth of social friendship, and the occasional companionship of his brother Peter, we are called upon for another ten years to accompany in his wanderings.

Chapter VII

THE WANDERER SETS FORTH

In the album kept at Deep Dene, Thomas Hope's country seat in Surrey, Irving on June 4th, 1822 wrote some verses that not without pathos suggest the fate of the chronic wanderer that he knew himself to be, the

> "Strange tenant of a thousand homes
> And friendless with ten thousand friends!
>
> Yet here for once I'll leave a trace,
> To ask in aftertimes a thought;
> To say that here a resting place
> My wayworn heart has fondly sought."

Less than a fortnight later "the poor pilgrim" had set forth for Aix-la-Chapelle, hoping to find in its baths and waters relief from his ailment. The place, however, in more ways than one disappointed him. He continued to be disabled by inflammation in his legs, preventing him from full enjoyment of the lovely gardens and environs of Aix; and, altogether, those were dull weeks. His chief amusement was to observe the people at or near his lodgings. Of some of these the first few pages of his note-book give vivid word pictures—the nervous gambler and the old gentleman followed by his dachshund being masterpieces in miniature.

The birthplace of Charlemagne, "that monarch so renowned in history and song," had the element of historical appeal for Irving, who did not fail to visit the old Town Hall where, in 1748, the treaty was signed, ending the "War of the Austrian Succession," so largely fought on the American continent. In

this hall, also—and only a few years before Irving visited it—
had met the Congress which settled European affairs after the
Napoleonic upheaval of conquest had subsided. Frederick
William III who, in 1806, had been so drastically defeated by
the Corsican at Jena, now included Aix-la-Chapelle in his Prussian domain, while its former ruler lay in his almost neglected
grave at St. Helena; and Irving's final entry before leaving Aix
on August 5th, concerns a dinner in honour of the King of Prussia's birthday, at which Irving sat near "young Blucher," son of
the famous Field Marshal who shared the laurels with Wellington at Waterloo.

In an open carriage Irving set forth accompanied by an old-
time American acquaintance, Thomas Brandron, for Wiesbaden.
Cologne, Coblenz, Bingen and all the lovely intervening Rhine
country with its castles and verdant vineyards were in this delightful manner seen. Irving was much interested in the looks
and manners of the officers whom he met, some of them "in the
costumes of the time of Turenne." Turenne is a name Irving
jotted down more than once in his diaries; "the great Turenne"
whose descendant, De Latour d'Auvergne, Irving commemor-
ates in "The Crayon Papers." And indeed of the heroes among
Napoleon's officers, none is nobler than that nobleman who,
refusing all recompense for his brave deeds, received from the
Emperor the title of Premier Grenadier de France, and whose
place, long after his death, "was always retained in his regiment, as if he still occupied it; and wherever the regiment was
mustered, and the name of De Latour d'Auvergne was called
out, the reply was, 'Dead on the field of honour!' "

From Wisbaden, Irving made an excursion through the heart
of the wine country, tasting at its source the Johannesburg, "the
nectar of the Rhine." He arrived at Mainz (to which he still
gives the French spelling of Mayence, although it was no
longer a French possession) on August 10th. His abode there,
the Hotel de Darmstadt ("John Ardnot, the landlord a fat jolly
publican") has its niche in literary history, for in this hostelry
Irving wrote the Introduction to "The Tales of a Traveller."

There he received from the landlord's sixteen-year old daughter, the pretty Katrina, daily lessons in French and German. Irving notes that the Hotel de Darmstadt was formerly named the "Ville de Paris—very flourishing in time of the revolution—fallen since. Mine host says the fall of Bonaparte cost him 400,000 francs." I think it likely that when Irving later wrote his keenly humorous, kindly satiric, sketch of "A Contented Man" he had recourse to these days in Mainz for his prototype of the hero of that tale, the hotel-keeper who had lost his fortune.

Even more likely is it that the charms of Katrina, who, in this note-book, our bachelor author (not yet quite forty years of age) calls "la belle Catherine," had something to do with a stay protracted well into September, although the attractions and amusements of the city itself shall be sufficient explanation for the unromantically-minded. Mainz, in a letter of August 21st to his sister, Mrs. Van Wart, Irving called "one of those old battered warrior towns that enjoy the advantage of being knocked about, and battered, and taken, and retaken in every war." If the reader would here see one of the most amusing and deft of re-wordings (based on a paragraph in his diary, and showing how these diaries served Irving in his correspondence) let him observe how in the diary Irving writes: "These little old German towns taken and untaken by sack and ravaged in every war seem to have the fate of the unfortunate Miss Cunigonde who was ravished at every turn," and chuckle over the way Irving has, for his sister's eyes, given Mainz a brave warrior character instead of the frail feminine of Voltaire's heroine in "Candide."

Among the guests at the Hotel de Darmstadt was a Russian Colonel who had been in the army of General Kutusoff, Napoleon's intrepid opponent in the Campaign of 1812. This Colonel, who is portrayed by Irving in a dozen words—"malade imaginaire—room littered with books—Col. in robe de chambre"—reminds us how even to this day Russian literature has not wholly thrown off the mood which took intellectual as well as sentimental hold of Europe after the publication of Goethe's "Leiden des Jungen Werther."

On the 13th of September, Irving (in company with a young English officer, Capt. Wemyss of the Dragoons), left Mainz for Frankfort. The great annual fair, where merchants from all over France and Holland, as well as Germany, assembled, made the question of lodgings difficult. Two rooms were finally obtained at a shoemaker's. After three days in that city, whose new streets and general air of success impressed Irving, he drove on to Darmstadt where he first heard Weber's opera, "Der Freischütz," originally produced in the preceding year. From Darmstadt the traveller's road wound along the base of the lovely range of the Odenwald mountains, through little villages buried in orchards and surrounded by vineyards, in the fertile valley of Baden. At Erbach, the armour of Goetz von Berlichingen and of Wallenstein arrested his attention in the Knights' Hall, and were, to the man of letters, of all the more interest because the two warriors who wore these suits of armour had been made the heroes of poetical dramas by Goethe and Schiller —Goethe's "Goetz von Berlichingen" having been translated by Irving's friend, Walter Scott.

To the golden September days belongs an unrhymed poem, autobiographically one of the most significant lyric expressions from the pen of Irving. It begins with a line:

"We look forward to better hours"

suggesting that the "kind of intoxication of the heart" which has taken hold of him, evokes new visions of happiness through love. Then, characteristically, comes the mood of doubt in these verses:

"What better times can I hope?
My sunny days of youth are over."

And as the poem ends there is the indubitable reference to his romance with Matilda Hoffman in this long and lovely line:

125

"The happy bowers, the rosy chambers, the evening walks, the morning greetings—the early days of love."

After this poem, the note-book's connected memoranda of travel close with picturesque notes concerning Heidelberg's famous castle, the thirteenth century structure whose beauty as a ruin is due in part to the attacks of the French in 1689, and in part to the damage done by lightning just three quarters of a century later. Strange it is to consider how over the hostile forces of man and of nature beauty should have won so enduring a victory!

At Heidelberg his leisurely little diary ends as a record of travel. But the book contains some additional jottings. "The luxury of lying on grass and looking up to the sunset sky—Swallow high up, turning up yellow breast—Owl that lived in a hollow tree, like a decayed gentleman in his old tottering castle."—Such are a few of these delightful notes. But the most important is the paragraph reading "A weight rested upon my mind,—there was a soreness of heart as if I had committed some hideous crime and all mankind were justly irritated at me. I went about with a guilty look and sought to hide myself. It was not without some effort that I occasionally threw off this weight and recollected that my only crime had been an unsuccessful attempt to please the world." Although this may be a note for a story (Hawthorne similarly jotted down such notes in his diaries) there is in it the suggestion of how deeply the gentle heart of Washington Irving was grieved by the criticisms directed against him by some of his countrymen for having so long stayed away from his native land.—But then, in lighter vein, this final jotting: "French woman dips into love like a duck into water,—'tis but a shake of the feathers and a wag of the tail and all is well again, but an English woman is like a heedless hen venturing into a pool, who is drowned."

The second of Irving's notebooks in Germany contains a few pages of entries that chronologically belong in the first diary, and as these commence again with his boating tour from Mainz to Coblenz, we conjecture that at the moment of departure the proper book was not at hand, and Irving slipped a fresh volume into his pocket. In any case, on September 6th, he began his sixty mile voyage down the Rhine in company with Lieutenant Humphreys (a young English officer of the Royal Artillery), and for the first time saw the romantic scenery from the waters of the river itself. The return to Mainz was made by carriage, past the high Taunus Mountains and through little towns. In many ways the Rhine reminded Irving of the Hudson, beside whose banks he spent early days of sad reverie after Matilda Hoffman's death. It is of her, assuredly, that he was thinking when he wrote on September 7th, "My summer is nearly over —the shadows of autumn begin to come—the leaves of past pleasures are strewn around me—the joys of youth, how have they passed away—friendships faded—loves untimely fallen— hopes blighted—what fruit is there to repay this ill-spent summer?"

On the road from Nassau to Schwalbach one of the post horses of a carriage preceding Irving's fell dead, whereupon Irving invited into his own carriage the gentleman in the other vehicle. They dined together that evening; but not until they parted did Irving learn that the man whom he had befriended (as Washington Irving would befriend any traveller in difficulties) was none other than the distinguished diplomat, the Baron de Berstatt, Prime Minister of the Duke of Baden. The Baron invited Irving to be his guest in Baden, won by the charm and kindness of the American. Another instance of how Irving was even more than (as Thackeray called him in one of the "Round-about Papers") "the first Ambassador whom the New World of Letters sent to the Old," but indeed our unofficial Ambassador in spheres other than literature's.

After Mainz had been left and the carriage tour with Captain Wemyss had proceeded as far as Heidelberg, some twelve days were spent at this town. Irving's note-book gives no details of his stay, but from a letter of September 20th to his sister, Mrs. Van Wart, one gathers that the attentions shown to Irving by Count Jennison, formerly Grand Chamberlain to the King of

Wurtemberg, and once Minister to the Court of St. James, contributed largely to Irving's enjoyment of Heidelberg, whose neighbourhood abounded in "old castles, famous in legend and goblin tale."

On September 30th, Heidelberg was left behind. Carls-ruhe, the charming little capital of the duchy of Baden, was the next stopping place. A few days later, the travellers drove on —past the village of Sasbach where Turenne met his death— to Strassburg, on the frontiers of France. That same evening (October 3rd) Irving is busy with his diary at an inn in the Black Forest village of Hansach, and with his customary enthusiasm for old inns he writes of the "huge room where waggoners are boozing—great dusky kitchen— Hostess in peasant's dress,"—and "the simple good-looking girl, mine host's daughter." Morning and evening drives, wild mountainous drives by moonlight, figure in these jottings, which bring us on the 5th of October, after "peeps at Lake of Constance," to the "little principality of Hohenzollern." Here in the ninth century had Count Tassilo built his high castle at Zollern in Swabia, little reckoning that after a thousand years one of his descendants would be the central figure in a world at war.—And so comparatively brief a while ago as Irving's day, the castle of the Hohenzollerns was merely like an "English country squire's establishment."

A long night's ride and Irving reaches Ulm, at half after four in the morning, only to find the gate closed. But the gate was opened for the travellers (how remote, yet cosy it all seems!) and the "postillion wound his horn through the quiet streets." Irving, his interest no doubt quickened by his military companion, was anxious to see the field of Blenheim, and he includes in his diary many historical notes concerning the battle where Marlborough achieved the "famous victory" over whose worth the verses of the poet Southey have cast much—shall we say humorous, or tragically sorrowful?—doubt.

At Augsburg Irving arrived in time for the fair. Dürer's painting in the Hotel de Ville especially attracted his attention;

but his most enthusiastic note has to do with the "snug smoking supper of mutton chop, pigeon and woodcock & bottle of Bordeaux." From Augsburg the journey continues on the road to Munich. By the time Munich was reached, Irving's health had so greatly improved that he was able to walk as much as he wished, and so he visited palaces, libraries, gardens, churches, galleries—indeed everything that the "charming little capital" of Bavaria had to offer. His comments are amusing in many fields: of music, for instance, where he writes of an orchestra as "a number of grave looking persons seemingly employed in the art of making pleasant noises"; of art: "How sad that so many fine paintings should be doomed to galleries to be only glanced at by the world"; of the little royal courts of Germany, where "the people seem to look on their amusements as matters of such importance." But the music and the drama, the great library of half a million volumes, with its treasures (The Gutenberg Bible, the Nibelungen Mss., etc.) impress him mightily, and the palace of Prince Eugene, with its splendid collection of paintings, and its furniture that had once belonged to Napoleon and Josephine.

Eugene Beauharnais, the former Viceroy of Italy, for whom Napoleon had gained as wife the King of Bavaria's daughter, was a great favourite at Munich. Him Irving sees on the occasion of a grand fête in honour of the King's birthday. But it is more from the Munich prison than any Munich palace that the traveller brings back the most interesting jottings in his note-book. He describes the conditions and regulations in this "Maison de force," and records the crimes and sufferings of several criminals. The officers of the prison are, Irving notes, "armed with cutlasses and have something of a military air—according to the passion of the country."

After a week's stay, Irving left Munich on October 17th, again travelling in an open carriage with Captain Wemyss. To those of us who have thus driven through the lovely Tyrolean country, Irving's sketches of "glimmering meadows, dripping forests, blue mountains"; of views with "pigeons, fowls and dogs"; of singing postillions and ribbanded peasant women, bring delightful reminiscences; although in those days the landscape lacked that element of princely romance with which the magnificent imagination of a later insane King of Bavaria endowed it in the form of grottoes, castles and palaces.

In less than two days the carriage brought the travellers to Salzburg, in Austria. Here Paracelsus died, the Swiss physician, alchemist, and chemist who still lives in the pages of Robert Browning. Here, too, are the famous salt works in their mountains of subterranean passages and lakes; and the towering Untersberg, within which, according to the firmly held belief of the peasants, "Emperor Charles V and all his army remain spell-bound." Several legends having to do with the famous Emperor and his army (the story of the waggoner, and of the old man of Tiesdorf) Irving preserves in his note-book; and he records the then current talk among the country people of how the English, in league with the Turks, were about to oppose the Greeks (who were Catholics) and how Charles V, as defender of the Catholic faith, would issue from the Untersberg in time to overcome the foe.

One line among Irving's notes of Salzburg and its surroundings gives forth unusual and winning music—"Carillon of Salzburg performing a waltz." In this ultra-Catholic little city the convent and church bells were continually ringing to prayers; but one of the church towers had a chime of bells that thrice daily played a waltz. "And I presume," writes Irving to his sister, "all the street devotees are expected to dance to it."

Salzburg was left by Irving and Captain Wemyss on the 21st of October, and Vienna reached on the 23rd. Irving's first note concerning the Austrian capital has to do with the erstwhile King of Rome, son of the Emperor of the French, and now merely the Duke of Reichstadt, grandson of the Emperor of Austria. "In driving thro town pass young Napoleon in carriage & six," Irving records in his note-book; while, in a letter to his sister, he amplifies his comment on Prince Metternich's captive eaglet into "a very fine boy full of life and spirit, of most engaging manners and appearance, and universally popular. He has something of Bonaparte in the shape of his head and the lower part of his countenance; his eyes are like his mother's."

About a week after arriving at Vienna Irving visited the famous Lichtenstein galleries. It was while walking through the gardens of this Prince that the thought came to Irving of "preparing a collection of tales of various countries—made up from legends, etc."—a jotting of interest in connection with the "Tales of a Traveller." Not impossibly the great collection of paintings from various countries may have had a subconscious influence in the germination of this idea. At any rate, the Lichtenstein canvases made a great impression on Irving. His selections are numerous as he goes from room to room, and his eclecticism is shown by the pictures he chooses for special notation. The list begins with a guitar player by Caravaggio, the first of the great Italian realistic painters, and ends with Weninx, a master in the delineation of fruits and animals; while between these exponents of altogether different schools, Irving finds place, among others, for Van Dyck and Rubens, the Flemish; for Ribera the Spaniard; for the Frenchman, Chardin; and for Rembrandt, after whose colossal name it seems almost trivial to add: "of Holland." Perhaps it was with some such thought in mind that Irving saw the pictures of this gigantic genius, this Titan in the world of art. He omits all description, all comment and merely records the name "Rembrandt."

At the Imperial Gallery Irving found other paintings specially to attract his attention, and his notes show perspicacity. The rich sensuousness of Jordaens; the mellow colouring of Van Dyck; the Dutch quietness of Teniers; the great strength of Caravaggio; the loveliness of Carlo Dolci; the sweetness but "insipidity" of Rafaelle Mengs, do not escape him; nor various anachronisms in costumes.

Music as well as art contributes to the pleasure of these Vienna days, during which Irving hears "Fidelio," noting that Beethoven's style is rather out of fashion—"Rossini has introduced a different taste." Rossini, then only thirty years of age, had already written some twenty operas that were played throughout Europe. "The Barber of Seville" was Irving's favourite of all operas, if overwhelming preponderance of attendance be proof; Beaumarchais' wit being probably as delicious to Irving as Rossini's music.

With constant interest in all aspects of life, Irving's notebook carries us from opera-house and Imperial palace to many classes of people: the long-bearded Polish Jews, the leather-jacketed Hungarian peasants, the phlegmatic Sclavonians, and the Gipsies. When, early in November, Irving leaves Vienna, for a two days' tour amid Danube scenery, he takes us again into romantic legend, as where, in the Castle of Durstein, with its "dungeon cut out of solid rock" and "savage mountains around," Richard the Lion-Hearted was kept prisoner. We are again in the days of the Crusades, with a King of England seeking to escape a King of France, and falling into the hands of an Emperor of Germany.

At the little village of Stein Irving had crossed the Danube and driven to the convent of Gottreich, "its vast buildings and lofty towers looking dim and shadowy, like a great palace of enchantment, just rising into existence." The treasures of the convent, with its library of rare manuscripts, "the cabinet of natural history, etc." were shown to Irving by a young monk acting under the instructions of the Superior, "a round, sleek, jolly-looking friar"; nor does Irving, whose interest in viands and beverages contributes so human a note to many pages of his memoranda, overlook the fact (which he includes in a letter to his sister, written a few days later) that the cellars of the convent of Gottreich are "as well stored with old wine as the library with old books."

Returning to Vienna after this little tour, Irving, we fancy, must have derived amusement from the situation of his room in the hotel. On one side of the American humorist was an Irish Colonel, "who keeps a mistress partly through ostentation," and on the other side a "Dutch Dandy who plays the piano and rides in the Prater."—With what enjoyment Irving must have overheard the conversation and the music by which he was flanked! Yet it is not to Irving, but to an unknown woman, that we owe perhaps the most delicious page in this Vienna diary. Under the title of "He Is Gone," and with a note to the effect that this is "an attempt at an English lament by a young German lady, in the absence of her lover— Vienna 1822," Irving transcribes a poem that leads one to reflect how swiftly his sympathetic approach must have won the confidence of the young lady poet during Irving's brief stay in the Austrian capital. In any case, the verses are so enticing in phraseology that the temptation to quote them cannot be withstood; and so here they are:

I

When the lark
In the Spring
Song will sing
never hark
on his sung
In the spring
He is gone!

II

In the wood
in the plain
on the road
O in vain!
of the rest
will none
he's gone!
As he soon
gone was
more moon
more sun
Did me shun
He is gone.

III

Glow the rose
appear violet
under moose (*sic!*)
on rivulet
forget me not
for him none
he is gone!

IV

Calm and peace
Stranger are!
Unhappy is
Fool with care
grief and smart
my poor heart
he is gone!
Poor little heart
To thine ache
To thine smart
does not break?
die, die, poor heart,
I will none.
he is gone.

WASHINGTON IRVING ESQUIRE

One more quotation, and we shall have ended with the memoranda jotted down by Irving during his Vienna days. "Nations," he writes, "are fast losing their nationality. The great and increasing intercourse, the exchange of fashions, the uniformity of opinions by the diffusion of literature are fast destroying those peculiarities that formerly prevailed. We shall in time grow to be very much one people, unless a return of barbarism throws us again into clans."—Is there not in this concluding sentence one of the first expressions by an American man of letters of the spirit of internationalism?

The tour through Moravia and Bohemia, almost entirely unrecorded in any Life of Washington Irving, forms the subject matter of the note-book that commences with the departure from Vienna on November 18th. Irving's travelling companion was Willoughby Montague, a lieutenant in the Royal Artillery, and a member of a family distinguished in English annals.

The gaunt hills and monotonous grain fields of Moravia appeared unattractive to one whose recent memories were enwrought with the beautiful scenery of the Rhine and the Tyrol; nor until Iglau was reached did Irving meet with any pleasing village architecture. Thence the journey, at the pace of some forty miles a day, continued into Bohemia, where, on November 21st, we find him in the quaint and ancient town of Teutch Brod, in the windows of many of whose houses bread was displayed for sale. Later on, at midday, Irving stops at Jenikau —a fair is being held in the main street, offering colourful opportunities. The Bohemian peasant women are "generally ugly," but Irving observes "a pretty black-eyed Jewess" tending a booth.

Czeslau is reached in the afternoon. Here the tomb of Zizka, the intrepid commander of the Hussite army after, in 1415, Huss, on the charge of heresy, had been burnt at the stake, was less a reminder of a soldier's death than of the ever-increasing life of religious liberty. But recollections of a conflict of far different nature were evoked when, that same evening, Irving and his companion reached the town of Kolin where,

134

in 1757, Frederick the Great was defeated by Count Darin. And interesting it is for us of to-day to recall that in that Seven Years' War England was the only supporter of Prussia, against whom were arrayed Saxony and Sweden, as well as France and Russia, in alliance with the Hapsburgs.

Before reaching Prague (on November 22nd) Irving passed through the "old-fashioned village" of Bömische Brod, the scene, as he notes, of one of the Tales of Grimm who at that time—an author of nearly the same age as Irving—was in the alkahest of his genius transmuting into golden literature the legends and the fairy-stories of Europe.

Prague offered a fascinating contrast after the days among "sombre mountains" in a "country of boors and rude villages." The excellent opera and theatre delighted Irving. As Rosina in the "Barber of Seville" the beautiful actress Henrietta Sontag charmed Irving. A mere girl, less than seventeen years old, the future Countess Rossi was then on the threshold of her bewitching career.—Irving witnessed an excellent performance of "King Lear," in the "very good exact" translation of August William Ifflau, on whose activities as dramatist, actor, and Director of the Berlin National Theatre, death had only a few years previously rung down the curtain.

Many of the great nobility of Prague had left that old city of the Bohemian Kings to take up their residence in Vienna, then the supreme city of the continent, not only in the sphere of politics and diplomacy, but also in the alluring realm of fashion. The palaces of Prague were deserted; among them the princely Czarnin, whose fallen estate Irving portrays in its contrast with its ancient splendour—vividly in his notes on ruined statues and fountains dry, but even more vitally in that paragraph where a ragged boy drives cackling geese about the courts.

The Cathedral, with its tombs of Ottocar and other warrior Kings; the Chapel of St. Wenceslaus, the tenth century Duke whose attempt to convert his land to Christianity won him the title of Patron Saint of Bohemia, after his assassination by his brother; the prison of King Wenzel (Wenceslaus IV), Holy Roman Emperor and strangler of his wife, whose cruel reign ended in imprisonment when his nobles rebelled in 1394,—all these Irving notes; and the portrait of yet recent or ruling sovereigns—the great Maria Theresa; Maria Carolina's husband, that Ferdinand of Naples whose throne Napoleon had taken first for his brother Joseph Bonaparte, and then for Murat, his brother-in-law; Louis XVI of France and his ill-fated Austrian bride, Marie Antoinette; and other portraits that, could they have spoken, might have voiced deep things to Irving of the French Revolution and the then so triumphantly ended era of Napoleonic domination. For was not the Hapsburg monarch, who had lost the title of Francis II, Emperor of Germany, when the Corsican adventurer founded the Confederation of the Rhine, now wearing, unchallenged and no longer tremulous, his new title of Francis I, Emperor of Austria?

From all these vast terrestial conflicts Irving brings us, with the name of Tycho Brahe, to the vaster and quiet region of the stars. Unappreciated in his home country, and driven thence by envious enemies, the great Danish astronomer had accepted the hospitable invitation of Emperor Rudolph II and, at the close of the sixteenth century, established himself and his tools of observation, at Benateck, near Prague. Here to learn from him came Kepler whose discovery of the great laws of astronomical motion was in large measure due to the counsel he received from Tycho Brahe.

Irving's hotel at Prague (its name, the "Stadt Wien," being evidence of the attraction that Vienna held for all that part of the Continent) was a curious, rambling building, in one of whose rooms "a remarkably fat child 11 years old" was exhibited; and wax works in another. Music had its representative in an Italian female singer; Parisian fashion in a French "marchande de linge," and card-playing coachmen and servants added to the general hodge-podge of the hotel's promiscuous life.

On November 26th, after a five days' sojourn, Irving and

Montague left Prague for Dresden. Their drive of two or three days brought them through the little villages of Schlau and Laun and Torplitz into Kulm, where, in 1813, the Austrians defeated Vandamme, one of those loyal generals of Napoleon who enlisted under the banner of the Emperor during The Hundred Days. At Peterswald the Austrian frontier was crossed, and the Kingdom of Saxony entered. That same evening the travellers drove into Dresden under a moon "in full splendour in a deep blue sky." Thus fittingly did nature set the scene for Irving's entrance into weeks of glitter, and of romance.

Chapter VIII

THE DRESDEN PERIOD

IN a preceding chapter the note-books that Irving wrote during the six or seven months at Dresden and in its vicinity were drawn upon to throw new light on Irving's love affairs. They showed him flirting slightly with Madame de Bergh, and seriously caught up in increasing devotion to Emily Foster, to whom, in the month of March, he proposed. But now there shall be recourse to these diaries rather for the general view of his pleasures and pursuits, his social relaxations and his literary activities during the period when Irving first came into warm relationship with European diplomats and with royalty itself.

On December 3rd, 1822, just a week after his arrival, the dated entries of his Dresden life begin; but before this he makes us acquainted with that circle of friends whereof he was to become so welcome a segment. Irving records the names in a list beginning with that of John Philip Morier, the British Minister at the Court of Saxony, a diplomat who in 1810 had been Secretary of Legation at Washington. To his son, Captain Morier; Campugano, the Spanish Minister; General Conicoff, the Russian; Count Jordan, the Prussian; Count de Rumigny, the French; Count Luxburg, the Bavarian; Count Palffy the Austrian Minister, as also to their ladies, and other members of the diplomatic corps, Irving's list introduces us. A score or more other names appear and re-appear in these note-books. Mrs. Foster's cousin, Col. Livius, who had done some writing for the London theatres; Mr. Corkran, a young officer; Captain Trotter of the Lancers; young Walter Scott; John Cockburn, an English officer of artillery with whom Irving was to tour Bohemia

138

and Silesia; Richard Airey, son of that General who later became Governor of Gibraltar; Böttigar the antiquary, to whom
Irving in 1827 addressed a letter of introduction for Longfellow; Count Blome of Denmark, "with his Countess a pretty little girl—only married six weeks"—these are some of the personages of Irving's Dresden days.

Then, of course, the royal household. The elder group includes that "excellent old gentleman," King Frederick Augustus,
and his excellent old wife; his amiable brother, Prince Max; and
his lively little brother, Prince Antoine, devoted to religion, hunting, and dancing, and to his stately spouse, the sister of the
Emperor of Austria. Frederick and John, sons of Prince Max
and brothers of the Queen of Spain; Frederick's wife, the Princess of Austria, and John's bride, the Princess Amelia of Bavaria, are among the younger royalties with whom Irving becomes on the same terms of cordiality that obtain between him
and the elder Princes, and to whom, in his ever modest and
charming way, he brings new information concerning the young
Republic overseas. This especially to the Saxon Princess
Amelia, daughter of Prince Max, who was "a little of a Blue
Stocking" and liked to speak to Irving about his writings and of
America.

Of the word-portraits Irving draws in these surroundings so
different from anything in his past life, two especially arrest the
attention. Irving's description of General Conicoff is as perfect
a characterization as is to be found in his note-books in its swift
presentation of appearance and personality and of the milieu in
which the idiosyncrasies of the old diplomat found play: "C.
the R.M.—little old bachelor beau—seventy years old—very
gallant—fancies himself in love often—yellow—somewhat
shrivelled—lively eye. Hotel elegantly furnished—formerly
Fouche's [1]—gives elegant entertainments—superb suppers—fid-
gets at them—is surrounded by knick-knacks and trinkets—buys
bad pictures and expects you to praise them—is lively, a little

---

[1] *Joseph Fouché, Duc d'Otrante, was a French statesman who took part in the overthrow of Robespierre.*

capricious and very vain—writes little poems—sonnets, epigrams, etc.—compliments the ladies."

It would have been good fun to know "the little old bachelor beau," but even more delightful to meet Jean Paul Richter, whom Irving saw for the first time at the Christmas Night "rout" at Count Knobelsdorf's. In no Life of Irving is there any mention of Jean Paul, and the comment that the foremost of American humorous authors of his day makes concerning the foremost of German humorists, is one of those choice nuggets that the unexplored passages of these note-books reveal to the reader's eager spade.—"Jean Paul—" Irving begins—"a comic or rather humorous German writer—about 50 years old."— Note the critical acumen in the modification of the term "comic" into "humorous." For though Jean Paul's writings, which, a hundred years ago, were household works in Europe, have those elements of extravagance, grotesqueness even, that are the superficial attributes of comicality, his eccentricities never declined into vulgarity, and the essential humour of his writings flowered from his recognition of what is permanently ridiculous in human nature. Though Jean Paul used the jester's bells more than he did the whip, with no less intense scorn than a Carlyle he attacked the masked face of sham.

There is quaint humour in the anecdote Irving relates of Jean Paul. The famous author "carries a poodle dog with him wherever he goes." At the Dresden gallery the attendants told him civilly that his dog could not be admitted. "Then," said John P., "I cannot see the Dresden gallery, and in fact he went away without seeing it."—The Dresden Gallery, with its world-renowned Madonna by Raffaelle, its glorious Correggios, its superb Vandyck! But the poodle could not enter; therefore neither could "John P." Good old philosopher, true, in however comic a manner, to his feelings of loyalty! Yet even so, we wonder whether any but an American humorist (writing in however private a diary) would have called the famous Richter (as Lowell or Mark Twain might similarly have done) "John P."

Although Irving's happiest hours went by at the home of the Fosters and in preparing for and in acting in those amateur theatricals wherein Emily participated, there was no phase of enjoyment Dresden could offer that he did not share with a zest reminiscent of his early merry days in America. He played at commerce for pool—"at which no one could lose more than one half dollar—great noise and laughing"; he attended small musical parties where Captain Morier performed on the flute, Colonel Livius on the piano, and the Prussian Minister on the violoncello; he listened to (but with generous unwillingness to believe) the scandal concerning Madame Novocheska, a Polonaise Princess suspected of having stolen the diamond necklace of the Princess Theresa; he went to skating parties on the Elbe, to balls, dinners, dances innumerable given by the various diplomats, some of these parties being in honour of the nuptials of Prince John and the Bavarian Princess. On more than one occasion he attended boar hunts, once with young Walter Scott as his companion. Prince Antoine the King's old brother, who was to succeed, four years later, to the throne of Saxony, broke off the branch of a bush and gave it to Irving to wear in his hat—"as everyone does when present at a successful chasse." Often he went to theatre or opera; sometimes we find him in clothes warehouses choosing costumes for the theatricals and tableaux at Mrs. Foster's. A great favourite at court (the Queen on one occasion sent the Master of Ceremonies to bring Irving to her; told him that she had not seen him for a century and paid him many compliments on "The Sketch Book" which she was then reading in a French translation), he had the royal gardens to walk in. He heard Carl Maria von Weber playing his own music on the piano; he talked with the King of Bavaria about Benjamin Franklin whom the King knew in Paris and whose horse and cabriolet the Bavarian monarch had bought after Franklin's departure; he discussed with the younger princes the future of Europe, with Russia as its vast and dangerous factor. There were gay luncheons at inns and at hunting pavilions; country excursions; sails on little lakes; dinners under trees on the lawn. And through it all the songs and whispers of Madame de Bergh, and the surging music of the heart so deeply stirred by Emily Foster.

Writing to his brother Peter, on March 10th, 1823, Washington refers to his "casual career of dissipation," and though he confesses that he has done nothing with his pen he finds consolation in the idea that he has *"lived into* a great deal of amusing and characteristic information; which after all, is perhaps the best way of studying the world." And yet during the Dresden period Irving did not wholly give himself up to pleasures, for he was becoming proficient in both German and Italian. The beauties of Goethe and of Schiller and of Guarini's "Il Pastor Fido" (which he read with Mrs. Foster) were now accessible to him in their original languages, and he could grasp the merits of German translations of Shakespeare. His study of German had begun during the dark days at Liverpool, perhaps, like the flute-playing, as a mental distraction. In Dresden he advanced so rapidly (at the moderate expense of forty-four dollars for over five months of tuition with a Herr Keysler) that, before he left, he was able to begin the translation of the German librettos for two of Weber's operas. With French, also, he was becoming increasingly familiar; but probably, as he suggests in his letter to Peter, the greatest benefit of those days accrued from the easy terms on which they placed him among diplomats and in circles of royalty. When later, under circumstances of great difficulty, he represented his country at the Court of Spain, the grace and discretion with which Irving exercised his functions were doubtless to some extent attributable to his Dresden experiences.

Of the esteem in which Irving was held, and the privileges accorded him in official as well as in royal circles, there is an instance in the leniency shown him on the single occasion of his infraction of Saxon law. A pistol which he was to use in the performance of "The Wonder: A Woman Keeps a Secret," he found, by chance, loaded; whereupon, opening a window, he fired it off. Instead of the legal penalty of twenty dollars and confiscation of the weapon, the President of the Court imposed the nominal fine of some two dollars, and courteously returned the pistol to Irving. Whom the King treats with friendship, Justice is apt to regard benignly.

But all the courtesies and attentions that he received, all the splendid entertainments, of the Prince de Lippe, the Baron, Loewenstein and so many other cordial hosts, began to pall on Irving when, in March, Emily refused the offer of marriage from the delightful American who was, after all, so much her senior. Study also lost its flavour for him; restlessness seized upon him, and there were hours of unmistakable dejection. It very possibly was Mrs. Foster who (on the theory that the heart grows fonder with absence), suggested to Irving that his temporary withdrawal from Dresden might lead on his return to a more receptive Emily. In any event, he determined upon a tour among the Giant Mountains—the Riesen Gebirge—and on the 20th of May, with the two young Foster boys at hand to wish the traveller godspeed, Irving set forth accompanied by John Cockburn, the English artillery officer, in the carriage of his good friend, Mrs. Foster's cousin, Col. Livius. The horses at the fair pace of some six miles an hour brought them safely in the evening to Bautzen. Here, strangely enough on May 21st, they rode over the scene of one of the last of Napoleon's victories. It was on May 21st, 1813, that the Emperor of the French defeated, not without severe losses of his own, the combined forces of Russia and Prussia. Here too, during the Thirty Years War, Wallenstein had achieved one of the most brilliant of his successes.

The scenery through which Irving passed reminded him of England, largely because of the cottages "surrounded by garden and grass plot, so buried in trees, and the moss-covered roofs almost mingling and blending with the surrounding vegetation." Lovely is the mountain valley with its "rich foliage & flowers"; lovely the ruins of the convent of Oüwein; lovely the moonlight walk into the little town of Zittau, as, late at night, Irving returns under its arched gateway.

The touches of gay colour enlivening his memoranda are in pleasant accord with the Bohemia of operettas. Pretty peasant girls, the white and green plumes of uniforms, holiday pastimes,

143

"people spinning under trees with brooks tinkling near," even graveyards gay with their painted tombstones, all these Irving notes before, on May 22nd, he passes the boundary and arrives at Friedland, where Wallenstein's castle beguiles him. But I question whether the historical and literary associations of the ancient structure which the great warrior purchased in 1622— more than six centuries after its tower had been erected—interested Irving as strongly as the recollection that Emily Foster had made a sketch of the castle; and it is to her mother (but for the daughter's eyes) that he writes his only letter from this place of great events, and of sieges as unavailing as Irving's own.

Into Silesia, through various straggling towns and pleasant valleys, the notes then lead us. Here we come to the highest mountains of the Giant Range—Schneekopfe and Riesenkopfe rising a full mile above sea level. The scenery grows bolder, wilder the crags. Here was the legendary home of Rübezahl, a figure of old German folk-lore, a curious imp mingling mischief with kindness. Irving does not relate the legend, but his easy familiarity with it is shown where, on May 26th, he characterizes his landlord in the single phrase, "old Rübezahl."

The notes of these days have numerous amusing passages; none more so, perhaps, than when, at Königgratz, Cockburn introduced Irving to the sergeant of police as an American Colonel; whereupon the sergeant's guard turns out in honour of our gentle officer. But reminiscences of a less pleasant military nature are enwrought in the name of that little town, for at Königgratz, in 1866, Austria's defeat, establishing Prussia's hegemony in Germany, was the beginning of events whose culmination was reached in the World War of our own days.

Towards the end of May the travellers arrived at Prague where they were to stay for almost a month, because of the scarlet fever that attacked Cockburn. The illness of his friend and his own mood of reaction after the festive (and restive) months in Dresden, led Irving to abstain from society. He walks through the old and the new parts of the city—Altstadt and Neustadt; rambles on the slopes of the Lorenzburg; writes on his "History

144

of an Author" (his novel that was never to be finished, and in which Buckthorne and his friends would have had further adventures) ; begins the first English version of "Der Freischütz"; goes to the theatre; hears operas of Weber and of Mozart; and awaits, in his correspondence with Mrs. Foster, the message of hope that does not come. He is "sick of fashionable life."— "I have never let myself into the current for a time but I have been ultimately cast exhausted and spiritless on the shore."

These gloomy weeks of the unsuccessful suitor ended with the return to Dresden on June 27th; but before we follow Irving thither, let us pause for a moment in the Austrian town of Kulm.—"So poor a scrap of earth," writes Irving, "a little hill so fought and struggled for—yet how enormous the amount of human suffering that must have taken place there."—Then he philosophizes on the scene of the battle where, with the capture of Vandamme and ten thousand of the French Army, Napoleon's hold relaxed on the highest rung of his victorious ladder.

On his return to the Saxon capital Irving's first calls were on the Fosters and Madame de Bergh. In the course of the fortnight that preceded his final departure from Dresden he visited the other friends whose names appear so often in his note-books of that period; but of dinner parties, routs, gaiety in general, there is no mention. Emily had not changed her mind. The notes are in a quiet key. He takes, on his last Sunday, farewell of the King and Queen.

Here, then, we reach an end to social doings and to romance during those eventful six months. They had been abortive in original work, the "American Tale" which Irving read aloud to his friends the Fosters being presumably one of the manuscripts that he later destroyed, and little else of literary composition remaining to his credit save the librettos which shall engage our attention in the succeeding chapter. Yet for the literary historian there remain to be culled a few notes, aphorisms and observations, some of them very decidedly with the personal touch; others indicative of Irving's manner of reflection; still others characteristic of his facility to paint with few phrases a sentient portrait. For instance, there is the Captain of a sloop of war—"Old bachelor—had his rooms in upper part of house—used to carry everything there—books, music, etc. He was a musician—played flute—blows hard—amused himself with algebra—had no occupation and fell often in love—children sent up to his room—told them stories—when any one was cross he sent it away and requested that it might have its head changed." There is the remark of an advocate at Aix-la-Chapelle, a remark gaining fresh significance in view of the early events in the World War through which civilization has so recently staggered: "The Prussians have done in two years what Bonaparte for the French could not in twenty-five. They have caused the French to be loved."—There is, in corroboration of Irving's comment that "great men are generally more anxious to have the reputation of talents which they do not possess, than to be extolled for those on which their greatness is founded," the note that "Cuvier would be thought a great politician and is little elated by any praise as comparative anatomist. Wellington makes light of the science of war, but values himself on a talent for science; and Bonaparte was continually aspiring to the name of a great legislator, instead of great captain." There are jottings, possibly for stories, concerning an old soldier at Metz who showed his contempt for the Bishop, and of an old gentleman who used to have his pew "well lined and stuffed as he did his carriage. He took his nap there twice on Sunday very cosily, and thought to travel comfortably to Heaven as he did to town, dozing comfortably all the way." There is an anecdote of a "furious quarrel between two Frenchmen," and some lines concerning the virtues and the charms as well as the faults of the French. But most noteworthy, because autobiographical, are the closing note of the second Dresden diary and one of the last notes in the third. "A man's amours and his maladies are generally the most interesting topics to himself and the most tedious to the rest of the world"; and then: "Love cooled down into Friendship which is Love retired on half pay."

Mrs. Foster, not as the last gesture of friendship, but, as subsequent incidents prove, with the unquenchable optimism of the maternal matchmaker, invited Irving to travel with her and her children on their road of return to England. Amid the romantic beauty of the Hartz Mountains, and in the intimacies of little inns, there might arise situations, sentimental moments, that would yet cause Emily to change her mind. One questions whether Irving, with his habitual lack of self-confidence, was hopeful of so favourable an issue, and the journey must have been for him that "mixture of pain, pleasure, fondness and impatience" with which he wrote of looking back on Dresden.

The party set forth in sunshine, Irving in an open carriage with Mrs. Foster; Emily, her sister Flora, the two young boys and their German tutor following in a post-chaise. After they had left Leipsic a terrible storm arose. The rain was driven by a hurricane with "incredible violence"; hail, "large as hazel nuts," hurling itself against the travellers. The horses became panic stricken and the carriage, dragged down a steep bank, was overthrown. In helping the women out of it, in running to a smith's shop some half mile off and sending workmen to repair the damaged carriage; in escorting the drenched and slightly bruised women to a nearby inn, Irving had opportunity to display his quick sympathy and his courtesy. But neither then, nor during the two days in the little town of Cassel, was he able further to advance his suit; and after (having accompanied the Fosters not only to Rotterdam, but as far down as the Brille) he left them waving to him from the boat, it was a man lonely at heart who, travelling night and day save for a few hours' stay at Antwerp, made his solitary way to Paris.

Chapter IX

THE WRITER OF PLAYS

THE months spent mainly at Paris from August, 1823 to the following May were given over by Irving largely to a little known phase of his literary activities, and to it this chapter, somewhat in the nature of an interlude, will be devoted.

There has among American men of letters of the first rank been none who cared more for the theatre. As a boy Irving stole away from his father's home for surreptitious attendance at such dramatic performances as little New York could offer; hardly more than a boy he contributed, under the name of Jonathan Oldstyle, those letters to the *Morning Chronicle* which have a place among the earliest of worthwhile American dramatic criticism; as a young man, especially in his correspondence with Brevoort, he pronounced intelligent judgment upon the gifted English actors who visited our country. At the opening of the Park Theatre the verses recited by Cooper were from Irving's pen. During his seventeen years in Europe he saw that vast number of plays whose titles, recorded in his diaries, constitute a list—English, French, German, Italian, Spanish—unparalleled in the record of any other American; and as an older man, after his return to the United States, his interest continued so unabated that he would spend winter weeks in New York in order not to forego theatre and opera.

This keen attitude towards dramatic entertainment was, in more ways than one, in accord with Irving's temperament and his philosophy. To him as a pleasure-lover the appeal of the theatre is obvious. The theatre offered him, with its comedy, that merriment—with its drama, that romance and those poignant touches of sentiment—for which his nature craved. These, of

148

course, as to many of us. But Irving sought there also the particular alleviation of his frequent moods of dejection, and particular intellectual incentive for his critical faculties, and the more general withdrawal into the realm of imagination.

After his disappointment in love Irving was in no mood for the finest kind of creative work. He had, moreover, during the Dresden days not only taken the part of Sir Charles Rackett in "Three Weeks after Marriage," of King Arthur in "Tom Thumb," and of Don Felix in "A Wonder: A Woman Keeps a Secret," but had also made his first attempt at the translation and adaptation of plays. The manuscripts of these he took with him to Paris where, shortly after his arrival, he again met John Howard Payne, still engaged in the selection and revision of French plays for London. Payne lost no time in urging Irving to collaborate with him. The author of "The Sketch Book," his name now honoured both in Europe and America, felt some hesitation in entering into the less dignified field of adaptation; but his passion for plays, his entire willingness to add to a purse somewhat depleted by the monetary demands of the unsuccessful steamboat enterprise, and last, but assuredly not least, his desire to be of service to a friend and a countryman more hardpressed than himself were the determining factors in an acquiescence which included the condition that his participation should remain secret.

While Irving gave advice, and probably more than advice, in connection with many of the plays that Payne worked upon during the years 1823 and 1824, two of these were very largely his handiwork—"Charles II," and "Richelieu." With them we may consider "Abu Hassan" and "The Wild Huntsman" [1]— adapted by Irving from the German—as the four finished pieces of Irving the playwright. And after that there shall be a glance at the germinal ideas of a play whose writing Irving contemplated but never carried out.

---

[1] *In this chapter the author, without resorting to quotation marks, has with appreciated permission drawn upon his introductions for the recent, and initial publications of "Abu Hassan" and "The Wild Huntsman" by the Bibliophile Society.*

WASHINGTON IRVING ESQUIRE

When, towards the end of the year 1822, Irving arrived at Dresden, the chief figure in the musical life of the attractive capital of Saxony was Carl Maria von Weber. As manager and conductor of German opera at Dresden, and as himself a composer of operas and symphonies, he had achieved a reputation which became greatly enhanced after "Der Freischütz," originally produced at Berlin in 1821, appeared with enormous success in London in 1824. About a dozen years earlier Weber had composed at Darmstadt his opera of "Abu Hassan," using as the libretto therefor the German of Franz Karl Hiemer. All Dresden, as indeed all Germany, was familiar with the music; and early in the year of 1823 Irving decided to write an English libretto—part translation, part adaptation from the German. Irving's diary shows that he began this work on Sunday morning, the 20th of April; and that on that very evening, at a concert in the Queen's apartment in the royal palace, he heard Weber playing his own music. During the next five days Irving wrote steadily, finishing the rough draft on April 25th. On the 26th his friend Col. Livius played him the music of "Abu Hassan"; and journal entries during the first half of May indicate how rapidly the writing went on, Irving working with Livius on the songs, until the 18th of May when the alterations were finished.

For nine months Sheherazade, the Vizier's daughter, had entertained King Shahriar with many marvellous tales. All who love the Arabian Nights will remember how the King, after having discovered the infidelity of his wife, continued for three years to consort each night with a virgin who was slain when the morning came; how then the people of his city fled with their daughters so that at last no virgin was left when the Vizier went forth to search for the doomed bride, and how, thereupon, Sheherazade insisted that she herself be brought to the King. Him she so beguiled with fascinating legends chosen from "a thousand books of histories, and works of the poets" that when a thousand and one nights had gone by, and she had borne him three sons, her prayer that the mother of his children should be spared

150

from death, King Shahriar granted. Whereupon "joy spread through the palace of the King until it became diffused throughout the city, and it was a night not to be reckoned among lives: its colour was whiter than the face of the day."

On the two hundred and seventy-first night Sheherazade began "The Story of Abon Hassan the Wag, or the Sleeper Awakened," in some ways the merriest and most amusing of all her recitals. Abon Hassan was the son of a wealthy merchant of Bagdad. When his father died Abon Hassan divided his inheritance into equal parts, and one of these portions he expended so lavishly that before long there was nothing left of it. Then he found—it is no uncommon experience in a selfish world—that the boon companions to whom he had been so generous, and who were unaware of the fortune he had laid aside, fell away from him. He determined henceforth to associate only with strangers, nor with any person for more than a night. This went on for a year, each guest after a night of munificent entertainment being dismissed the next morning—a procedure suggesting that of King Shahriar with his brides of a night.

At the end of a year there came to Abon Hassan the Caliph Haroun-Al-Raschid, disguised as was his custom when he set forth on his adventures among the people. With what wealth of hospitality—food and drink, slave-girl and music—the merchant's son entertained the ruler of Bagdad, we may find recounted in the Arabian Nights. The Caliph, intent on an amusing requital of his host's generosity, placed into Abon Hassan's cup a lozenge of bhang and, after the young fellow had become drugged thereby, had him conveyed to the palace where, when Abon Hassan awoke, he was addressed by all the attendants and slaves of Haroun-Al-Raschid as "Prince of the Faithful." The comedy was so well enacted that Abon Hassan, at first believing he was caught in some trick of evil genii, finally believed himself to be the Caliph. The predicament into which this belief led him after he had been again drugged and returned to his home; the second adventure with Haroun-Al-Raschid that terminated in Abon Hassan's becoming the boon companion of the Caliph and the husband of the favourite of Zobeide, the Caliph's wife, lead up to that portion of the narrative which provides the material for the play adapted by Irving.

Matrimony did not change the extravagant habits of **Abon** Hassan, and the time came when he and his wife, after a delightful life of carousal, found his creditors pressing hard upon him. The Caliph had played more than one merry trick upon him. He decides to play a trick upon the Caliph, which shall serve the purpose of replenishing an exhausted exchequer. How Abon (whose name Irving writes as Abu) and Nouzatalfuad (renamed Fatima) alternately feign death, gaining thereby rich purses of compensation from the sympathetic Caliph to the bereaved widower and from the affectionate lady Zobeide to the disconsolate widow; how the Caliph and his lady become involved in an amusing altercation and a considerable wager as to which of their two favourites really is dead; and how amid general rejoicing and forgiveness (after the chief of the creditors had been neatly tricked) Abon Hassan and his wife come to life again, Sheherazade related to King Shahriar with such dexterity that the story remains one of the wittiest of farces.

While the credit for the construction of the play belongs to its original author, it is full of delicious phrases showing Irving's own whimsicality. When Abu Hassan reveals his scheme to his wife, "I only ask thee," he says, "to assume the mask of death; and I hope the mummery will bring thee more profit than fifty acts of twenty Tragedies wherein twenty times as many heroes and heroines give up their mighty souls." To which Fatima answers: "Oh, that's quite another thing. A theatrical death gives me as much pleasure as a real one is my abhorrence." When the Caliph looks with sorrow upon the supposedly dead Abu Hassan, "Ah, poor fellow," he comments, "they say he kept his accounts admirably. The only trouble was he never discharged them. . . . No gentleman could run in debt more intrepidly." When the play comes to its happy ending, "Am I not the shrewdest of all dead men?" its hero asks. "The simple folks let themselves be laid upon their bier without any future object; but I knew well what I was about. I had not the slightest inclination to remain dead, but only died—to gain a living!"

But the wittiest and merriest portions of the play are those where Fatima tells Abu Hassan of her interview with Zobeide to whom she has brought the news of her widowhood; and where Abu Hassan reports to Fatima his similar interview with the Caliph. After Fatima has shaken at Abu Hassan's ear the purse of consolation, with its clink of the hundred gold pieces given by the Caliph's wife, this is the dialogue that follows:

FATIMA: *Zobeide heard my lamentations at a distance and came to meet me in the door of the antechamber. What has happened to you, said she? Ah, cried I with broken voice, what greater misfortune could happen to me than the loss of my beloved husband? Yes, dearest protectress, Abu Hassan, the poor Abu Hassan, he whom your majesty honoured with your power and made happy with my hand—Abu Hassan is no more. He is dead—he is dead!*

ABU HASSAN: *Faith, you move even me!—Well, and what answer made she?*

FATIMA: *Why—after a long pause of silent sympathy the Sultana tried all she could to console me for my loss.*

ABU HASSAN: *Ah! You see what a treasure you have in me. —How others know my value though you don't! Well, the good Sultana, bless her soul! did the best to console thee.*

FATIMA: *She did indeed. My own Fatima, said she, thou hast lost one of the merriest of men.*

ABU HASSAN: *Ah! dear, good Sultana!*

FATIMA: *But then, added she, his jokes were growing sadly stale.*

ABU HASSAN: *Hm! hm!*

FATIMA: *No man could be more generous than he!*

ABU HASSAN: *The good old Zobeide!*

FATIMA: *For he demanded more than belonged to him.*

ABU HASSAN: *Pshaw!*

WASHINGTON IRVING ESQUIRE

FATIMA: *He was of a loving disposition.*

ABU HASSAN: *Did I not tell thee so?*

FATIMA: *For he made love to every woman he met with!*

ABU HASSAN: *Nay nay—that's scandal!*

FATIMA: *Take him for all in all, my dear Fatima, said she, he was such a man as thou wilt not readily meet with again.*

ABU HASSAN: *By the Prophet but the Sultana was in the right after all!*

FATIMA: *But thou mayest meet with a better man any day in the week!*

ABU HASSAN: *Out upon thee, baggage! This is all thy own joking. The Sultana is a woman of too great discernment to make such a speech. But come, it is my turn to play the mourner, though I doubt whether the Caliph will think my loss worthy of such a heavy purse full of consolation, as the Sultana has given thee.*

From his interview with the Caliph, Abu Hassan returns with another hundred pieces of gold and with a magnificent brocade. "Now say," he asks, "whether I have not outdone you in the art wherein the strength of your sex consists, the art of crying!"

FATIMA: *A hundred gold pieces—a very pretty sum. Ah you see how the Caliph valued me—he knew that so heavy a loss needed consolation.*

ABU HASSAN: *Yes truly, and there was another consolation he offered me—which dried my tears in a twinkling.*

FATIMA: *Ah! And pray what was that?*

ABU HASSAN: *Six beautiful slaves! Abu Hassan, said he— loving tender Abu Hassan—thy heart is too kind and fond to be suffered to withdraw in loneliness—thou hast given a proof in thy fidelity to thy wife what a vast flock of affection thou hast in thy disposition. Take now to comfort thee a score of the fairest of those Slaves just brought to my harem!*

FATIMA: *A score of beautiful Slaves!*

ABU HASSAN: *Do not alarm thyself my dear. Said I—Com-*

154

mander of the Faithful, with a mighty potentate like thee it is meet to have hundreds of mistresses. I am a philosopher—I have learnt to moderate my desires—once indeed I should have thought a score of mistresses a score of blessings—but now I am fain to content myself with half a dozen! Oh Nature, Nature, how easily art thou satisfied!

FATIMA: *Half a dozen mistresses! Let them not come here though—or you'll find one wife too many for you!—Ah rogue, rogue! I see by that twinkle of the eye, you are at your jokes again.*

"Abu Hassan," composed in 1810, was Weber's first operatic success. In 1816 he accepted the King of Saxony's invitation to take charge of German opera at Dresden, but there the intrigues instigated by Morlacchi, the director of Italian opera at the Saxon Court, led to petty and major annoyances that to some extent account for the length of time taken in the completion of "Der Freischütz," which was not finished until May, 1820, some three years after its inception. The next year, on the anniversary of the Battle of Waterloo, "Der Freischütz" had its first performance at the New Royal Opera House in Berlin. So popular has it been that to follow its career in Europe and America were to become involved in far ramifications of singers, stage managers, musical directors and librettists; but one may stress the fact that the first version in English of a libretto for the first great German opera was written by the first famous American man of letters.

Legends having to do with the purchase by Satan of a human soul in exchange for some extraordinary favour granted by that temporarily complacent monarch are to be found in the literatures of many lands and ages. One of these, a legend that had a very particular vogue in the central Europe of the fourteenth, fifteenth and sixteenth centuries, related to magic bullets. As to the method of making these bullets, folk-lore offers various choices; but the surest way involved sacrilege and posited affiliation with the infernal powers. The aspirant towards their ownership would, at Divine Service, instead of swallowing the Sacramental Host, secrete it. Later he would affix it to a tree, and then shoot at it. Drops of blood, we are told, would fall on a cloth prepared to catch them. This cloth would then be burned and, with the proper incantations, its ashes, mixed with lead, would result in the magic bullets. Seven in all, so runs the legend, would be the fruit of this curious labour; and six of these seven bullets were "free"—free to reach whatever mark their owner might desire—but the seventh had a supra-magic quality. It remained peculiarly in the power of the Devil himself, and the destination that he chose for it in the majority of the legends was fraught with dramatic surprise and grim tragedy. On this point it is interesting to consider how drastically our friend Satan became the exponent of poetic justice.

In choosing this legend for his opera Weber conferred with his friend Friederich Kind, a lawyer who was to some extent a man of letters, and from the pen of this writer came the initial libretto. Kind placed his story in the dominions of Duke Otto-kar, and chose as its hero a huntsman who in the original version is called Max and is, by Irving, renamed Albert. This hunts-man is a noted marksman and the affianced of Agatha (renamed Bertha by Irving), the daughter of Cuno, the Prince's chief for-ester. According to the custom of the country Albert will suc-ceed his future father-in-law as Chief Forester if he succeeds in the test of marksmanship set by the Duke.

Another forester, Caspar, is the villain of the story. He has sold himself to the Devil for worldly advantage, and, as the play begins, the time is approaching when he must fulfill his part of the contract unless he can redeem his own security by bringing to the Evil Spirit a victim in place of himself. The Devil in the original version goes by the name of Samiel; in Irving's manu-script he is called Urian. He is the Wild Huntsman, the dire agency through whose favour unerring marksmanship can be attained.

A third forester—or peasant rather—is Kilian, who appears in Irving's version as Andreas. The change in name is, of

156

course, inconsequential; but with Irving's treatment of Andreas
we come to psychologically, philosophically and dramatically
Irving's most important departure from the original version.
In the initial German version, in the first acted English version,
and indeed in all subsequent versions, the hero of the play, after
meeting with disaster in the preliminary contest, and fearing not
alone his failure to succeed the Chief Forester but even more the
possibility of losing his bride, succumbs to the villain's temptation and accompanies Caspar into that wild glen where he hopes
to obtain, consciously through infernal aid, the magic bullets
which shall assure his victory in the final contest of marksmanship. Irving, however, decided to change the plot of the story
in such a manner as to keep Albert's character free from the
taint of infernal association. In a few pages of preliminary
notes he writes: "In the present Drama the hero is never to
raise suspicion to temptation; to spurn at all base and underhand means of securing success, and by his steadfastness and
faith to merit and receive the protection of heaven."

"To carry on the supernatural part of the story," Irving goes
on to write, "another person is made to yield to temptation and
to seek the assistance of infernal agency. He is represented as
inflated by the vanity of temporary success and the moment of
successful temptation is when he is in the midst of dissolute
revelry." So Irving develops the character of Andreas—a man
far more the vain peasant than the sturdy marksman—along
these lines. Irving begins the play with the usual scene where
Andreas, through the agency of Caspar's magic bullets, succeeds while Albert fails in the preliminary contest. He then
builds up a scene in which Andreas gets drunk, boasts, becomes
a little too intimate with Marion, the daughter of Christopher
the inn-keeper. The drunken Andreas listens to the arguments
of Caspar who promises him the position of Chief Forester,
and hints that Bertha also may become the peasant's prize. It
is Andreas who then accompanies the villain to the wild place
where the Wild Huntsman will preside over the making of the
additional magic bullets which Andreas believes will bring him

victory in the final contest with Albert that is to take place the next day. Caspar, having failed to capture Albert as the victim who shall be his substitute in the compact with the Devil, must content himself with bringing the foolish peasant into the presence of his Diabolic Majesty. Irving's treatment of the character and the actions of Andreas are such that—to quote Irving's own words—"Andreas is ultimately left in doubt how far he had committed himself in his half-soul'd dealing with the Fiend —whether he was to be saved or damned, or whether indeed, from his weakness and indecision of character, he were worthy of either."

Having, in Act I, preserved the spiritual integrity of his hero, Irving, it must be admitted, lessens the dramatic content of Act II by this substitution of the peasant, a secondary character.

The scene of incantation still remains one of considerable effect. A gruesome glen—blasted trees—craggy mountains surrounding it—a steep and dangerous path on one side—weird moonlight that succumbs later to the thunder clouds—a circle of charred stones in whose centre, with perhaps a skull as a receptacle, Caspar begins to mould the fateful bullets. In the course of their creation Satan appears, preceded by the wailing of invisible spirits, and followed by all manner of dire and terrible events. The moulding of the bullets is accompanied by ever wilder phenomena, the climax being reached as trees fall and rocks split open when the seventh bullet brings about a veritable convulsion of nature.

The third act begins with the discussion between two huntsmen as to the approaching trial of skill. Albert enters in cheerful humour, for the evil spell that was over him the preceding day when he had shot so amiss seems now to have been broken. His rifle is "once more true to its master." This recurrence of skill is in consonance with Irving's change in the plot and may be regarded as an evidence that the forces of Good are now fighting on the side of the hero who refused to accept the aid of the Evil One. But when Albert goes to the cottage of his beloved he finds her in a state of unhappy premonition, and in the scene between Bertha and her confidant, Nina, the wreath that should have been her wedding-wreath appears as a death wreath. Nina thereupon takes some white roses to make a bridal wreath of them, for these flowers have had the blessing of the good Hermit, who is symbolic of Divine intercession. We are thus prepared anew for a dramatic scene where, much as in epic poetry, supernatural agencies will contest in deciding the fate of the hero.

Caspar, realizing that "the spell of Urian is over and something holy blesses Albert's aim," has one resource left—the fatal seventh bullet. He determines that this shall find its mark in the heart of Albert's bride. But when his dupe Andreas fires the last bullet at the white dove in the distant tree, it does not strike the white-clothed Bertha, but the hiding Caspar who pays with his death the penalty of all his treachery. The Duke announces to Albert that he has won the coveted place as Ranger, and then places in the hero's hand the hand of his beloved. At this happy juncture—vice punished, virtue rewarded —the play fittingly comes to an end, everybody this side of Hell satisfied; and even there we may imagine the Wild Huntsman partially content through his irrevocable capture of the soul of the villanous Caspar.

Irving's version of "The Wild Huntsman" is notable not only for its interesting reconstruction but also, and especially, for the felicity of its diction. The language fairly flows, often with that stream of simple melody characteristic of his style. The dialogue offers so many examples one hardly knows which to choose; but take, for instance, the words wherewith Conrad, the Chief Forester, addresses Albert who is downcast at the inexplicable falling-off of his marksmanship. "Rouse thee then, Albert; shake off this heartless desponding mood, which is the whole cause of thy ill luck— Rouse thee and be thyself, and the event is certain! And now, Brother Huntsmen, remember— the place of rendezvous for tomorrow's hunt is in the meadow by the mill. His Grace will be there by sunrise— We'll show

159

him sport, I'll warrant, and make the forest echo with the music of our horns."

Or again, with that light touch which is an element of Irving's humour, we find him portraying Andreas with a skill that may well have been based on memories of the gay days when the Irving boys and the Kemble boys and Brevoort and Paulding and the others had such convivial times at "Cockloft Hall":

ANDREAS: *'Sblood, this strange talk of Caspar has somewhat sobered me. I don't half like this business of the Wolf's Glen. Not that I'm afraid, damme. Dare-devil Andreas afraid—that would be a good joke! But I don't like this cooking in the night air, and I've not been long enough in the conjuring line to feel easy in it. Egad, I'll e'en have another pull at of the bottle (Fills.) If I am to be a conjurer, damme, it shall be a bottle conjurer. (Enter Christopher in nightgown and slippers.)*
CHRISTOPHER: *What—still at it, Master Andreas? Shall I bring you another bottle?*
ANDREAS: *No, good Christopher. It's time for sober people like me to go home to bed. (Looking out of the window.) Zounds, what a storm is gathering. Harkee, good Christopher, no more wine but a cloak, good Christopher—a good mantle to keep out the rain. Your wine is dry wine, good Christopher, and I wish to keep it dry—so give me a mantle, good Christopher, to keep out the rain. I've no idea of making a flask of wine and water of myself. A dry body and a wet soul—that's my motto—so give me a mantle, honest Christopher. 'Twere a pity good liquor should be spoiled.*

Irving is just as happy in portraying the sprightly Nina. When Bertha expresses fear that something has happened to Albert who is more than an hour late for the love tryst, "This comes of one's getting a character for punctuality," Nina answers. "Give me a lover that never keeps an appointment—one that never comes when the door is open, but climbs into the window when I least expect him." And again when Bertha on her wedding day is heavy-hearted with strange forbodings, her cheerful companion says to her: "Dear, dear Bertha—for heaven's sake don't look so gloomy on your wedding morn. Upon my word, you frighten me—I had no idea marriage was such a terrible thing. Why, lud, my dear, 'twill soon be over, and then you'll think no more of it than all the married folks one sees."

The two librettos we have been considering John Howard Payne brought to the attention of English managers; but he had not been empowered to use Irving's name. If the authorities at Covent Garden had been aware that the manuscripts were from the pen of the famous and popular author of "The Sketch Book," very probably they would have been accepted, instead of remaining unknown, and unpublished for over a century, until their recent issue by the Bibliophile Society.

Payne was more fortunate in negotiating with the management of Covent Garden the two plays that he had selected for adaptation from the French originals by Alexander Duval. The former of these, in its French version first performed at the Théâtre Français under the title of "La Jeunesse de Henri V," and in turn, based (as Mr. Arthur Hobson Quinn notes in his excellent "History of the American Drama") on Sebastien Dercier's published but not acted play entitled "Charles II, Roi d'Angleterre," was far more the work of Irving than of Payne. When Payne, at London, received from Irving the manuscript of "Charles II, or the Merry Monarch" he wrote: "I consider it one of the best pieces of the kind I ever read; there is a never diminishing vein of wit running through it, which coming in aid of situations eminently dramatic, gives it a claim to rank with the best works in the language." This praise, none too high, is of a nature indicating that Payne was writing of work by Irving, not by himself; and indeed the wit and the grace of the play are Irving all over.

The Earl of Rochester is in love with Lady Clara, one of the ladies of Charles's court—seriously in love this time and eager for marriage. Frowning on the amatory escapades of the King and his boon companion the Earl, Lady Clara agrees to become the wife of Rochester on the condition that her suitor effect, or at least seek to effect, the reformation of the Merry Monarch. A young page is devoted to the niece of a retired sailor, Captain Copp, who presides over a tavern at Wapping. Rochester takes the King to this tavern, introducing himself as a seaman, Tom Taffrel by name, and the King as his messmate, Jack Mizen. He counts, and rightly, on Charles engaging in flirtation with lovely Mary Copland, the Captain's niece, and he manœuvres to involve his adventuresome liege in a situation which shall teach him a good lesson. The two supposed sailors run up quite a bill for exhilarating potations. When time for payment comes the Earl leaves the King in the lurch. Charles's purse is missing; he offers his jewelled watch as security to the irate Captain, and Copp, suspecting that the watch is stolen property—for how could a seaman have so magnificent a piece of jewellery?— locks the King in the room while he goes off for the authorities. They recognize the time-piece as belonging to the King of England. The worthy old tar returns to his tavern, only to find the prisoner flown, Charles having leapt out of the window with a final kiss of the hand to Mary. Copp and his niece present themselves shortly thereafter at the palace to present the watch to the King. There Charles and Rochester are recognized by Copp as the seamen who made so merry at his tavern; and there Mary, who is in reality the kin of the preceding Earl of Rochester, comes finally into her own, with, for good measure, the young page as her husband.

The characterization is splendid, and the dialogue sparkling, throughout the play. Captain Copp is the outstanding figure, as fine a piece of humorous delineation as anything in "Knickerbocker's History of New York." His language, with its metaphors borrowed from the life of the sea, is more engaging than anything else we can think of in literature of the kind. When Mary comments on the demeanour of Charles and Rochester in the tavern and says: "By their swaggering about so, they must be very rich," Copp answers: "Pooh, child, 'tisn't the deepest

Theatre Royal, Covent-Garden

This present THURSDAY, October 7, 1824,
Will be performed the Comedy of The

SCHOOL for SCANDAL

Sir Peter Teazle by Mr. W. FARREN,
Sir Oliver Surface, Mr. FAWCETT,
Sir Benjamin Backbite, Mr. JONES,
Joseph Surface, Mr. COOPER,
Charles Surface, Mr. C. KEMBLE,
Crabtree, Mr. BLANCHARD, Careless, Mr. BAKER,
Rowley, Mr. CHAPMAN, Moses, Mr. YATES,
Snake, Mr. CLAREMONT, Trip, Mr. HORREBOW,
Lady Teazle by Miss CHESTER.
Lady Sneerwell, Mrs. VINING, Mrs. Candour, Mrs. GIBBS.
Maria, Miss LOVE, Maid, Miss GIFFORD
In act III a SONG by Mr. TAYLOR.

To which will be added the new Comedy in two acts, (with some Musick) called

Charles the Second

OR THE

MERRY MONARCH.

The Musick composed by Mr. BISHOP.
King Charles the Second, Mr. C. KEMBLE,
Lord Rochester, Mr. JONES,
Captain Copp, Mr. F A W C E T T,
Edward, (the King's Page) Mr. D U R U S E T,
Lady Clara, Mrs. FAUCIT,
Mary (Copp's Niece) Miss HAMMERSLEY.

PLACES for the BOXES to be had at the Box-Office, Hart-street, from Ten till Four ; where PRIVATE
BOXES may also be had for the Season, or Nightly.

The Publick is respectfully informed that

The Theatre will be opened Every Night this week.

Tomorrow, the Comedy of PRIDE SHALL HAVE A FALL.
Count Ventoso, Mr. W. FARREN, Torrento, Mr. JONES, Lorenzo, Mr. COOPER,
Major O'Shannon, Mr. CONNOR, Cornet Count Carmine, Mr. YATES, Countess Ventoso Mrs DAVENPORT
Victoria, Miss PATON, Leonora, Miss LOVE..
After which (in consequence of the unprecedented applause from all parts of the Theatre,) will be
repeated the Comedy of
CHARLES the SECOND; or, The MERRY MONARCH.
On Saturday, (in consequence of the repeated enquiries at the Box-Office) the Comedy of The
INCONSTANT will be repeated.
Old Mirabel, Mr. W. FARREN, Young Mirabel, Mr. C. KEMBLE, Durætete, Mr. JONES
Bisarre, Mrs. CHATTERLEY, Oriana, Miss JONES.
With The IRISH TUTOR.
And the Melo-Drama of A TALE of MYSTERY.
On Monday, the Play of The MOUNTAINEERS.
Octavian, Mr. C. KEMBLE, Virolet, Mr. MASON, Kilmallock, Mr. CONNOR, Roque, Mr CHAPMAN
Lope Tocho, Mr. BLANCHARD, Bulcazin Muley, Mr. EGERTON, Sadi, Mr. DURUSET,
Floranthe, Miss F. H. KELLY, Agnes, Miss LOVE, Zorayda, Miss LACY,
With the last new Pantomime of HARLEQUIN and POOR ROBIN.
On Tuesday will be revived *Beaumont and Fletcher's* Comedy of
RULE A WIFE AND HAVE A WIFE.
The Duke, Mr. BENNETT, Juan, Mr. EGERTON, Perez, Mr. JONES, Leon, Mr. C. KEMBLE,
Cacafogo, Mr. FARLEY, Margarita, Mrs. FAUCIT, Altea, Mrs. VINING,
Estifania, Miss CHESTER. (her first appearance in that character,)
Old Woman, Mr. FAWCETT, Daughter, Mr. KEELEY.
To which will be added,
PRESUMPTION ; or, The FATE of FRANKENSTEIN.
On Wednesday, Mr. YOUNG
will make his first appearance this season, in the character of SIR PERTINAX MACSYCOPHANT
in *Macklin's* Comedy of The MAN OF THE WORLD.
After which, (4th time) CHARLES the SECOND; or, The MERRY MONARCH.
⁎⁎⁎ *The Publick is respectfully acquainted that*
SHAKSPEARE's Comedy of AS YOU LIKE IT,
With additional SONGS, DUETS, &c. selected from his Works, and composed for this Play by Mr. H. R. BISHOP,
is in rehearsal, and will be immediately brought forward.

DER FREISCHUTZ

has been in preparation the whole of the Summer, and will be produced as early as possible with the attention
necessary to the beauty of its Musick—the splendour of its Scenery—and the intricacy of its Machinery.

Printed by W. Reynolds, 9, Denmark-court, Strand.

PLAY-BILL OF "CHARLES THE SECOND
OR THE MERRY MONARCH"

laden ships that make the most rolling." "But they spent their money so freely," suggests his niece. "A sure sign that it's running out," answers Copp. "The longest cable must come to an end. He that pays out fastest will soonest be brought up with a round turn."

Then again when the King, unable to foot the bill, lays the blame on Rochester, "Come, come, messmate," says the Captain, "I'm too old a cruiser to be taken in by so shallow a manœuvre —I understand all this—your companion makes sail—you pretend to have been robbed! It's all a cursed privateering trick— clear as day." "Friend Copp," Charles offers, "if you will wait till tomorrow, I'll pay you double the sum." Double the sum!" exclaims Copp. "Thunder and lightning! What do you take me for? Look ye, neighbour, to an honest tar in distress, my house and purse are open to a jolly tar who wants a caper and has no coin in hand. Drink today and pay tomorrow, is the word; but to a sharking landlubber, that hoists the colours of a gallant cruiser, to play off the tricks of a pirate, old Copp will show him his match any day."—And, finally, when the bluff old Captain realizes at the palace that it was the King of England whom he had locked up as a thief and so drastically bawled out, he makes no apology but characteristically observes: "Ah! Your Majesty knows, that he who cracks a joke must not complain if he should chance to pinch his fingers."

But what more than anything else made the hilarious success of this comedy was the song that Captain Copp began over and over again, only to have his niece stop him before he came to the conclusion of its first stanza. Here we have Irving's humour at its broadest, but no thought of decorum shall keep us from setting down the verses:

> "In the time of the Rump,
> As old Admiral Trump
> With his broom swept the chops of the channel;
> And his crew of Big Breeches,
> Those Dutch sons of——"

Mary (putting her hand on his mouth) : "Oh, Uncle, Uncle, don't sing that horrible song."

Charles Lamb told John Howard Payne that "he can't keep Copp's song out of his head, and is very anxious for the rest of it. He says the hiatus keeps him awake o'nights."

No less satisfactory is Irving's treatment of Rochester. The Earl's quality as wit and poet (and as moral instructor) is suggested in sentences such as that wherein he gives advice to the young page who has just confessed his love for the tavern-keeper's niece: "But I told thee to skim over the surface of beauty, just dipping your wings, like a swallow, not plumping in like a goose. I told you to hover from flower to flower like a butterfly, not to bury yourself in one like a bee."—The goose simile Irving adapted from the jotting in a note-book of 1822 where he observed that French women dip into love like ducks while English women plump in like heedless hens.

Again dealing with the amorous adventures of court personages, but essentially different from the farcical character of the play relating to Charles II, is the tragedy, "Richelieu," the drama whose adaptation from the French of Duval was also the joint work of Payne and Irving. The episode which furnishes its theme revolves around Richelieu's passion for a woman of the middle classes who, in the cast of characters, appears under the name of Dorival. After she has been lured to his palace and seduced against her will she resorts to suicide, a grim ending to, on the whole, an unconvincing drama, whose chief interest lies in the opposition in the characters of the profligate Duke and his uncompromisingly honourable if somewhat Puritanic secretary, Dubois. It is from Richelieu's palliation of his romantic adventures and the phraseology of his argumentation that the flavour of the drama arises for the student of Irving, as many sentences in these parts of the dialogue are clearly his. This, for instance: "I know you're a handsome fellow; but spare me that growling virtue that runs at the bottom of every speech like the drone of a bagpipe." And this: "Bravely spoken, Sir Oracle! but don't let your virtue boil over to scald your neighbours." And this:

164

"Every paltry cynic; every phlegmatic moralist whose chilly constitution keeps him virtuous must ring dull changes on the
faults of Richelieu! And what forsooth are Richelieu's mighty
crimes—his vivid feelings, his joyous temperament, his love of
beauty, his gallant devotion to enchanting women, in short the
mighty sins of youth and generous blood!" A little later there
comes a sentence distinctly reminiscent of a metaphor jotted
down by Irving in one of his earlier note-books when he may have
been thinking of Byron. "We notice," he makes Richelieu say,
"every stoop and pounce of the eagle, as he soars aloft in the full
blaze of sunshine, while the owl mouses securely in the dark
and nobody knows of his peccadilloes."

These, then, are some of the many passages wherein is evident
the specific work of Irving. That in a general way he contributed largely to the entire play is made manifest by various
entries in his diary, and by Payne's grateful acknowledgment
in the dedicatory letter to Irving when, in 1826 at New York, the
drama was published in book form. Irving did not always
agree with Payne concerning his choice of dramatic material, and
we find him unwilling to work on "Azendai," but he does go to
the trouble of correcting Payne's play of "The Spanish Hero,"
(as is proved by the diary entry of January 14th, 1824);
helps him in "Beaux and Stratagems"; and is in other instances
his friend's literary advisor and aid. More than that, Irving
turned his attention to Payne's business interests, and was successful in having the English manager, Price, raise the remuner-
ation from one hundred pounds to one hundred and fifty pounds
for the services of Payne in obtaining plays for the London stage.
Irving did acts of kindness to many men of letters—Bryant,
Prescott and Hawthorne among them—but there is no one on
whom he conferred more generosity than on the unfortunate son
of Sarah Isaacs, the author of the immortal "Home, Sweet
Home," by the irony of fate most homeless of American poets.

Charles Kemble, who took the part of Charles II, may possibly have been let into the secret that this play was largely the
product of Irving's pen. At any rate, on September 11th, 1824,

165

he asked Irving to write a play for him. The diary does not reveal either an assent or a refusal; but in the following month Irving conceived the plan of a play to be entitled "The Cavalier," and during the following week wrote almost feverishly. After this all trace of the play is lost. Nothing remains of "The Cavalier." But loosely placed between the pages of a diary of that year have been discovered the notes for a play based on a suggestion given to Irving the preceding March by Lord Byron's friend, Captain Medwin. "El Embozado"—The Cloaked Figure—is a drama of the dual nature of man. The plot that Irving worked up from Medwin's note reveals an aristocratic and dissolute young man who seduces a peasant girl. After having given her love, she learns that her hero is engaged to a young noblewoman. She kills herself. The night before the marriage her seducer is carousing with his boon companions. Later, when he is alone, he is confronted by a mantled figure that accuses him for his evil ways; will hear nothing in extenuation; threatens and commands. The spoiled young fellow becomes enraged and is about to attack the stranger when he realizes that the unknown visitor is himself. His other self— his better self—stands in the way of his career of riches, happiness, and of cold and selfish vice. But how shall a man get away from himself? The keenest sword cannot cut the strings of conscience; and in Irving's play—as later, although differently evolved, in Stevenson's "Dr. Jekyll and Mr. Hyde,"—the solution is the hero's death.

Irving's interest in "Faust" (a drama that Irving remarks Goethe apparently took from the "Magico Prodigioso" of Calderon, a play which Irving read in the original), was a motive which undoubtedly led him into deeper thought concerning man's dual nature, and to the desire of embodying his reflections in a work of literature. Only the other day, when I was seated at Irving's desk in the little study of Irving's home at Sunnyside, I found in a drawer containing books and papers for many years unstudied, Irving's autographed copy of "Faust." Six francs, twelve sous he had, on September 17th, 1825, paid for this favourite literary treasure.   But whatever may have been the intensity of Irving's spiritual and intellectual reaction to that masterpiece of German literature, it is not surprising that "El Embozado" was never completed.   For such drama of the soul Washington Irving was not equipped.   His mind was not great enough, his experience not poignant enough, his imagination not sufficiently deep.   He may indeed have been able to achieve a production theatrically successful, but not a play of such psychological, embracingly intellectual and convincingly dramatic content as to satisfy his own critical sense as a writer of fiction and as a student of plays.

Chapter X

TRANSITION

IRVING'S life, both as man and as man of letters, falls, roughly speaking, into two divisions—"roughly speaking," because even after his return to America in 1832 he gave play to his instinct of the wanderer, and, too, his pen brought forth (mainly along the lines of legends mingled with history) various imaginative writings. But with his departure for Spain in 1826 there began not alone his career as pre-eminently the historian and the biographer, but also, in its personal aspects, his more stable, assured and unemotional period. The two or three years following the Dresden days may thus be regarded as the transition epoch. The determining factors that led to the romantically calmer and, in authorship, less imaginative stage, were his disappointment in love and his chagrin at the comparative failure of "The Tales of a Traveller."

The hesitancies and doubts that assailed him during this period find frequent expression in his diaries, and the different kinds of literary work that he then attempted, generally with little satisfaction to himself, give evidence of that uncertain state of mind which did not come to an end until he became engaged at Spain in the insistent and meticulous task of historical research. There for the first time as a man of letters he was to have proof of Thoreau's aphorism that routine is a wall to retreat to.

Irving's occupation in writing for the stage, with "Charles II" as the one notable success (but, even so, an anonymous success) has been reviewed in the preceding chapter. But how many were the abortive literary attempts of those days! He had begun at Dresden the manuscript of "Buckthorne and His Friends" which, for a brief while, he intended to develop into a novel; but the novel never came to fruition. Irving realized that a lengthy piece of fiction was not his métier, and that the short story, or the story-essay, was the field for which his talents best qualified him in imaginative literature. In 1824 he gathered together a sufficient number of such pieces for "The Tales of a Traveller," containing in addition to "Strange Stories by a Nervous Gentleman," "The Italian Banditti," and "The Money Diggers," the completed portion of his unfinished novel, that "History of an Author," into which "Buckthorne and His Friends" had failed to develop. For the "Tales" he received the considerable sum of fifteen hundred guineas from Murray, but this satisfactory financial arrangement did not compensate his disappointment at the book's unfavourable reception by critics on both sides of the ocean. The author of "The Sketch Book" and of "Bracebridge Hall" had not added to his reputation, and the ever-sensitive Washington Irving felt this very keenly. He attempted other stories in those days whereof his diaries record the titles. "The Bold Dragoon"; "The Mysterious Picture"; "The Story of My Uncle and the Marquis"; an unidentified Italian story; a robber story (presumably "The Adventures of Popkins"), are some of his discarded excursions into fiction. "I wish, in everything I do, to write in such a manner that my productions may have something more than the mere interest of narrative to recommend them, which is very evanescent; something, if I dare to use the phrase, of classic merit." Here, in Irving's own words, we have the explanation for the destruction of these tales. They did not reach so high a standard; and one wonders, with amusement, what would happen to the magazines of to-day if American short story writers, of whom Irving was the first to be successful, were to maintain the literary ideals to which he gave expression and, at real cost to himself, adherence.

With equal self-rigour and therefore with like futility he entered the sphere of essay writing, especially during his sojourn at Bordeaux in the late months of 1825 and January of the succeeding year. There he conceived the idea of "a work on manners and morals as connected with manners—suited to

America." Suavity of Manners," "On the Treatment of Strangers in America," "National Prejudices," "The Union," "American Rural Life," "Public Prosperity," "The Navy," "Essay on Education," "National Character," "The Probity of Dueling," "The Theatre"—these are the papers on which Irving wrote at some length, or "scribbled a bit," and finally "gave up in despair," destroying a series of manuscripts which, one may feel certain, would be a rich treasury for the student both of Irving's life and of the development of American civilization. For however unsatisfactory these writings may have seemed to their sensitive and self-critical author it is impossible not to believe that, when Irving wrote his "comparison patriot and demagogue"; when (recalling early associations with Aaron Burr and Commodore Decatur, protagonists in two of the most famous of American duels) he set down his views on the evil and illogicality of duelling; when, with that generous broad-mindedness that made him so great a figure in the reconciliation of the English-speaking peoples, he engaged on the theme of international courtesy, he lodged into these howsoever fragmentary papers, nuggets of the pure gold of his mind and nature.

The marked contrast between the early gay period in American cities and the years of commercial harassment in Birmingham and Liverpool has its parallel in the years of 1824 and 1825 as contrasted with the festive Dresden days. There is, however, in this later time of dispirited moods an element of pathos peculiarly its own—the pathos of a middle-aged writer seeking not only the means of support but also the anodyne for sorrow, and casting about, none too hopefully, for the kind of literary work which should maintain the fame that he had achieved. When a man begins to doubt himself, to consider himself a failure—and especially such a man as Irving—he shrinks within his shell. There is evidence of this tendency in Irving's almost entire cessation of correspondence with Brevoort during these two years. His first letter in 1824, dated December 11th, begins: "I have suffered an enormous time to elapse without writing to you; but I cannot help it. I seem no longer master of myself and my leisure"; and in this letter is his defence of his own manner of writing, brought forward because he had observed in recent letters from his brother Ebenezer that Brevoort was joining in the advice that Irving should write a novel. "For my part I consider a story merely as a frame on which to stretch my materials. It is the play of thought, and sentiment and language; the weaving in of characters, lightly yet expressively delineated; the familiar and faithful exhibition of scenes in common life; and the half concealed vein of humour that is often playing through the whole—these are among what I aim at, and upon which I felicitate myself in proportion as I think I succeed." But Brevoort does not seem to have sent any encouraging reply, it may be through the impatience of the man of affairs with a friend whose early indolent habits were so well known to him, and to whom he may now have wrongly ascribed indolence as the explanation for unwillingness to go through the arduous task of novel-writing. Not until Irving was engaged on his important biographical work in Spain, in 1827—Irving happy in his new labours and Brevoort certain of the seriousness of this literary effort—did the correspondence between the two friends take on much of its old-time fluency and cordiality.

Most significant of Irving's literary discouragement during the transition period were the letters written by him in 1824 to his nephew Pierre Paris Irving. He speaks to Pierre of the "Pernicious effects of early publishing." He hopes that the boy's literary vein is "but a transient one," and that he is preparing to establish his fortune and reputation "on a better basis than literary success." He hopes that "none of those whose interests and happiness are dear to me will be induced to follow my footsteps, and wander into the seductive but treacherous paths of literature. . . . I have a thousand times regretted with bitterness that ever I was led away by my imagination. Believe me, the man who earns his bread by the sweat of his brow, eats oftener a sweeter morsel, however coarse, than he who procures it by the labour of his brains." At the same period that he was addressing his nephew in this vein, Irving was writing to his friend Leslie: "I am isolated in English literature without any of the usual aids and influences by which an author's popularity is maintained and promoted. I have no literary coterie to pry me up; no partial reviewer to pat me on the back; the very review of my publisher is hostile to everything American.—I have one proud reflection, however, to sustain myself with—that I have never in any way sought to sue the praises nor deprecate the censures of reviewers; but have left my works to rise or fall by their own deserts."

Thus, sufficiently unhappy, but always with quiet dignity and stainless integrity Irving went his way. The hope which had rearisen in his heart after he had been some months in Paris, leading him to visit the Fosters at their home in England in 1824, was to be frustrated. His diaries show that he met in Paris in 1825 both Mrs. Foster and Emily and that, a little later, he wrote to Emily a letter which took him two or three days to perfect. Nor even may that have been the final plea, later visits to the Foster household in England perhaps reviving the old hope. The French and English months of 1824 and 1825 went by in a manner summed up in the closing entries for those two years. "This has been a dismal day of depression," he wrote on December 31st, 1824, "and closes a year, part of which has been full of sanguine hope, of social enjoyment, peace of mind, and health of body—and the latter part saddened by disappointment and distrust of the world and of myself; by sleepless nights and joyless days— May the coming year prove more thoroughly propitious." When that "coming year" ended we find: "So closes the year—tranquil in mind, though doubtful of fortune and full of uncertainties—a year very little of which I would willingly live over again—though some parts have been tolerably pleasant."

The social enjoyment to which Irving alludes in the former of these notations was of a subdued nature. Irving's frequent attendance at the theatre has already been observed; but there is no mention of even a single dance, or any convivial dinner party remarkable for its gaiety, such as he had attended in Dresden or in former Paris days with Thomas Moore. Much of his leisure time was spent in the family circle, at Auteil, of his niece, Mrs. Storrow. In Paris he consorted mainly with the English and Americans. We find him on one occasion the guest of the Russian Ambassador, Pozzo di Borgo, Napoleon's Corsican adversary who was to become a signer of the Treaty that established the neutrality and inviolability of Belgium. After the entry of Charles IX, Irving is at an even statelier affair, a banquet given by the Duke of Northumberland. He is frequently a welcome guest at Lady Granard's. Among the notables that he meets here and there are Prince Leopold, later the first King of Belgium; Prince Ferdinand of Saxony (with memories of the Dresden days); and Baron Humboldt. With Talma he again discussed the drama, and with Pasta—the Jewish-Italian actress then at the height of her fame—he discussed her own acting. But, by and large, Irving led a retired life, writing sporadically, reading a great deal. The rooms that he had taken over from John Howard Payne were within a five minutes' walk of the Bibliothèque Nationale, and Irving had the privileged use of whatever volumes he might desire. In the sequence shown by his memoranda, among the books that he read were Metastasio, Johnson's "Rasselas," Boileau (notably the "Essay on Criticism"), Boccaccio's "Decameron," Lives of Oliver Goldsmith, of Racine (and various of his plays), of La Fontaine, of Piron, the dramatist; the Orations of Bossuet, the Memoirs of Henrietta Wilson, writings of Voltaire, Thomas Moore's Life of Sheridan, the plays of Calderon, the Memoirs of Irving's friend Sir Edgerton Brydges, a History of the Moors in Spain, and (though of course not for the first time), Molière, Milton and Gibbon. The list is significant. We may pass by, with a fleeting comment on Irving's un-Puritanic nature, the libidinous memoirs of the notorious Miss Wilson—but we must pause to reflect upon the considerable number of formal biographies, for here we find strong evidence of the turning of Irving's mind towards that field of literature which he was to enter upon, with his Life of Columbus, as the chief vocation of his later years. Worth noting, also, is Irving's entry for July 31st, 1825, recording that the Scotch publisher, Constable, desired him to write a Life of Washington. Irving did not assent; yet, a Life of Washington was, some thirty-four years later, Irving's final achievement.

Plays, also, Irving read in considerable number, while the poet in whom he was then most interested was Lord Byron. Byron is more frequently mentioned in Irving's note-books of this period, than any other writer. Irving's writings delighted Byron, and Thomas Moore had doubtless shown Irving Byron's letter of July, 1821, wherein the English poet had written of his enthusiasm for the writings of "your Mr. Irving." On the other hand, Irving took such pleasure in Byron's poetry that he sent him—the only gift ever presented to a man whose acquaintance he had never made—a copy of "The Sketch Book." He inscribed the first of the two volumes: "Lord Byron with the author's high respect and admiration. Washington Irving, Dresden, May, 1823." The phrase to be noted is "high respect." The manner in which Byron had conducted his life aroused so much censure in England that the poet was then living, self-expatriated, at Genoa. There, at the very time that Irving's gift reached him, he was preparing for the journey to Greece, where, a protagonist in the cause of Greek independence, he was so soon to die. How proud and solitary a figure was then Lord Byron, how deeply he felt the animadversions of the English, is shown by his unwillingness to have anything to do with the English in Italy, save for a few friends. The Earl of Blessington and his Countess were among these few, and to Lord Blessington he wrote during those days a letter that now lies before me. There we find him saying that he wishes to sleep quietly "in some of my old glens where I used to dream in my former excursions"—those excursions described in "Childe Harold's Pilgrimage." "I should prefer a grey Greek stone over me to Westminster Abbey—but I doubt if I shall have the luck to die so happily."

It may be that Byron's devotion to the cause of liberty evoked Irving's phrase, but this surmise is not necessary to explain the "high respect." Irving was neither an "Early Victorian" nor a

PORTRAIT OF IRVING BY WEDGEWOOD
AFTER SICURAC

New Englander in his attitude towards sex. In Irving's philosophy love for woman was not a vice. The virtues that counted most were generosity and mental integrity. Byron's genius Irving could, of course, appreciate, and in an entry for October, 1824 (six months after the poet's death), Irving writes of Byron as an eagle "in the heaven of narration." "Nothing is easier than the flight of an eagle—he soars up to heaven without an effort and sails about in the clouds without labour"; but the lesser birds—the imitators—"every owl and buzzard and crow and chough . . . soon forsook the mission and flapped heavily in mid air." Easily could any American man of letters of those days appreciate Byron's genius; but not many could so readily, and with "high respect," evaluate the fineness that mingled with the evil in Byron's nature. Irving could; and after Byron's death it was the understanding New Yorker, and not a London or an Edinburgh critic, who was—a fact hitherto unrecorded— asked by the publisher Galignani to write a sketch of Byron for the only Continental journal printed in the English language.

With William E. West, the American artist best remembered for his portrait of the English poet, Irving "had much conversation about Lord Byron whom he describes as simple, kind and affectionate." When, on another occasion, Irving heard the opinion of a narrow-minded Englishman reflecting on Byron's courage, his indignation at such stupidity was marked. The episode of the poor Greek who accompanied Byron's corpse to England and was in an "agony of grief" during the funeral services, led Irving to write: "A nature that could inspire such attachments, must have been generous and beneficent." And there is among Irving's writings no paper more appealing in mood, more happy in the approach to its theme, more sustained in style than "Newstead Abbey," the recountal of the three weeks Irving spent in 1831 at the ancestral home of Byron.

Washington Irving is no longer very much read. His is too quiet a flavour for the palate of our generation. His fame is accepted; a set of his works stands in the best selected libraries; but he is not much read. Yet let no one forego the pleasure of

175

"Newstead Abbey," especially no person interested in Irving the man; for here are shown in those passages which relate to Lord Byron and his sister, Augusta, for whom Byron's affection was so loyal, and in those fascinating pages that have to do with Byron's love for Mary Chaworth, rare glimpses into Irving's own heart. Like Byron, Irving was a devoted brother; like Byron, the memory of a beautiful romance of early days shone throughout life. When Irving thrilled to Byron's phrase concerning Mary whom Byron used to call "his bright morning star of Annesley," Irving was thinking of Matilda Hoffman; and again of her when he wrote: "An early, innocent, and unfortunate passion, however fruitful of pain it may be to the man, is a lasting advantage to the poet. It is a well of sweet and bitter fancies; of refined and gentle sentiments; of elevated and ennobling thoughts; shut up in the deep recesses of the heart, keeping it green amidst the withering blights of the world, and, by its casual gushings and overflowings, recalling at times all the freshness, and innocence, and enthusiasm of youthful days."

In "Newstead Abbey" also, there is frequent recourse to the theme of the supernatural. Irving revels in superstitious legends associated with the Abbey—the traditions of the goblin friar who walked its cloisters at night time, and of the hairy apparition which Byron saw and decided was the Devil—but when Byron repeated these tales, or brooded over the skulls of his ancestors, it was, Irving decided, for the sake of "poetical enjoyment," and no foible of the reasoning mind. Such was Irving's own approach to the supernatural and the legendary; and his journals of the years 1824 and 1825 give (as do also many of his earlier and later diaries) indication of how keen a hunter he was in these fields. On November 8th Irving is dining at Lord Granard's, and Lady Charlotte Fitzgerald tells him of the bleeding head that Earl Grey (the Whig statesman who, in 1833, had the bill passed which abolished slavery throughout the British Empire) saw "at several times and in several places." Once it was at the end of his table, once at the end of a room, again on the pillow of a bed. Lady Charlotte also told him of the haunted room that led the noted English Admiral, Earl St. Vincent, to advise the owner of the house to dispose of it.   Then, too, in Irving's note-book we find the gruesome legend of Littlecote Hall, referred to by Walter Scott in "Rokeby."   It seems that one night an old midwife was summoned by a stranger to come to the immediate aid of a lady of high degree.   A rich reward was promised, but the woman had to consent to be blindfolded. The cunning dame counted, however, the number of steps leading up to the castle, and cut out a piece of the cover of the bed on which the lady lay.   A male child was born, and this so infuriated the stranger that he seized the infant and flung it into the fire.   The next morning the midwife was able to identify Littlecote House (an old feudal hall in Berkshire) as the scene of the murder, and the infant's uncle as the criminal.   Let us continue in Irving's own words: "Darrell was tried before Judge —— who was well known to be venal.   As Darrell had no children, he promised to make the judge his heir if he acquitted him.   The Hall has contin[ue]d in family of the Judge and is still owned by one of the house.   From the time of his acquittal Darrell continually saw ghost of his sister and her child.   If he opened a window, they were there—saw them night and day. He was riding in hunt and was going to leap a stile when she and child stood the other side and forbade him.   He told her to stand out of the way or he would ride over them—tried to leap, but the horse who saw the ghost reared, recoiled, threw him and broke his neck.   The place is called Darrell's stile to the present day."

At Bordeaux the next year, Irving jots down various strange anecdotes: here, however, with rational explanations for the ghost.   In one case a man who had been terribly alarmed by a dark figure, discovers that a woman just out of a mad house had been put in the same room with him, and that "he had been held back in bed by the circumstance of there being but one sheet —which was doubled—and that he was entangled in the fold." In another instance the sudden breaking of a great mirror that fell from the wall, and the arising of a dim figure from a cloud

177

of dust, was afterwards explained to the landlady who had fainted, by the old chimney sweep "who had come down the wrong flue of the chimney and as the wall above the fireplace was old, of one thickness of brick, had fallen thro'."

With all his reasonableness that led Irving to give little credence to the supernatural, and to attempt explanation of his own curious dreams, he was yet, in his Spanish days, to be a participant in a strange experiment with the other world. A young Englishman, John Nalder Hall, a companion to whom Irving had become warmly attached, had died. His friend, confident in the belief that the spirits of the dead could communicate with the living, had obtained Irving's promise to give him the opportunity of verifying his belief, both for Irving and for himself. So one evening, setting forth on the horse that had belonged to Hall, Irving rode from Seville to Casa de Cera where they had resided together. There the strange tryst was to be kept. There, doubting, yet eager for the message from the dead, Irving "breathed an appeal for the promised presence of his departed friend." If ever a message could come from the dead to the quick, surely it would come now, so passionate had been the belief of the young man he cared for so dearly. The sun went down. Irving mounted his horse and rode homeward through the silence that had remained unbroken.

In the spring of 1824 literary and theatrical business took Irving to London in time to see the second performance of "Charles II." The most interesting of his memoranda of this period have to do with Thomas Moore and Samuel Rogers. Irving was then intending to write biographies both of Rogers and of Thomas Campbell, for a series to be published by Galignani; but neither of these works ever got beyond the preliminary stage of the consideration of material. The Life of Campbell might have turned out successfully, as both in the biographical sketch that he had previously published in the *Analectic Magazine,* and the Introduction that he was later to write for the American edition of Beattie's Life of Campbell, Irving showed his sympathetic interest in his subject. As for Samuel Rogers, I hardly think that Irving would have been the right biographer. The two men remained on friendly footing for long years; they exchanged copies of their works (presentation volumes of "Italy" and other poems of the banker-author, still stand on the shelves at Irvington); after his return to America Irving gave various of his friends—FitzGreene Halleck and Henry T. Tuckerman among them—letters of introduction to Rogers. But Irving was too kind and gracious a man to be in sufficient sympathy with the caustic old Englishman to qualify as his biographer. Thomas Campbell said that the best way for a person to escape the sharpness of Rogers' tongue was to borrow a hundred pounds from him: that Rogers would never say a word against that man until the debt had been repaid. Irving, however, was prone to accept the acidity of Rogers at its surface value. He notes in his memoranda for August, 1824 how "very critical and censorious of Moore and others" Rogers had been at dinner, and writes to Thomas Moore in a letter of August 14th: "He served up his friends as he served up his fish, with a squeeze of lemon over each. It was very piquant, but it rather set my teeth on edge."

During his same period in London, Irving's memoranda show Rogers discussing famous gossip: "When Lord Byron and Caroline Lamb quarrelled, Lord Byron told him when men and women fell out the one that keeps the ground longest wins. Lady Caroline gave in two minutes before me. Lady Caroline took all Lord Byron's letters, made a funeral pyre of them, put his miniature on top, and burned them; but mark you they were only copies, and what made the ridiculousness complete was that there was no one present to be taken in by it but herself, and she was in the secret. He said that when Lord and Lady Byron separated, Byron told his friends, and Rogers among the number, that he alone was to blame."

Byron's executors persuaded Moore to burn the memoirs which the English poet had left in charge of the Irish poet, but Moore was soon engaged upon his "Life and Letters of Lord Byron," still the most valuable book concerning the author of "Don Juan." Irving was enormously interested in this work of his friend who showed him some of Byron's journals when Irving, in June, went to Bath to meet Moore. During the few days that they spent together at Bath, Moore took Irving to visit various of Moore's friends, but the modest, and now much tired and disillusionized American, was no longer the merry addition at social festivities that he had been in his younger days. In his diary for June 17th, 1824, Moore writes: "Took Irving after dinner to show him to the Starkeys, but he was sleepy and did not open his mouth; the same at Elwyn's dinner. Not strong as a lion, but delightful as a domestic animal . . . only in the easy familiarity of domestic life could he be seen to the greatest advantage. It was not more in what he said, than in the way he said it; the play of feature, the eye, the tone, the gesture. There was a natural, easy delightful sportiveness about his conversation when under no restraints or form of ceremony, a mixture of wit, whim, fun and drollery, of which few could resist the fascination."

A few days with the Van Warts at Birmingham; a few days with the Fosters at Brickhill near Bedford,—these were the brief vacations Irving allowed himself during July. The rest of that month and the first half of August were given over to altering, correcting, and adding to the "Tales of a Traveller," before its London publication on the 25th. It was arduous work for an indolent man, and on his return to France he went to the attractive village of Auteuil "that," as he writes to his sister, Mrs. Paris, "I might be quiet and might keep clear of the crowd and dissipation of the metropolis." In the final week of August he spent a few days at Fontainebleau, whose trees and flowers and animal life in the way of squirrels, partridges, lizards and bees all came in for notation in his diary, with other pictures of jovial blacksmiths and gay young Lancers. Near the old Château Passy Irving observes "lovers strolling by moonlight"; and altogether these few pages that lead us on the last day of August to the lodgings which Irving had taken at Auteuil, are full of delightful touches—brief phrases conjuring up sunset and

180

moonlight scenes amid the woods and gardens of the Kings of France.

September finds Irving partly occupied in his retreat near Paris, where his brother Peter, the Aspinwalls and other friends come frequently to visit him. In a French servant woman, Marianne, he has a combination of "cook, butler, valet de chambre and footman." He studies Italian, reads descriptions of German travel, sits for his portrait by a French painter of miniatures, does a little writing, sees a great deal of the Storrows, and now and then goes to Paris for the day. One of the occasions that brought him there was the funeral of Louis XVIII, concerning whose last days Irving writes at considerable length. The entry for the 16th of September discloses a slight but not uninteresting fact unknown to Irving bibliographers. It seems that Galignani wished to have Irving "translate from the French into English an article on the King's death to insert in the newspapers." Irving assented, and the article was forwarded to the publisher the same day. We are here reminded that it was in a translation from the French that Irving made his first appearance in the world of books. On the 27th of September Irving is again in Paris for the day and sees the entrance in state of Charles X, that reactionary monarch whose folly of intolerance brought on the Revolution of 1830 and the final overthrow of the elder branch of the Bourbons.

In the second week of October Washington and Peter started forth on a ten days' trip through Touraine, "the centre and garden of France," prior to going to Paris for the winter. His memoranda of Orleans, Tours and other little villages of that lovely region have all his characteristic charm; and of this charm it is the human note that is the essence. If we find him writing on one page of Louis XV and Madame de Pompadour, we shall find him on the next page describing with equal zest his landlady, the "little, yellowish, fattish woman with snubbed and snippy nose." If he pauses to comment on Gothic architecture, reveling in the loveliness of some stone tracery, he is equally certain to note the onions and white sauce, the roast pigeon, cheese and pears, not to mention the bottle of wine and glass of brandy, that make the inn vie in appeal with the cathedral. And if Irving the historian records at Chinon the important fact that Rabelais was born there, Irving the poetic chronicler does not fail to remember the vibration of the clock in the old tower.

Not far from Chinon stood the castle of the Duke of Duras, the ancient Château d'Usse, on the river Inere, a tributary stream of the Loire. The Duchess, a woman "idolized in the world of taste and literature and extolled for her exemplary and amiable character," had given Irving a letter which threw wide open the doors of her castle to him and his brother. For two days they enjoyed the hospitality of the great ducal estate, rambling amid its old apartments, plucking figs from the luxuriant trees, and spending evenings before the blazing fire that the concierge made for them in the library of Catherine de'Medici. The castle itself had been built in the time of the First Crusade and the old tapestries hanging on its walls had looked down upon many kings and princes. Never was Irving more in touch with the romantic history of France, than during this brief stay at the Château d'Usse.

The next month appeared those comparatively adverse critiques concerning the "Tales of a Traveller" that led Irving to give up for many years the kind of writing which had established his fame abroad. On November 23rd he met at Galignani's an unnamed person whom he calls "my evil genius" and who told him that "the critics were attacking me like the devil in England. Returned home for a short time but could not work—remained downhearted." Peter came in and dined with him, and afterwards Irving went to see Pasta as Desdemona, but it was "a black day" for him. Another evil genius sent him, from time to time, anonymous letters from America, containing clippings from newspapers with disparaging comments regarding Irving's long absence from his native country, or relating to the inferiority of the "Tales of a Traveller" to "The Sketch Book" and

"Bracebridge Hall." Even so, in this discouraging year, Irving had merry moments. He was amused when Rothschild (whose hospitality he later accepted) came into Lady Harvey's box at the opera and told Lady Harvey that Pasta was "with a child." On December 15th, five days after he had begun those Spanish lessons which were to be of such service to him during his months of research at Madrid, he indulged in an excellent pun: "My Spanish master was not punctual so I went out to give him a lesson." On Christmas day at West's studio, where he found Dominick Lynch sitting for his picture, he sat for several hours chatting with these American friends about New York, talking about the "Dutchman, etc, laughing heartily till past three"; but as Irving writes in an entry a few days later, "Tho' laughed a good deal both at West's and at dinner—a merry head may sometimes go with a heavy heart."

Dominick Lynch, the jovial wine merchant who sang so beautifully the songs of Thomas Moore, and to whose initiative is due the introduction of Italian opera in America, was the most cheerful of Irving's companions of these days. Much as Payne had intensified Irving's interest in plays so Lynch brought Irving into greater liking for the opera. He is in frequent attendance at the Paris Opera House, going there, and to the theatre, on an average of two or three times a week. The playhouses of Paris at that time included the Académie Royale, the Théâtre Français, the Opéra Comique, the Gymnase Dramatique, the Ambigu Comique, the Porte St. Martin, the Gaité, the Panorama Dramatique, and the Cirque Olympique. Without these places of amusement Irving's days would have been much greyer. He had temporarily lost all enthusiasm for authorship, and his nights were restless with "broken sleep and uneasy thoughts."

Politics, we have seen, never much interested Washington Irving. International relationships did. The decade ending in the early thirties witnessed the eighteenth century's most important forward step in the liberalization of countries both in Europe and in America, with a brave struggle for independence in other nations that were later to achieve it. Between the years

183

1810 and 1825 the Spanish and Portuguese colonies in Central America and South America became independent states; Greece kept up its long fight from 1821 to 1829, and, in 1830, there were revolutions in France, in Belgium and in Poland. The Holy Alliance, which sought to repress republicanism in America as well as in Europe, had found its strongest opponent George Canning, the English Prime Minister who, in 1823, called,—in his own famous phrase—"the New World into existence to redress the balance of the Old." There were many Englishmen not in accord with their Minister's attitude towards the Bourbons. At Lady Thomond's, on March 6th, at Paris, Irving met perhaps such an Englishman in the person of Colonel Alcock. The details of their discussion are not given, but Irving's philosophy as to the manner in which countries should approach one another is shown in this excerpt from his note-book: *"I maintain: until nations are generous they will never be wise; true policy is generous policy; all bitterness, selfishness etc., may gain small ends, but loses great ones—it may appear chivalrous, but it is true; expedience may answer for the moment—they gain a point, but they do not establish a principle—there is a return of the poisoned chalice."* This sentence deserves italics.

More to Irving's taste than any discussion were hours spent with young people. Among his companions of these days were the children of the Storrow family, and the "two girls and two very fine boys" of his old friend Charles King, who had large old-fashioned apartments at Versailles. Then, too, the Van Wart boys were at Paris for a while. A Mr. Carter of Virginia was there also, and asked Irving to what school he should send his daughters. Irving, after consulting with Mrs. Storrow, takes him to Madam Clement's where Irving notes, with his old time interest in the sex, a "pretty blonde taking lessons at piano in one room—a beautiful brunette taking singing lessons in another"; nor does he fail to record the "languishing, half open eyes" of the eighteen-year-old Carter girl, while the younger is "very pretty and lovely with long, auburn ringlets."

But in spite of lovely children, of his cordial friends among the English and the Americans, the mild dissipation of theatre and opera, and the warm letters that reached him from his brothers and sisters and such old friends as Captain Nicholson and James K. Paulding; despite even the loyal affection of Peter, the year 1825, much as the year 1824, went by in a desultory and unsatisfactory way, with now and then a bit of travel to break in upon those fruitless months. In June, on the 14th, he "set off in carriage with Mr. and Mrs. Meyers for Havre," arriving there two days later after having spent the previous night at Rouen. The next week Peter met him there, and the two brothers—still interested in their unfortunate venture—"went out on a sail of experiment in the new steam-boat, the 'Duchess of Angoulême.'" Frequently sailing on the river, now to La Maillerie, now to Rouen, Irving spent a few quiet weeks at Bordeaux until the 10th of July again saw him in Paris. He arrived there just in time to meet, at Versailles, Colonel Thomas Aspinwall, the American Consul who frequently acted as Irving's business adviser and representative in connection with the publication of his books. The end of the next month he again left Paris, this time with the Storrows, his brother Peter, and his artist friend Newton, for a five days' excursion which took him through Ermenonville (where Rousseau was buried), Senlis, Compiègne, Chantilly, and Ecouen. Chantilly, with its old castle that belonged to the Montmorency and Condé families, and with its magnificent stables (stalls for one hundred and fifty horses), seems to have interested him most. The first morning after his return to Paris, Payne told him of Kemble's desire to have Irving write a play; and that afternoon, at Sir Thomas Lawrence's, Irving met the famous Scotch painter, Sir David Wilkie, who was to become one of Irving's best friends.

Still restless, and able to do little writing save for corrections and changes in Payne's play of "Richelieu," Irving, after a fortnight in Paris, brought to an end his residence in the metropolis and its environs. On the 19th of September he jots down that he is "very nervous." Directly after that he records that he "received letter from the Fosters." Obviously he had been waiting for this letter, obviously his fate is definitely sealed. He must have a change of surroundings; if possible, of thoughts. On the 22nd he and Peter leave Paris "at six o'clock in the morning in *Berline de Commerce* for Moulins." A sister of Charity has the third place. The Irvings come too late with their luggage, but will not be delayed and leave their trunks behind. They pass through Fontainebleau, through Nemours, with its "picturesque little castle on the banks of the Loire." At Moulins they visit the tomb erected by the Princess of Ursins for her husband the Duke de Montmorency whom Irving confuses with the Count de Montgomery who accidentally killed the King of France in a tournament, the Count's lance entering the eye of his monarch. At Saint Pourcain Irving is annoyed by a "scolding bitch trollope of housemaid," but at their next stop, Rion, he enjoys chatting with the pretty landlady, and about America with a young mercantile traveller. A nearby castle (the Château Tournelle) leads him to resort, as during the tour in Wales, to the pencil of the amateur artist, and he makes a pleasant little sketch of it. At Clermont he enjoys hearing "mine host" tell stories of the country, and relishes the "dish of trout fried in wine and passed out on sliced bread" which forms the repast at the mountain inn. Aubusson, famed for its tapestries, offers him an old ruined tower. The next morning Peter and Washington are joined "by preceptor of Limoges, who sings, chatters, plays the droll to great delight of the blacksmith, who mounts the front of Cabriolet." Leaving Limoges by moonlight at one in the morning, the brothers, after breakfast at Chalus, visit the tower of the ruined castle of Chebrot where Richard the Lion-Hearted was killed. Then a lovely drive through Perigord—"country covered with chestnut trees"— dinner that evening at Perigueux; all night travel through beautiful country, and so, the following afternoon, into Bordeaux.

The four months that Irving spent in this city of southern France mark the end of the transition period. They include, on the side of literary endeavour, in addition to those abortive attempts at a volume of essays and an original drama already noted, some retouching of "Richelieu" and other plays wherein Irving aided John Howard Payne. There is also considerable reading of Italian authors, especially Dante and Alfieri, while Machiavelli interests Irving to such an extent that he copies out his maxims. As to more personal occupations and amusements, chess is now and then indulged in; music is enjoyed in private, and in public Irving hears "young Litz"—this being the fourteen-year old but already famous Hungarian pianist, Franz Liszt. The theatre, of course, is visited—though not so frequently as at Paris—and riding to the hounds becomes the foremost diversion.

Irving and Peter had quite a few American and English acquaintances at Bordeaux. The Scotts and the Johnsons and the Bartons are names that often figure in his note-books. Yet most at home he seems to have been in the French household of Mr. Guestier, a considerable owner of vineyards. On October 8th he rides with him to the "estate of the Wine de la Rose—Chateau with white tower in which a former proprietor, who had gained the wine its reputation, used to live—had flag-staff on the tower on which he hoisted a flag according to the quality of his wine. In the best years he hoisted an English flag—the next best a Dutch—the third best a French flag—as a signal for the wine brokers." The next day, again on horseback, Irving visited Battalia,—"the seat and vineyard of Mr. Guestier the elder." Two days later, rising at four, Irving again mounts his horse and goes out "with Mr. Scott's harriers—found a hare on the borders of The Landes—after two hours chase killed it on the vineyard of Battalia—Scott's huntsman a small, dark, sallow man with bright eyes." Irving obviously enjoyed this mild hunting (perhaps with memories of those boyhood hours when, fowling-piece in hand, he sought for rabbits in Westchester County). Twice more that same week does he go a-hunting. On Wednesday he follows the hounds of a Mr. Calarousce. "His pack made up of a mixed breed—large, as they have occasionally to hunt the boar and wolf. Dogs deep-mouthed—give a rich, rolling note like distant thunder—start one hare, but after chasing it for some time, lose it in the wood—get on the traces of others, but the dogs are idle and we do not start them. Returning home we start a hare in The Landes—after half an hour's run we kill it." On Thursday Mr. Barton's hounds lead the chase, this time without success, save for the amusing word picture that Irving's note-book reveals of "one of the huntsmen with us, a fat, round man with little coat with peaked skirts that looked like the index of a sun-dial on his broad breech." He had a "hunting horn slung round him which he tooted continually if permitted. Mr. Scott kept him in check and he swelled like a bladder with repressed wind."

On another occasion Irving's horse—a pony he calls it—takes him to Libourne, a town near Bordeaux especially attractive in its wide streets and shady trees. Here a fair is going on in a public place under a low arcade, and "horse jockies, farmers, etc.—vagabond dogs and vagabond boys lounging about after scraps," countrymen arriving "in blue cloaks that cover their horses to the rump," bring life and colour to the hotel where Irving and his friend Nathaniel Johnson have with difficulty managed to get accommodation. On the ride back to Libourne Irving stops at the chateau belonging to the Duke de Berry and visits the room in which Henry IV had slept.

The mood of Irving during this Bordeaux period varies. At times he is downcast—"rather *abattu*," "quite *abattu*,"—but on the whole he is more tranquil than at Paris. He regards with sufficient quietness the prospect of the entire loss of a considerable sum which he has put into a mining proposition that turned out even worse than the steamboat speculation. His moments of greatest excitement come when, with his customary fervour in the initial stages of literary creation, he is writing those essays which were to end in disappointment. The one really lucky stroke resulted from the letter that he sent to Alexander Everett, then the American Minister at Madrid, asking Everett to attach him to the Legation; for Irving now contemplated a sojourn in

188

Spain. Of course Everett was glad to grant this favour to his distinguished compatriot, and in his reply suggested that Irving should translate the work of the "Voyages of Columbus," recently completed by the Spanish historian Navarette. Irving was immediately intrigued by Everett's suggestion.

Chapter XI

THE WANDERER TURNS SCHOLAR

A FORTUNATE day for Washington Irving when he entered Spain, though an unfortunate country during his early years there as an author, and his later years as the American Minister.   The Peninsular War, one of Napoleon's most selfish moves on the chessboard of his ambition, had done much to divide the Spanish people into factions, and Ferdinand VII, re-assuming the throne on which Napoleon had placed his eldest brother, Joseph, was too weak a ruler to contribute to the strength and prosperity of his country.   His reign is remembered chiefly for the repeal of the Salic Law, whereby, in 1833, it became possible for his little daughter, Isabella II, to succeed him; an event so resented by her uncle, Don Carlos, that the country was for years rent by civil strife.

It was not, however, the Spain of his own day that so much interested Washington Irving during his initial sojourn in the Peninsula, as the romantic land of greatness under Ferdinand and Isabella.   Briefly after his arrival at Madrid, in February, 1826, Irving reconsidered his intention of translating Navarette's "Columbus," but came to the decision that this book was a treasury of data to which he now desired to add the fruit of his own research for a Life of Columbus that should be of more general appeal.   Such important fruit was Everett's suggestion to bear.   Then, after a period of arduous labour in the field of material relating to the great discoverer, some collateral reading caught Irving up in the fascination of the history of the Moors, and he left Columbus aside for the "Conquest of Granada."   Next he turned to a more intense study of the legends associated with the Alhambra; and so between the arrangement of historical
190

data and the elaboration of romantic legends Irving was continuously passing forward and backward over the shadowy dividing line between these adjacent territories. How intense were both his interest and his application is evident when one considers that during the first forty-three years of his life, he had written really only four books—"Knickerbocker's History of New York," "The Sketch Book," "Bracebridge Hall," and "Tales of a Traveller"—while during the years 1828–1832 were published his "History of the Life and Times of Columbus" (and also an abridgment of the same), his "Chronicle of the Conquest of Granada," his "Voyages and Discoveries of the Companion of Columbus" and "The Alhambra."

At a stage of his life's journey when Irving was eager to throw himself into work that might dull the pain of his disappointment in love, and lessen the humiliation that his sensitive soul felt so keenly by reason of disparaging criticisms of the "Tales of a Traveller" he found himself all at once translated into a world of high events and of glamorous, though often cruel, deeds. The year 1492, known to every Western school-child however otherwise remiss in dates, as symbolic of a new hemisphere, was for the Christendom of the fifteenth and sixteenth centuries even more significant as the date of the expulsion of the Moors from Spain. The long and bloody struggle between the followers of the Cross and the followers of the Crescent was now, in Europe, concluded; and ended with acts more rich in daring and in romance than many a drama can boast. Religion, poetry, chivalry, the gesture of the knight, the strategy of the warrior, the cunning of the diplomat, were all inwoven in the events that reached their climax when Granada, queen-city of the Moors, fell before the warrior-queen, Isabella of Castile. And for Irving all these struggles that reached their apex at the time when Columbus enlisted the aid of Isabella, took on a nearer relationship as he came into acquaintance with the lineal descendants of more than one of the heroes who fought under her banner.

The most famous of all these heroes, or at least the one most popularly adored, was Hernando del Pulgar, whose direct descendant, the young Marquis of Salar, Irving found so charming a fellow when he met him at the hospitable table of the Duke of Gor. "El de las Hazanas," "He of the Exploits," was the name by which all Spain knew the intrepid nobleman who engaged upon such astounding adventures. Of these one still furnished the subject matter for frequent festivals—his midnight ride into Granada where, with his dagger for nail, Hernando del Pulgar affixed to the gate of the chief mosque the inscription "Ave Maria." Of course this challenge could not be unanswered by the young Moorish knights who vied with the young Spaniards in deeds of daring, and the next day the Moorish warrior, Tarfe, confronted the Christian army with the holy inscription tied contemptuously to the tail of his horse. His triumph was brief. Immediately he was challenged by Garcilaso de la Vega and slain in single combat, and it was the Spaniard's turn to parade the "Ave Maria" before the line of warriors, the inscription now raised at the end of the avenging lance. After Isabella had captured Granada the mosque became the city's chief cathedral. The right was accorded to the lineal descendant of Hernando del Pulgar to ride into the church on horseback and to keep his head covered at the elevation of the Host. Irving does not, however, record that the Marquis of Salar availed himself of these extraordinary privileges.

In celebrating the deliverance of Spain from Moorish rule annual performances in Spanish villages had recourse to legends of many combats in addition to those wherein "El de las Hazanas" figured. Always the Spanish warriors emerged as the final victors, and at the climax the image of the Virgin was borne in triumph. Gonsalvo of Cordova, known to all historians as "The Great Captain," was the leading hero in many of these revivifying performances; and with *his* lineal descendant, the old Count of Luque, Irving became on friendly terms during those days at the Alhambra when they took their meals together in the Court of the Lions; sometimes, with the Duchess, playing at tressilo in the evenings. It was Gonsalvo who, acting for Isa-

192

CHRISTOPHORVS COLVMBVS LIGVR. terroribus Oceani superatis dubiusque genti Orbis regiones à se inuentas Hispanis regibus addixit. An salutis ꝏ. VIID.

CHRISTOPHER COLUMBUS

bella, effected the capitulation of the last of the Moorish Kings in Spain, that Boabdil whose final days at the Alhambra so fascinated Irving. To Gonsalvo also belongs the credit for having been one of the first generals (as astute in diplomacy as in military strategy) to use artillery with commanding success. Beautiful in person, perfect in his knightly manners, eloquent and splendid, Gonsalvo de Cordova combined qualities which won for him among his compatriots the title of "The Prince of Youth;" while that keenness and subtlety of mind which directed even his exceedingly extravagant adventures in arms qualified him to become "The Great Captain" in the most important period of the conflict between the Spaniards and the Moors. The unreliable though doubtless brave Boabdil, whose ambitions had led him into disloyalty to his father the King, was no match for Gonsalvo. The Moor was forced to yield to Isabella. The gateway through which he departed from the palace of his ancestors formed the quarry of the most interesting of all of Irving's quests into the by-ways of Spanish history. The one favour that Boabdil asked for when he gave up the keys of the Alhambra was that no one should ever enter the palace through the portal by which he had left. In an old chronicle Irving found this anecdote and "set a poor devil at work" to find the gate which had been walled up. Finally it was discovered in a ruined tower that had been destroyed by French artillery during the Peninsular War.

From many directions Irving received special courtesies in his research. The friendship of Everett, to whose legation Irving was nominally attached, brought the American author into contact with the intelligentsia as well as the diplomatic and social sets of Madrid, and his always ingratiating personality quickly made friends for him. Add to this that the country itself, and the life of both the peasant class and the people of the cities, appealed to various phases of his nature, and it is easy to understand under what interesting auspices he passed his years of initial scholarship, whether in the enjoyment of study and of writing, amid the gayer scenes of the capital, the historic associations of Seville, the sheer beauty of the Alhambra, or the intervals of picturesque travel.

As soon as Peter and Washington, in February, 1826, had left Bayonne in the diligence for Madrid, and, passing the French frontier had come to the town of Vittoria (the scene of Wellington's triumph over the French in 1813), the good looks of the Basque women and the engaging qualities of a true Spanish dinner—"fowl, pork, buck sausages all together"—aroused Irving's enthusiasm. In old Castile, the impoverished village of Corvo spoke to him with the note of antique pride, for on its ramshackle houses were still displayed the coats-of-arms of the knights of old; and a little later Irving observed a Castilian "seated on his mule, with his great wrap and mantle flowing around him, his montero cap, and his swarthy face looks with vast hauteur on all the world." Thus even before reaching Madrid Irving had come into appreciative touch with the physical and spiritual flavour of Spain.

At Madrid Irving had the luck to find an apartment in the home of the American Consul, Obadiah Rich, a passionate collector of rare books, a student, and the possessor of a library with many items of special interest to Irving. His first week was given over largely to paying calls upon members of the diplomatic corps, a task that Irving undertook at Everett's request, and that constituted his fulfillment of whatever obligations may have been entailed upon him by virtue of his title of attaché. The French Minister, the Marquis de Moustier; the Prince of Cassaro, the Neapolitan Ambassador; Baron Liebermann, the Prussian Minister; Mr. Debel, the Dutch; the Austrian, the Swedish, the Sardinian representatives, the Minister from Saxony (who had been an acquaintance of Irving's at Dresden), the Pope's nuncio, Bishop of Tyre,—a "tall, thin, pleasant man, quite willing to play cards on Sunday evenings"—with all these he soon became on friendly footing, dining at their houses, going occasionally to theatre and opera, and now and then engaging with them in confidential discussions on the condition of the country to which they were accredited, where "nobody about the King dares to tell him the truth." (Despite the impoverished state of the treasury, Ferdinand VII was talking of sending one hundred thousand men to South America to halt the destruction there of the Spanish power.) But that household of a foreign diplomat in which Irving felt most at home was where the adorable children of Madame d'Oubril, wife of the Russian Ambassador, walked into Irving's heart, and where her niece, Antoinette Bolvillier, may indeed have lost her own heart to Irving. To that household also belonged the young Prince Dolgorouki, Secretary of the Russian Embassy, with whom Irving formed a friendship of many years.

In playing games with children, in teaching them to draw, in telling them stories, Irving, past the age of forty, was the same engaging fellow who had romped with the young folk of New York families twenty years earlier, and who had been the favourite uncle with the children of the Van Warts in England. With the little d'Oubrils, including Constance, Marie, and a baby boy, Irving was on such affectionate terms that he would write to or for the children, and they to him, when he was away from Madrid. On one occasion, in a letter to Prince Dolgorouki, he says: "The precious line from my dear, dear little Marie was a happiness beyond all hope. I can fancy the little woman leaning with her whole body over the table, her ringlets hanging all around her charming face, as she achieved that prodigious manuscript, every letter of which is almost as big as herself." To Antoinette Bolvillier, Irving writes: "Tell me anything about the children . . . I would give all the money in my pocket to be with those dear little women at the round table in the salon, or on the grass plot in the garden to tell them some marvelous tales . . . Tell my little Marie I kiss her hand and hold myself her loyal and devoted knight. If she wishes, at any time, the head of a giant, or the tail of a fiery dragon, she is to call upon me. My arm and my court sword are always at her command." In still another letter to Antoinette: "Give my love to all my dear little friends at the round table from the discreet Princess down to the little blue-eyed boy. Tell la petite Marie that I still remain true to her though surrounded by all the beauties of Seville, and that I swear (but this she must keep between ourselves) that there is not a little woman to compare with her in all Andalusia." What a pity it is that the tales Irving recounted to young people died away on the air of America, of England, of France, of Spain, though we have some hint of their fantastic nature in a letter that Colonel Aspinwall wrote in 1826: "The children desire to be remembered to the chocolate merchant, and assure you that they have not forgotten Hempen House nor the German Princess with the long nose." In another letter Aspinwall writes: "All the young fry send their kindest remembrances . . . They have picked out a tree for you to lie under and tell them stories when you come to Highgate next summer."

The only note in contradiction of that gentleness which pervaded Irving's nature in his relations with old as well as young is observable in his interest in bull fights. Sometimes at Madrid he goes as often as three times a fortnight, although he confesses to Antoinette that he is a little bit ashamed of his predilection. The sight of slaughtered horses and bulls seems, during the early period of his stay in Spain, to have excited him pleasurably. Apart from the novelty and picturesqueness of these combats, Irving, however unconsciously, was caught by their deeper fascination arising from their commingling of beauty and brutality, and of the opposition between the mental and physical forces so symbolic of life as a whole. And Irving, it must be remembered, was for all his feministic temperament never devoid of courage. He had of his own volition gone into the War of 1812. On one occasion in France, he stopped a brutal driver from lashing his tired horses; and on another, in Spain, he interfered in a very rough street brawl begun by a ruffian's too insistent attention to a young girl. Irving, even when personal risk was involved, followed his path of courtesy and kindness.

Irving's first visit to court was with Everett. A few weeks after his arrival in Madrid, he saw the Besamanos, the ceremony of the kissing of hands that always took place on the

Queen's Saint Day, the Queen herself being Ferdinand's third wife, Marie Amelia of Saxony. The King of Spain, as previously the Kings of Saxony and Bavaria, and as subsequently the Kings of England and of France, showed liking for the quiet and gracious American. Later in the year when (in company with the Everetts) Washington and Peter were at St. Ildefonso, Ferdinand guided Irving through the royal gardens with their fine exhibition of playing waters. The treasures of the royal library were equally open to Irving, and of the royal armoury, where the suits of armour of Ferdinand and Isabella, of Gonsalvo, of Boabdil, of Charles V, and of the Cid (whose fame is perpetuated in the poetry of Corneille), intrigued Irving's imagination. At High Mass, held by the Pope's nuncio, Irving saw Ferdinand washing the feet of the poor and waiting on them at table, one of those curious religious ceremonies harking back to the Middle Ages. That early impatience with Roman Catholic ritual which Irving displayed on his first visit to Rome, seems now to have disappeared, and on Good Friday he feels the impressiveness of the silent streets, the cessation of the church bells and the "sentinels on duty with reversed arms. Next day the bells ring jubilantly in honour of the Resurrection."

Thus a multiplicity of new interests—among them the companionship of the Marchioness de Casa Yrugo and her daughter, Narcissa, who danced the bolero so delightfully, and of the Marchioness Santa Cruz, and her especially handsome daughter, Mlle. d'Alvay, brought Irving pleasant diversion in the hours that he spared from work on "Columbus" and the "Conquest of Granada." Emily Foster was not yet forgotten, and Irving had his off hours; but on December 31st, 1826, after commenting that this had been a "year of the hardest application and toil of the pen that I have ever passed," he could add: "I feel more satisfied, however, with the manner in which I have passed it than I have with that of many gayer years, and close this year of my life in better humour with myself than I have often done."

The next year was given over very largely to the completion

of the "Life and Times of Columbus." Never before had Irving been so devoted a scholar and so intense a labourer. He rises at two in the morning and writes for twelve hours uninterruptedly; he rises at three; at five. Dolgorouki lends him books; Navarette is of aid; the Duke of Veraguas arranges for his examination of archives that no American had ever studied. Entries in the diary tend to become monotonous in their reiteration of "all morning at Columbus," "all day Columbus." Society sees little of him, though in the evenings he is often at the d'Oubrils, or with some of the very few Americans then at Madrid. Everett and his family, the Secretary of the American Legation, John Adams Smith, Rich, the American Consul, Peter and Washington, Henry W. Longfellow, then just twenty-one, and Lieutenant Slidell of the Navy, made up the little American colony. Slidell, who later assumed the name of Mackenzie in honour of his mother's brother, had a nice talent for writing and though he is most remembered in connection with his action as Naval Commander in having hanged for mutiny the son of the Secretary of War, Slidell has a place among American biographers as the author of Lives of John Paul Jones, Perry and Decatur. Then, too, he wrote various volumes of experiences of travel, the publication of the first of these books, "A Year in Spain," having been arranged for through the friendly interest of Irving.

Longfellow, to whom also Irving took a great liking, wrote to his father that Irving "is one of those men who put you at ease with them in a moment . . . He makes no ceremony whatever with one and of course is a very fine man in society, all mirth and good humour." Such blue moods as Irving still had—one comes across such entries as "terribly nervous and low spirited today"—no one knew of save Peter, who shared all Irving's confidences. Talks with his friends, long walks with his brother, an occasional game of chess at the Ryans, or a game of whist at home, were the milder diversions in a year of scholarship that found its financial reward in the more than three thousand guineas Irving received for the "Life of Columbus."

This large sum was due to the successful efforts of Colonel Aspinwall, then American Consul at London, who (as Gilbert Stuart Newton wrote to Irving) deserved "credit as a sharp bargainer with the publisher Murray." Newton also wrote that Thomas Moore's latest work, the Life of Sheridan, was not likely to raise its author's fame, and that Scott's "Napoleon" was "quite a failure," so that the public would probably prove receptive (as, indeed, it did) towards Irving's "Columbus," "a work uniting entertainment and information."

The only vacation Irving seems to have allowed himself in 1827 was an excursion to Toledo in company with Peter, Lord Mahon and David Wilkie. With Wilkie he had gone to bull fights and to galleries of paintings. A sincere friendship had sprung up between the two. Distinctly noteworthy is it that in the early days at Rome and Paris, and in the later days of London and Madrid, Irving's close friends among artists were more numerous than among writers. This is to be explained not so much by reason of Irving's unfulfilled ambition to become an artist, as by the fact that when Irving consorted with Newton or Leslie or Wilkie there was no question of rivalry or envy. In an address delivered before the Massachusetts Historical Society, after Irving's death, Longfellow, in speaking of their days together at Madrid, said that he had "found the author whom I had loved repeated in the man. The same playful humour, the same touches of sentiment; and, what I admire still more, the entire absence of all literary jealousy, and of that mean avarice of fame which counts what is given to another as so much taken from one's self." Of course, with the great-hearted Scott and the merry-hearted Moore, there could be no question of any petty sentiments, but Irving's reluctance to get into intimacy with authors as a general class was due to his aversion from the little motives that in those days of often venomous criticism rose to the surface in the stream of clique life. However bitterly he himself was attacked by fellow-wielders of the pen (as on the occasion when he changed the line in "Marion's Men," "And the British soldier trembles" to "And the foeman trembles in his camp," in order to avert the antagonism of the British public, after Irving had arranged for the issue in England of a volume by Bryant) he never, even in self-defence, said an unmannerly word against a fellow-writer. *"Aucun fiel n'a jamais empoisonné ma plume"* was the simple claim of the dramatist Crebillon in his speech on being received into the French Academy. Irving's pen similarly remained ever uncontaminated; nor was it ever used to more single-minded and scholarly purposes than in the year which saw the completion of the Life of Columbus and which ended with the satisfactory entry in his diary: "A year of labour, but much more comfortable than most I have passed in Europe, and leaves me in a state of moderate hope as to the future."

On the first of March, 1826, Peter returned to France, whose climate was more suited to the troubled conditions of an almost always ailing man. That same day Washington left Madrid for one of those tours towards which he was impelled by his latent spirit of the wanderer. He had as companions the Russian Consul General, Gessler, and Stoffregen, Secretary of the Russian Embassy. The pleasure of their travel was greatly enhanced by Gessler's "two magic gifts," as Irving called them: "a leathern bottle, curiously wrought, which is never empty though continually in use," and a sack equally miraculous from which issue "hams, sausages, fowls, conserves" and, once, a pie containing "a monstrous fish equal to that which swallowed Jonah." After Cordova had been left behind and La Mancha —the realm of Don Quixote's exploits—traversed, the bare and sterile country gave way to the fragrant loveliness of Andalusia. When the travellers had passed the bridge of Pinos, where Columbus, when about to abandon Spain in despair, was overtaken by the messenger of Isabella, and when Granada, "with its towers, the Alhambra, and its snowy mountains," came gloriously into sight, the magic of Spain for the first time fully took possession of Irving.

Ten days were spent in Granada, days which went by in horseback rides about its delightful environs, and in exploration of the lesser known halls and ruined towers of the Alhambra. Before leaving the old Moorish palace, Irving plucked a flower from the Court of the Lions and sent it to Antoinette. Then, via Adra, along the coast of Malaga, the scenery "uncommonly grand, but stern and melancholy." From Malaga past the Rhonda mountains (the people of whose adjacent villages Irving considered the finest that he had seen in Spain), the travellers proceeded to Gibraltar where, during his four days' stay, Irving was "overwhelmed by hospitality which, on the part of the military messes at the British regiments, is in the jovial and tempestuous style of the old school." Over this conviviality presided Sir George Don, the Governor of Gibraltar, a combination of "the veteran soldier, the keen sportsman and the old English country gentleman." Merry nights spent with his young fellow-officers in the War of 1812 were recalled to Irving by these jolly messes, their memory further accentuated by his meeting, at Gibraltar, with Dick McCall who had been one of the "Lads of Kilkenny" at Gouverneur Kemble's old mansion, and who was now the American Vice-Consul at England's great fortress town.

A few days at Cadiz, and thence to Seville where Irving thinks he will probably stay for some weeks. He really remained for over a year, all told the most peacefully entrancing year of his life. The initial weeks were spent largely in the company of Wilkie, at whose studio Irving sat for a portrait. After the English painter's departure from Madrid, Irving took lodgings at a Mrs. Stalke's where he met young Hall whose death was to lead him into that strange experiment which has already been recounted. May and June went by in the city itself, with occasional work on the "Conquest of Granada," and with, now and then, excursions into the surrounding country, as to the Alcala de la Guadalia with its remains of the great capital in Moorish times. "It is impossible," Irving writes to Antoinette, "to travel about Andalusia and not imbibe a kind of feeling for these Moors. They deserve this beautiful country. They won it bravely; they enjoyed it generously and kindly."

To enjoy generously and kindly was of the essence of Irving's philosophy of life. "No lover," he goes on, "ever delighted more to cherish and adorn a mistress than did the Moors to embellish, enrich and elevate and defend their beautiful Spain."

The attraction of women for Irving was so inveterate that frequently in his correspondence he resorts to similes and metaphors relating to the sex, nowhere perhaps with more originality than in one of his letters, in May, 1828, to Prince Dolgorouki. The Prince and the author are alike in their enthusiasm for art, and Irving tells his friend of the great enjoyment he is deriving from paintings in the Spanish churches. That they are in general little known, adds to the zest; and he contrasts the pleasure derived from these out-of-the-way masterpieces with that obtained from the paintings of Italy, "admired and extolled and criticized and written about, by every connoisseur or would-be connoisseur who has made the grand tour. A celebrated Italian painting is like the belle of a metropolis who is so much admired and talked about that the imagination grows weary of her; she seems to grow stale and common both to eye and ear; but one of these Spanish masterpieces in an obscure convent seldom visited by the foot of the traveller, is like a beauty in a country village, fresh and sweet from being rarely seen or stared at . . . I have two or three delicious little Murillos which I have found out in obscure or almost remote chapels or convents, and which I in a manner keep to myself. I carry on a kind of intrigue with them, visiting them quietly and alone; and I cannot tell you what delightful moments I pass in their company . . . As to those renowned 'Virgins,' who are visited by all the rabble rout of travellers, they are not ladies for my money."

As for the flesh and blood women of Andalusia, Irving tells the Prince that their famed beauty is a myth. He admits that there are beautiful women in Seville ("God be praised for all his mercies"), but not more than in other cities; and he comes to the conclusion that the fascination of Spanish women is due less to their features than to the "fire and soul" which (when they are interested or excited) "beam through their dark and flashing eyes." But Irving is now not in a mood for romantic adventure, and he looks at the women of Seville merely "with the eye of a saunting observer," which is "like judging a fountain when it is not playing, or a fire when it lies dormant." Then, strangely enough, for we have never seen Irving didactic (except perhaps in a letter or two to his nephew, Pierre Paris Irving), he proceeds to tell the Prince, who has shown such interest in Andalusian women, to "use his talent in such a manner as worthily to shape and mould 'this gay chaos.' Fix your attention on noble objects and noble purposes and sacrifice all temporary and trivial things to their attainment. . . . Cultivate such intimacies only as may ripen into lasting friendship, or furnish your memory with valuable recollections. Above all, mark *one line* in which to excell, and bend all your thoughts and exertions to rise to eminence or, rather, to advance towards perfection in that one line. You will be surprised how soon you will become disentangled from the thousand petty cares, petty pleasures and petty troubles that are now spun around you like a spider's web, and you will be surprised also to find how full of really great objects the world is around you."

This advice was given by Irving in the month of July, when he was living alone with Hall in a cottage, the Casa de Cera, a few miles away from Seville. Intensely occupied on the "Conquest of Granada," he was now for the first time a scholar living practically in solitude, keeping himself remote from the social temptations of cities. Herein is the explanation for this rare excursion into the ways of the preacher. What he said was of course worth saying, but it is not the kind of thing which Washington Irving could have said had he not been so overwhelmingly impressed by the satisfactions of the scholar's life and the joy of that great peace which came to him in the little un-neighboured cottage. Over its porch clustered grapevines and jessamines, its garden was full of orange and citron trees, through its windows came the odour of summer nights, came the light of lonely stars shining over tranquil plains, came the far-off chiming of cathedral bells. From there he writes to Antoinette: "We are great cheats of ourselves, and defraud ourselves out of a great portion of our existence, filling it up with idle ceremony and irksome occupations and unnecessary cares"; and there he won into intimacy "with what ought to be our best and most cherished society, *ourselves*."

Now and then Irving would drive into Seville to use the library of the Cathedral. There he discovered in a work of cosmography (by the Cardinal Pedro Alico) marginal notes in Latin, written by Christopher Columbus and his brother, the Adelantado. These notes, antedating the discovery of America, had to do with the theories of Columbus concerning unknown lands, and previous to Irving's research no one had been aware that the autograph was the great voyager's. So fascinated was Irving by the finds his research was more and more revealing to him that he determined the next month to visit Palos, whence the ships of Columbus had sailed on the adventure which was to be crowned on the shores of a new continent. The archives inspected by special permission of the King, did, indeed, not shed any new light on the life of Columbus, and there are students who still believe that the whole mystery of the great Genoese will never be resolved; that he was a Jew who thought his real mission was to be the Messiah; the Anti-Christ whose fame the Roman Catholic Church must at all costs limit to the field of geographical discovery. These theories, with their insufficiency of historical data, may be left in abeyance. Irving, in any case, had the satisfaction of visiting the church wherein Columbus had read the order for the caravels and where, after his return from America, he had spent a night in prayer, the fulfilment of a vow made during a storm at sea which threatened destruction to him and his adventurous crew.

By the end of August Irving had dispatched a considerable portion of the "Conquest of Granada" to London where Colonel Aspinwall obtained two thousand pounds for it, Ebenezer obtaining in the next month four thousand, seven hundred and fifty dollars for the American edition. In October, Murray offered him a thousand pounds a year to edit a monthly magazine, but this offer was refused not only because, as Irving wrote Everett, "his review (*The Quarterly Review*) had been hostile to our country," but also because Irving was planning to resume before long his residence in the United States. "I am haunted," he writes to Peter, "by an incessant and increasing desire to visit America"; nor was this desire lessened by evidence of that unfairness in American publishing circles at that time still rendered possible by the American attitude toward international copyright. From Peter, Washington learned that some anonymous person in America intended to issue an abridgment of the Life of Columbus, and Peter, who always had a nice sense of humour, reminded Washington of the "story of the fat voyager who was to furnish a slice of his own bacon to support his shipwrecked companions but insisted on having the first cut himself." Irving, unable to "endure the idea that a paltry poacher should carry off the fruits of my labours," took Peter's amusingly phrased hint and wrote the abridgment which led to six thousand dollars for the American issue. To the English publisher Murray, who had paid so large a sum for the original "Life," Irving made no charge for the briefer and immensely successful work.

Renting at fifteen dollars a month a cottage near the town of St. Mary, about eight miles from Cadiz, Irving and Hall escaped the heat of Casa de Cera during the autumn. In November Irving returned to Seville for special research in the archives. There the quiet satisfactions of the scholar were saddened, not many weeks later, by the tidings of Hall's death. Even so, 1828 was, as Irving records in his entry for December 31st, "one of the most tranquil in spirit of my whole life. I look forward without any very sanguine anticipation, but without the gloom that has sometimes oppressed me. The only future event from which I promise myself any extraordinary gratification is the return to my native country, which, I trust, will now soon take place."

With this continually increasing desire to get back home,

Irving begins to display a keener interest in American political affairs. In February, 1829, he writes to Everett of his surprise at the decisive defeat administered to John Quincy Adams by Andrew Jackson. Irving had been "rather sorry" when Adams was elected to the Presidency, but he was much more sorry at his being now defeated, as Adams had "filled his station worthily"; this, although he "suspects that Jackson has good stuff in him and will make a sagacious, independent and high-spirited President." Irving did not guess that the old general was soon to offer him an appointment which for a few more years kept him abroad.

The first four months of 1829 went by uneventfully enough. Irving collected materials for the "Legends of the Conquest of Spain"; for papers relating to various characters famous in Spanish history; and for a sketch of the Life of Mahomet. He added to his previous studies of German, French and Italian, the study of Arabic, thus, although he was never proficient in any of these tongues, acquiring a smattering of more foreign languages than was then usual among American men of letters. This knowledge, however slight, of native tongues had from his earliest days in Europe served him well in inns and in palaces, increasing the opportunities for those friendly approaches that made him so delightfully an unofficial ambassador. His Arabic note-book is a rather fascinating thing to the eye, and that his study of Arabic was of use may be inferred from the fact that in the library of the Escurial alone there were two thousand Arabian manuscripts among its thirty thousand volumes.

During these months he had his moments of restlessness, and the desire again to turn wanderer. A visit to the African coast was abandoned only because the Austrians were blockading Tangiers. He had, despite the success of his recent books, hours of financial worry, for a mining gamble that he had taken as long ago as 1825, in Paris, in Bolivar mines, necessitated paying assessments that deprived him of all the monies coming in from the English edition of the "Life of Columbus." Irving was hardly ever a lucky gambler—investor, I suppose, is the

more dignified term—and in steamboat, mining and land specu-
lations, a great part of the revenue of his pen was lost.

Late in April, Dolgorouki had come from Madrid in a large
party headed by the French Ambassadress, a party which he
left in order to accompany Irving to Granada. A fortnight
later Irving and the Prince, by special permission of the Governor of the Alhambra, took up their abode in the old Moorish
palace, and the most entrancing period of Irving's life began.
The Prince stayed a few days with Irving. During these days
Irving's midshipman nephew, Ebenezer's son, Edgar, dropped in
to visit his uncle. This unexpected appearance brought a keen
touch of the old family life, as previously had a visit, a year or
two earlier, of Pierre M. Irving. When both Prince and
nephew had departed, Irving, alone in the Alhambra, felt lonely
for a brief while; but soon the enchantment of his surroundings
cast its full spell upon him, and until his own departure in July
he was like a being in fairyland. "A kind of Oriental dream,"
he called it, in a letter to Brevoort. "Never shall I meet on
earth with an abode so much to my taste, and so suited to my
habits and pursuits." He felt like "the Knight of Industry when
he was pleasantly enthralled in the Castle of Indolence." To
Peter he writes of his room in the old palace, one window looking into the gardens of Lindaraxa, with the fountains playing
among the flowers; another window looking down upon the valley of the River Darro, and facing a mountain-side covered with
gardens and groves, among which stood the old Moorish palace
of the Generalife. "I have nothing but the sound of the water,
the humming of bees, and the singing of nightingales to interrupt
the profound silence of my abode." Later he moved into a
suite of rooms in an apartment built by Charles V. Tia and little Dolores (who waited on his needs) remonstrated at his "remaining alone in such a remote part of the old building, out of
reach of all assistance," in the event of robbers. He had as a
combination of valet, messenger, guide and companion, Mateo
Ximenes, the historiador. Into Granada Irving would seldom
go, the theatre and opera being closed on account of the death

of the Queen. When, indeed, he did leave the Alhambra, it was generally for the purpose of making use of the library of the Duke of Gor, that delightful nobleman whose family of lovely children (especially the nine year old Dolores) so attracted the American visitor.

Irving's weeks of writing, strolling, and, above all, dreaming amid these scenes of magic, where the richness of flowering nature vied in friendly rivalry with the beauty of Moorish architecture, were broken into by the news of his appointment as Secretary of the American Legation to the Court of St. James. Some of Irving's friends were of the opinion that this office was, in view of his fame, not important enough; but, as he wrote to Peter, "Such objections have little weight with me. The only reputation of which I am ambitious is not to be increased or decreased by official station." He accepted the appointment because "it would gratify my friends and would link me with my country . . . I am perfectly content for a time to be Secretary of Legation . . . I care not who takes the lead of me in entering a room or sits above me at table. It is better that half a dozen should say 'Why is he seated so low down?' than that anyone should casually say 'What right has he to be at the top?'"

A special pleasure that Irving took in the offer of this diplomatic post arose from the source of the suggestion of his appointment. It had come from his old friend Jack Nicholson, who had written in the matter to Martin Van Buren, Andrew Jackson's Secretary of State, while another old friend, James K. Paulding, had also approached Van Buren on behalf of Irving. "That I should have that fat, jolly little tar, Jack N., for a patron! I confess there is something so extremely humorous in this caprice of fortune that I cannot help feeling in good humour with it. Little Jack has had a kind of dogged determined kindness for me now for about twenty-five years, ever since he took a liking to me on our getting tipsy together in Virginia at the time of Burr's trial." Thus Washington to Peter, whose approval of the acceptance led the younger brother to write to the elder: "I now feel assured and contented in the decision

I have made. Never hesitate to give me your advice in all matters, whether trivial or important. You are my better half and in most matters I feel more confidence in your judgment than in my own."

The only regret felt by Irving in the circumstances was Jackson's decision not to reappoint Alexander H. Everett at Madrid. Sorry though he was that his friend had "fallen beneath the edge of the old general's sword," Irving, in writing to Everett, assumed that the President's action still left the deposed Minister undisturbed in his philosophy. Everett's reply, in a wholly unpublished letter found among Irving's papers, is an especially fine manifestation of the spirit of the gentleman and of the scholar; and he seems more regretful that Irving has not received an independent commission than at his own recall. Like Irving, Everett's taste was rather for literary occupation than for politics, and, again like Irving, he had "picked up materials enough to employ my pen *tant bien que mal*" for the rest of his life.

On the 28th of July, Irving left the Alhambra. He had as travelling companion a young Englishman, Ralph Sneyd. The weather being too hot for horseback, they traversed the Mediterranean provinces of Spain in a kind of "rumble-tumble called a tartana on two wheels," their baggage guarded by corsarios following separately. Near Guadix an unexpected carriage awaited Irving and he and Sneyd were driven to the nearby estate of the Duke of Gor, where they were taken in hospitable charge by the servitors of the Duke. They were entertained, the next day, at the old castle of Gor. To Irving, however, probably the most interesting night during these final travels in Spain was passed at Orchuela in the ancient kingdom of Murcia. It was at Orchuela that "Tadmor of yore played off the trick of manning his walls with women armed with reeds."

Irving's note-book of this closing journey, beginning with the last day at the Alhambra when he breakfasted with Muriel, the painter, and where he said good-bye to the Duke of Gor, has much data not recorded in any of his biographies. At Guadix he sees four prisoners brought in heavily ironed, "part of a band of twenty-seven, who in various places exchanged their booty." He notes, with equal interest, a battle between an enormous spider and a large fly in which the former is killed. At Baza he passes the chapel erected on the spot where Isabella of Castile is said to have fired the last cannon when Baza was captured by her in 1489. The next day at Cullar, on the Irun River, Irving is much taken by the appearance of a young gypsy: "Olive complexion—slender ankles and feet—a string of pearls around her neck—long silver chain with relique—earrings with imitation diamonds—embroidered bodice." The African look of the towns of Murcia—their women with white woollen mantles—attracted him. His pencil is at times occupied in sketches, including a drawing of Antonio, the long-legged, musket-armed Portuguese escort, their defence against robbers. In words incisive and musical he depicts the rich valley of the Segura, with its fruits of varied character, grapes and olives, citrons and oranges, dates and pomegranates. He notes the "little sturdy Valencian, who smelt strongly of wine," and whose "rosy face showed him to be a bibber." With the felicity of the stylist, able to find the perfect adjective, he hears the locust or the cricket making "its sultry sound." He observes the "huts of reeds tied together to withstand earthquakes."

At Alicante where Irving stopped to visit the American Consul, Adams, stories of famous robbers were related to him, in particular that of "El Gato, who with his men in the disguise of soldiers, succeeded in capturing a village, whose mayor and curate he then had brought forth and shot." The next day, passing through a defile especially noted for attacks by robbers, the soldiers accompanying Irving and the young Englishman mounted the heights and flanked the defile. While the travellers went past many crosses indicating murders of their predecessors, and while in one village Irving saw, hanging in an iron cage, no less gruesome an object than the skull of a robber with some of the hair remaining on it, he himself was not attacked, and Antonio's musket never had to be fired.

Irving makes several sketches of this musket, yet the weapon which with most satisfaction he comes across during these days was a sword in the Posada of Villena, and whose inscription is recorded in his note-book, both in the Spanish and Irving's English translation:

> *No me saqueis sin rason,*
> *No me embargues sin honor.*

> Do not draw me without reason,
> Do not sheathe me without honour.

At Valencia we are brought by Irving into scenes so contrasting in human values and relations, it is a bit difficult to realize that less than a century has gone by since Irving depicted them. Visualize a "great array of galley slaves," officers arranging them in platoons and then driving them "into their prisons for the night." England was soon to do away with slavery in her colonies, but in 1829 men were still bought and sold among the nations of the world and chained to the oars as in the days of Rome. Then, only a few miles away from its seaport where human beings were thus treated, see the gay world of Valencia, assembled in the glorieta, its fountained promenade; or visit, with Irving, the market place, with its flirtations between soldiers and house-maids, and listen as Irving did, to that friar, "talking and laughing with the buxom wife of a farmer—a young woman observing them from behind the curtain of the opposite shop."

At Valencia also Irving records his having smoked a "segar." Trifling as this notation may seem to be, it is, if I am not mistaken, the first time a cigar was used by any distinguished American author.

The next day, August 11th, after having passed Murviedo (famous, under its ancient name of Saguntum, as the town that opposed the passage of Hannibal), Irving and Sneyd came in sight of the ocean. An especially good dinner seems that day to have decidedly aroused his enthusiasm:—"Fish, flesh, fowl and game—fine melons—tomatoes—sweet peppers—black wine." Certainly a meal full of flavour; and then, besides, there was at table a merchant of Barcelona, a Catalan, "gay and good-humoured," who spoke with pride of his country. The Catalans, Irving is informed, often reply to the question: "Are you a Spaniard?"—"I am a Catalan." The merchant and his companion (of what sex Irving does not record) amused themselves and Irving with "bantering" a young Frenchman who had been boasting of his "good fortunes among the Spanish women."

In less pleasant company Irving finds himself at Barcelona, when, on visiting its cathedral, he was shown the body of St. Olegarios, "a hideous relique—clothed in Bishop's robes—face like a mummy—nose gone—teeth grinning—black, withered hands covered with rings and precious stones." But from the life of this saint, Irving obtained an anecdote especially sympathetic to him both for its whimsicality and for its relation to things supernatural and miraculous. Let us quote from Irving's note-book: "When the French had possession of Barcelona and the Spaniards were approaching to attack it, there was a rumour throughout the city that the saint had raised one of his hands. It was hailed as a sure omen of deliverance from their invaders. General Suchet, an Italian general who commanded the French army, went to the Cathedral with a detachment of his troops. He stationed some around the building and entered with others. Summoning the canons, etc., he entered the shrine of the saint and found that his hand was actually elevated in a menacing manner. 'Come, come,' said the shrewd Italian, 'this will never do. I must have that hand down.' So saying he replaced the hand upon the breast. 'And now Saint—,' said he, 'let me assure you one thing—if you raise your hand again, I will not only have you hanged, but all these good people of the Cathedral shot!' The saint never lifted his hand afterwards."—That Irving had not made his own research in regard to this anecdote is shown by his error in referring to the "Italian general." The officer was Napoleon's marshal, Louis Gabriel Suchet, Duc d'Albufera, who first won distinction in the campaigns in Italy.

The week spent at Barcelona has as its one notable event the dinner at the Count d'Espagne, Captain General of the Provinces. This nobleman, generally regarded as one of the most cruel in Spain, was in merry and talkative mood. With the wit so often flashing through his note-book jottings, Irving writes: "He was a lion joking in his own den." After dinner the Neapolitan Consul at Barcelona came in and was introduced to the Captain General, to whom he wished to make the announcement of the intention of the Neapolitan Princess, Maria Christina (affianced to the widower King Ferdinand), of coming to Barcelona. With what extravagance of courtesy and manifestations of intense interest the Count d'Espagne received from the Consul news which was already in his possession, Irving describes in a letter to his sister, fifteen years later. The playing with and mimicking of the little Neapolitan dignitary "was altogether a high farce, more comic in the acting than in the description; but it was the sportive gamboling of a tyrant, and I give it to show how the tyrant, in his hours of familiarity, may play the buffoon." Irving, in 1844, now the American Minister to Spain, was again in the palace at Barcelona where the Count d'Espagne had presided. But the Count himself, after having turned traitor to the daughter of Ferdinand, had long ago been "murdered by those whom he had opposed, and hurried into a bloody grave."

Irving's baggage arrived on the 21st of August. The next day, at a quarter before three in the morning, he and Sneyd leave Barcelona in the diligence for Perpignan. In high spirits they and the others in the diligence drive through the well-cultivated country. There are merry doings at dinner, and Irving, much as Laurence Sterne would have done, observes the "fine looking waiting maids." At supper he gets into a talk with a "fine French lad lately from his college—talks of France, all in reference to his college—peche mortel—eating viands on certain days."—There is a glorious moonlight drive after Gerona has been left behind; and the next day, at Puenta Puerta, with the fortress of Belgrade commanding it, they come to the frontier. The early years in Spain are ended.

Chapter XII

CHARGÉ D'AFFAIRES

GEORGE IV, "by the Grace of God" King of Great Britain and Ireland, was now, for England more fortunately by God's grace, approaching the end of his voluptuous and ill-spent life. The closing year of his reign was of wide-spread misery throughout his realm, the destitution of the lower classes leading to sabotage, to the burning of hay-ricks, to a general defiance of the law. All phases of revolt were met by severe measures on the part of narrow-minded ministers unable to read the signs of the time. Organization of trade unions went forward, and many blind gropings towards a more equitable state of society, until with the passage of the Reform Bill in 1832, "rotten boroughs" were largely abolished and the balance of power swung from the landed aristocracy to the middle classes.

It was thus to a country more internally disturbed than it had ever been since the Revolution of 1688 that Washington Irving (after a few weeks in France where he had stopped off to be with his brother Peter) came in October, 1829, to take up his duties as Secretary of the American Legation. During his first nine months in London his diplomatic tasks were comparatively insignificant, and he had much leisure for the renewal of old companionships. He looked forward to diplomatic life, the labours, as he wrote to Peter, being not great, and introducing him to "scenes and affairs of high interest,"—in that way preparing him for "higher intellectual labours." But although at dinner at Sir Robert Inglis's, in November, James Mackintosh suggested Irving's joining Walter Scott, Thomas Moore and himself in their series of historical biographies—a suggestion which led Irving to consider the Life of Washington—our

214

THOMAS MOORE

intermittently indolent hero let the pen of the author lie practically idle. His idea was "not to drudge at literary labour but to use it as an agreeable occupation." Now that money was coming in from the books that he had written in Spain, he was inclined, as he advises Peter also, to "indulge in the passing pleasures of life and mingle amusements with our labours." So we see him much in the company of his old friends, the painters Leslie, Newton and West, and more than once with Stephen Price, the New York theatrical manager now active in the affairs of Drury Lane. With his customary kindness he arranges through Ebenezer for the American sale of Moore's Life of Byron, and, after that has gone through, acts on Moore's request: "Do, like a good fellow, poke him up a little about it, as if the cash doesn't come, I must—go." He dines at many houses, and writes in a letter of January, 1830, to his boyhood friend, Gouverneur Kemble, "I have a villanous propensity to grow round and robustious, and I fear the beef and pudding of England will complete the ruin of my figure." Another boyhood friend, Frank Ogden, he meets with joy in London and visits him at his rooms in the very lodging house where Peter and Washington had dwelt in earlier days. On his birthday, April 3, 1830, Irving receives the tidings that he has been voted by the Royal Society of London one of their two gold medals, carrying with it a purse of fifty guineas, for pre-eminent work in the field of literature; the other medal being awarded to the historian Hallam. The next month he receives from Oxford the degree of Doctor of Letters.

When this honour was conferred upon him it was at an occasion unparalleled in the annals of the venerable college. Students went wild over the well-beloved American, and cries of "Diedrich Knickerbocker," "Rip Van Winkle," "Geoffrey Crayon" and "Ichabod Crane" resounded through the halls. They shouted aloud the names of his books—"The Sketch Book," "Bracebridge Hall"—that had done so much to bring America and England into better understanding. Deeply touched though he was by the tribute, so deeply that he was

almost overcome, the modest Irving never used the LL.D—
the same degree which, as the files of Columbia College show,
was conferred upon him by that New York institution of
learning after the appearance of "The Sketch Book." "LL.D,"
he wrote many years later to Donald G. Mitchell (whose
delightful book, the "Reveries of a Bachelor" reveals on every
page the influence of Irving), was a "learned dignity urged upon
me very much against the stomach of my sense, and to which
I have never laid claim." Briefly after the ceremony at Oxford, Irving's chief, McLane, left London for a short while,
and Irving's responsibilities began to increase.

On June 26th, the selfish libertine, George IV, performed
one of the few acts of his life that is not open to criticism, and
the Duke of Clarence assumed the title of William IV. Of
the fifteen children of George III, the new King was temperamentally and in manners the least royal. He was the bluff
sailor who, as Irving notes in describing a ball at the Duke of
Wellington's, "has an easy and natural way of wiping his nose
with the back of his forefinger, which, I fancy, is a relic of his
old middy habits." An affable old gentleman, well-meaning,
but not over strong in mind or character, the King was more
desirous that, "it shall be merry old England once more," than
capable of effecting this consummation. When, in July, 1830,
the abdication of Charles X placed Louis Philippe at the head
of a constitutional monarchy in France, and conservative English
statesmen, led by the Duke of Wellington as Prime Minister,
saw in this event further cause for the suppression of liberalism
in England, William vacillated between the desires to be the
popular monarch and to retain for the crown and the aristocracy those prerogatives which blocked the way of reform.

With clearer vision Irving himself had expressed to Peter
the hope that no terms with the Bourbons should be made; and
after his return from the Chamber of Deputies, where he himself had seen the Duke of Orleans take the oath as King of the
French, he wrote with satisfaction to McLane that Paris was
"quiet and cheerful." On American affairs, in this letter, he
216

dwelt with more anxiety, for the slavery question (in the background of tariff discussion) had already raised its ugly head in the direction of Secession, and "God help the inflammable South."

In September, Irving is again in London, and McLane now in Paris. His chief absent, Irving as Chargé d'Affaires keeps him advised of those activities in which he now plays a somewhat larger part. The difficulties of the Duke of Wellington in forming a satisfactory cabinet come in for discussion, and there is interesting comment on the qualifications and the character of Talleyrand, recently appointed as French Ambassador to the Court of St. James. "The talents of Talleyrand," Irving writes to McLane, "are not of the kind suited to the day and the crisis. The policy is of the dissolute, heartless kind of the old school; the trickery and intrigue of cabinets and saloons; not the policy suited to a free country and a frank and popular government. I question the greatness of any political talent that is not based upon integrity." This is followed by a remarkably good simile when one recalls that Talleyrand had held office during the Revolutionary period under Napoleon, under the Bourbons, and was now representing France under the House of Orleans: "As to Talleyrand, he cares for nobody and nothing. His patriotism is a mere local attachment, like that of a cat which sticks by the house, let who will inhabit it." Granting the appositeness of Irving's comparison, Talleyrand, who had been the Grand Chamberlain of the Emperor Napoleon and who was now at the London Conference the representative of the Citizen-King, was not alone sticking to France but was also engaging in thoughts of general European pacification, that were to lead to his plan of the inviolability and permanent neutrality of Belgium. The overthrow of Charles X, after his final attempt to make royal absolutism indeed absolute in his country, was the most successful of those many nationalistic and liberalizing movements that had, during the preceding fifteen years, been largely thwarted by the interference of Austria, still true to the political philosophy of Metternich. The Revolution of July 1830, general in its influence on Europe, had directly led to the culmination of the revolt of the southern provinces of the Netherlands against the pig-headed rule of the Dutch King William I. During Irving's first months as Secretary of the American Legation, Russia, France, Prussia, Austria and England were (largely under the guidance of Talleyrand) considering measures ending in the creation of the Kingdom of Belgium with Prince Leopold of Saxe-Coburg as its first monarch. The crafty brain whose processes moved Irving to aversion brought about that pact which, some three-quarters of a century later, a King of Prussia was, as Emperor of Germany, to violate, and, in so doing, range against him the armies of the world. Strange that this crafty brain was, through an oversight of the famous chemist, Micard (who prepared the body of Talleyrand for burial), covertly to be flung into the same sewer opening through which the body of Robespierre made its ignominious exit from the scenes of his bloody triumphs.

Irving's affection for his brothers and sisters was the one unbroken motif that ran like warm music through his life, and as soon as he had a chance for a vacation, he left London for a ten days' stay with his sister Sarah. There, in the old Van Wart home at Birmingham, he did indeed do a little literary work, finishing three of his Alhambra legends, "The Moor's Legacy," "The Garden of Lindaraxa," and "The Three Beautiful Princesses," legends whose titles hold the flavour of the old Moorish palace. Peter, whose literary flair had continued ever since the early years when he had published the *Morning Chronicle,* had given Washington some hints in connection with these tales, and to Peter he writes with satisfaction of their completion in the "nice little study" where every evening during the Birmingham visit, he "chatted and laughed" with the elder and younger Van Warts, and "dozed in the necromantic arm chair" which Peter "must so well remember." Dozing was one of the favourite habits of Irving, and I have heard descendants of some of his old New York friends relate how he would go to sleep even at the dinner table.

218

When, towards the end of October, Irving was back at his post, he was happy to have as a companion in London Henry Brevoort, the most loyal of all his friends. With that affluent American merchant, whose letters reveal distinct style and whose tastes coincided with those of Irving's in so many ways, and with Prince Dolgorouki, now of the Russian Embassy at the Court of St. James, Irving would go for rambles in the quainter parts of the old city, or would drive out into the country for dinner at some inn. With them sometimes during these days was John Randolph, United States Minister at St. Petersburg, and one of the most interesting and eccentric characters among all American diplomats. His language was unusual, and he swore strange oaths. His clothes were even more unusual, and he wore whatever he wished to wear. When McLane and Irving took him to be presented at Court, his costume, with unusual breeches, hose and gold buckles, and with the little clack hat, made so awkward a figure of the lanky man, that the Duke of Sussex, the King's brother, could not keep from poking fun at him in Irving's hearing. Whereupon Irving (as Pierre M. Irving relates) took care to impress upon the Duke that he was speaking of the United States Minister to Russia, "and one of the most distinguished orators of the United States."

The Duke of Sussex took a liking to Irving, and a year or so later when they met as visitors at Byron's old home of Newstead Abbey, spending a few days there together as the guests of Colonel Wildman, they became on terms of cordiality such as never before had been experienced by an American writer in his relations with English royalty. The King also was friendly with Irving, and on one occasion in 1831, after McLane had returned to America to become Secretary of the Treasury, William IV and Irving had a very interesting and satisfactory conversation, in the course of which Irving was especially tactful in making the King's comment on Lord Palmerston—who was present—a point of departure for pleasant words concerning other royal ministers. In writing to McLane of this interview, Irving observes that William IV "has always treated me with marked attention ever since I have had charge of the Legation"; while already during the previous year Irving had received compliments and gracious treatment from the Queen, the intelligent Adelaide of Saxe Meiningen, whose marriage, in 1818, to the then Duke of Clarence was an event of State duty, which terminated William IV's twenty years of happy intimacy with Mrs. Jordan, the actress.

The Duke of Wellington was the great host in those days. Even when he went out of power and made way for Lord Grey and Lord Palmerston, his house was the scene of magnificent entertainments. To some of these, to receptions given by the Queen, to dinner and balls at the Duke of Somerset's, at the Duke of Devonshire's, at Lord Aberdeen's, Irving would frequently go. The tips presented to the servants of these various noblemen appear among the items recorded by Irving in the book he kept,—"Disbursements for the Contingencies of the Legation of the United States at London." One pound, one shilling as "customary Christmas presents to keepers, St. James Park"; a similar amount for the Duke of Wellington's servants, and for the Lord Chancellor's servants; twice the sum as "gratuities to the letter carrier of the foreign ministers"; and four pounds, four shillings as fees to door-keepers of the foreign office are among the items in Irving's autograph. Not unamusing are they in these days when such paltry sums would hardly evoke a "thank you" from a waiter at some large dinner at a restaurant. But the affairs themselves, especially those at the Duke of Wellington's, were splendid enough, although Irving enjoyed himself better in chatting with Wilkie, Newton or Leslie in their studios, or at the dinner to which his old Paris friend, Kennedy, invited him to meet "a few vagabonds," Macready, the actor, among them. And he enjoyed himself better when he again dined with John Howard Payne, for the first time in many years, and found him "fresh and fair as a rose," in "marvelous good spirits notwithstanding that he was as usual up to the ears with negotiations for some half dozen pieces of various kinds."

Early in 1831 Irving spent over a month at Mrs. Van Wart's,

intending to be busy with his pen there; but he had one of his "fits of mental inertness" and accomplished nothing. He consoled himself with the thought that "there is no help in these matters any more than there is in the winds and tides when they set against us." His entire literary accomplishment for that year was a review, for the *Quarterly,* of Slidell's "A Year in Spain," a volume which he had himself corrected for the press prior to its publication, at his suggestion, by Murray. Nor does he seem to have done much reading beyond the daily journals. He was engrossed by events that might so easily have brought England to civil war, by decisions that were occupying all Europe in connection with the relations of Belgium and Holland, and especially by the attitude of Louis Philippe towards the plans for the new Kingdom of Belgium. On March 31st, Irving writes to Brevoort: "This evening will determine the fate of the present cabinet, which is in a tottering condition. We are looking daily for decisive news from Paris . . . What a stirring moment it is to live in. It seems to me as if life were breaking out anew with me, and I rejoice to find my sensibilities, which were waning as to many objects of past interest, reviving with all their freshness and vivacity."

In September, Martin Van Buren, who had been named by Jackson as Minister to the Court of St. James, arrived at London, and briefly thereafter Irving retired from the Legation and left London to visit the Van Warts; not, however, before a final meeting with his old friend, Sir Walter Scott, at a family dinner at Lockhart's, an unhappy evening for Irving as Scott was now a broken-down old man. From Birmingham, after a few days' visit to his nephew Irving Van Wart at Sheffield, Irving went to the old Elizabethan mansion of the wealthy and eccentric Rev. C. R. Reaston-Rodes, "a kind of wet parson, if I may borrow that phrase from the Quakers, as he is a bon vivant, hunts, shoots, races." Here at Barlborough Hall, the old English customs, and especially the Christmastide customs, were kept up, and Irving lived the life which he had described in "Bracebridge Hall." With his host he visited nearby Hardwick Castle where Queen Elizabeth had stayed during one of her tours through old England, and where her unfortunate cousin, Mary, Queen of Scots, had once been kept a prisoner. With Mr. Rodes he also saw Newstead Abbey for the first time and made so delightful an impression on its owner, Colonel Wildman, that a few months later Irving was there again with Martin Van Buren and his son. After Van Buren's departure he stayed on, living in Byron's own bedroom and revelling in all the associations of the historic abbey, "in the centre of Robin Hood's country, what once was merry Sherwood forest."

It was Irving's characteristic kindness that led him to suggest to Van Buren the tour which took them to Oxford, Blenheim, Stratford, Warwick Castle, Birmingham and then Barlborough Hall, where they stayed a fortnight, enjoying the Christmas "mummers, morris dancers, the glee singers from the neighbouring villages, great feasting, with the boar's head crowned with holly, the wassail bowl, yule-log, snap-dragon, dancing and all kind of merriment." Van Buren was in a frame of mind when travel and diversion were especially welcome and salutary, for he was waiting, doubtless with some apprehension, for confirmation by the Senate of his appointment as Minister. Jackson had nominated him early in December and all through that month discussion had gone on concerning his confirmation. The opposition in which Hayne, the great orator among the Southern diplomats, joined with Webster and Clay, the leaders of the Whig party, was largely a political manœuvre, but Webster and other opponents of Van Buren, who feared that his appointment might be a step on the ladder of ascent to the presidential office, could make the special point against Van Buren that in his instructions as Secretary of State, to McLane, then Minister to England, Van Buren had intimated a reproach to his country in admitting that a previous American administration had not been justified in certain claims which had been made in respect to commercial arrangements between the United States and Great Britain.

Of course Webster was not sincere in contending that an

American Minister ~~~~ always insist on the absolute justification of all the acts—past as well as present—of his country; and he was less than usually far-sighted in not realizing (as Irving was one of the first to realize) that Martin Van Buren's rejection would lead to such a re-action in his favour that he must almost inevitably succeed Jackson. The Senate voted adversely, and early in February, at a party given by Prince Talleyrand, Van Buren heard of the humiliating decision. He went on with his life and duties in London, Irving advising him to take the position that until the Senate had decided on a new Minister, Van Buren, by virtue of Jackson's nomination, was the American representative at London. The English, with their characteristic love of good sportsmanship, treated Van Buren "with more respect and attention than ever before."

Both Irving and Van Buren remained in London until the first week of April. It was during these months, when the New York author was of such value and comfort to the later president, that the friendship developed which, after they had both returned to America, led to further travel together. Prior to Van Buren's departure for Holland on the first of April, and Irving's for France (of course to see Peter) on the second, another New Yorker, this time the poet Bryant, made his appearance before the British public in the volume which had been arranged for by Washington Irving. The poems were preceded by a letter of dedication from Irving to Samuel Rogers, and when Rogers read it, he wrote to Irving: "To have been mentioned by you with regard on any occasion, I should have always considered as a good fortune . . . If I was a vain man before, I am now in danger of becoming a proud one; and still I can truly say that never in my life was I made more conscious of my unworthiness than you have made me by your praise." This note of appreciation was from one of the most caustic of Britons, a man not easily given to praise. But from critical and noncritical alike; from the reviewers in the journals and the boys at college; from royalty and diplomats; from lodging-house keepers and country folk; in a word, from the high places and

223

from the by-ways of English life, praise and affection flowed forth to Washington Irving; and it was as the most affectionately regarded of Americans that he sailed for his native land. The last of his recorded visits to any friends in London was at the home of the Fosters. Did he—years after the Dresden offer of marriage—then make the final attempt to bring Emily as his bride across the waters? And is not the second half of his protracted and protracted stay in Europe explained in large measure by a suitor's persistence in a love affair whose intensity and significance have escaped due attention because of Pierre M. Irving's sentimental desire to perpetuate the Matilda Hoffman legend?

Chapter XIII

TEN YEARS IN AMERICA

THE reception given to Irving by his fellow citizens was cordial beyond his most hopeful expectations. He found himself "in a tumult of enjoyment . . . pleased with everything and everybody and as happy as a mortal can be." Seventeen years had gone by since his home town had seen its famous son. Its chief citizens immediately arranged for a public dinner which Irving could not well refuse, although he looked forward to it "with awe," and wrote Peter that he would be "heartily glad when it was over." Doubtless he would have preferred to assume the rôle of the maid servant described by William Irving, a man almost as shy as his younger brother. On the occasion of a large dinner given by her mistress the servant had asked permission to go to bed early on the ground that she did not feel at ease with so much company about. Yet when the banquet took place at the City Hotel, with Chancellor Kent presiding, Irving managed to acquit himself most creditably in one of the very few public speeches that he was ever able to get through with. He had been "too proud to vindicate himself" from the charge that his long absence had alienated him from his country, and the cheers and applause were prolonged when in simple yet beautiful language he spoke of his "pride and joy" in America.

It took Irving some time to recover from the "topsy-turvy condition" into which he was thrown by all these manifestations of enthusiastic affection. Invitations from Philadelphia and other places to dinners in his honour he refused, although in the course of his first year or two at home he spent various weeks in Philadelphia, Baltimore and Washington. He was not yet in the mood to settle down, and the wanderer in him led, in the autumn of 1832, to that tour through the West which resulted in one of the most delightful works descriptive of American life and scenery, "A Tour on the Prairies."

The diaries from which this book was drawn lie before me, and just as the sketches of a great master are often more fascinating than the completed painting, so do the quick pictures here inscribed have an appeal more direct than the rounded paragraphs of the published volume. Henry L. Ellsworth, resident Commissioner among the Indian tribes, had invited Irving to accompany him on an expedition having for its purpose governmental negotiations with representatives of the different tribes. Charles Joseph Latrobe, an English traveller and author, and young Count Pourtales, a Frenchman (both of them friends of Irving) were in the party.

The excursion into the forests and prairies of the Indian territories had as its starting point Fort Gibson on the Arkansas River. Prior to meeting Ellsworth there, Irving spent a few days at Cincinnati, where, one evening at the theatre, to his "astonishment and dismay, the manager came out between the acts," and announced that Irving was in the house. This episode coupled with the manager's invitation requesting Irving again to visit the theatre, caused Irving to induce his companions to hasten their departure. By steamboat, via Louisville, to St. Louis; a visit to Fort Jefferson where he saw the famous Indian chief, Black Hawk, now an old man over seventy (Irving found him with the skin of a black hawk in his hand, and fanning himself with its tail); nine days on horseback from St. Louis to Independence; a deer hunt in the neighbourhood; another ten days of travel, sleeping every night in a tent; and Irving met Colonel Ellsworth at Fort Gibson. From the record of those weeks these are a few of the vivid pictures in which his diaries abound:

At St. Louis. "Little, well-dressed negro girl brings in salver of peaches—fat negro wenches drying apples and peaches on board under trees—wild gorse, flowers, etc., about house. In neighbouring field negro boys exercising race-horses."

DRAWINGS BY IRVING, INCLUDING OLD HOUSES IN CINCINNATI,
AUSTRIAN PEASANTS, AND ANTONIO, IRVING'S GUIDE IN SPAIN

Evening scene on Ohio. "Steamboat aground with two flats on each side of her—we take part of cargo on board—moonlight—light of fires—chant and chorus of negro boatmen—men strolling about docks with cigars—negroes dancing before furnaces—glassy surface of river—undulations made by boat—wavering light of moon and stars."

"Old negro scolding young negro for lying—he aims at a monopoly."

"Stop for wood near Wabash on Virginia side—negro woman in log hut—who cooks for men who get wood—a cheerful, contented being—plenty to eat and drink—good whistling—no one to worry or trouble her—does not think she'll marry again. Mr. Ellsworth asked her about her children, but the tears started into her eyes—she got up, crossed the hut—'I am not allowed to live with them—they are up at the plantation.' "

"Aground near native's house—slow boat on the Illinois shore with flag—groups assemble there—rifle shooting—horse race along shore—negro laugh—sunset—party breaks up—some in boat across glassy river singing ballad—others on horseback through the woods—some on foot—some loiter on the shore—beautiful, clear evening sky—moon nearly full—rising over the Virginia shore above tufted forests—night hawks."

Then these, showing how in the early days of western immigration various causes led to the disappointment of the adventurers:

"Still aground—go to shore—log house with corn field in wood—man and his wife from Philadelphia County—good looking man and woman—children decently clad—been here fifteen years—if it were to be done over would not come here—no means of educating his children."

"Stop at log house on the shore—pretty, delicate woman from near Nashville, Tennessee—wishes herself back—no church in neighbourhood—people rude. If there comes a Quaker the rude fellows pelt him, cut his horse loose and play all kinds of tricks."

"Take on board a little Frenchman and his wife who are roll-

ing a big box through the country like a pair of tumblers. He
is a blacksmith—she kept a cafe in Touraine—natives of Tours
—beguiled out here by a Frenchman, the same Lucas who had
bought land in Kentucky and represented it as a paradise—
from turnpike could meet diligence every day—the very place to
set up blacksmith shop and cafe—tells her to bring all the linen
she could. Arrived at the promised land and found it a wilder-
ness covered with trees . . . they re-embark to return to New
Orleans."

The pages of Irving's diaries have many special touches both
of beauty and of humour.—"Moon, hand-maid a virgin star,"
is exquisite. For comic pictures we may turn to "two Kentuck-
ians were quarrelling—one says: 'Put down that rock and I'll
fight you.' The rock was a stone as big as an apple"; or again:
"Negro driving team of seven oxen in Louisville, exclaims:
'Get along, you fat, money-making rascals.'" "The merriest
people in these parts," Irving calls the negroes; "if you hear a
broad, merry laugh, be sure it is a negro; politest people, fine
gentlemen." This is a memorable phrase. Because of their
good humour and their courteous ways, Irving speaks of the
negroes as "fine gentlemen."

As Irving and his friends approach Fort Gibson, they come into the life of the hunter, partaking in bee hunts and wolf hunts,
and in all the experiences of camping. They come into close
touch for the first time with the Indians, especially the Osages.
Indian legends,—which had interested Irving from early youth
—now reach him at first hand. There is an amusing story of
the old squaw who had been left alone when her party had gone
hunting, and who "prayed the Great Spirit to make something
to amuse her—he made the mosquito." (The God of the red
men, it might appear to some, has a more delicious sense of
humour than the God of the white.) There is the touching
story of the little Indian girl who died—"they buried her with
her playthings—she had a favourite little horse—they killed and
buried her with it." There is the excellent rejoinder of the
Indian to old Father Vail, a missionary trying to impress upon

his auditors the necessity of industry as the road to happiness: "Father, I don't understand this kind of happiness you talk of. You tell me to cut down tree—to lop it—to make fence—to plough—this you call being happy—I no like such happiness. When I go to St. Louis I go to see Chouteau or Clark—he say 'hello'—and negro comes in with great plate of cake, wine, etc. —he say 'eat, drink.' If he want anything else he say 'hello'— three—four—five—six negro come in and do what he want— that I call happy—he no plough—he no work—he no cut wood."

"Ah, but he has negroes to do all that."

"Well, father, you go to our Great Father—tell him to find me one, two, three negroes to cut wood and plough for me and I'll be willing to be happy like white man."

The preceding dialogue, lifted bodily from Irving's note-book, is indication of his general attitude towards reform when imposed from without. He was not one of those who try to remake people in their own images; nor had he that shallow sense of superiority which is the basis of chauvinism, and which, in its wide application, leads the Occident to consider itself more advanced than the Orient. At a time when individual states were seeking to impose their laws on the Indians, and when the Federal Government (acting on the theory that the Indian tribes though not independent still had the character of states) obtained through purchase the lands of various of the tribes, Irving was well aware that the rule of might, not of right, was directing the progress of events. Whether he was equally certain as to right and might in his consideration of the other great struggle then coming to a head, one cannot be sure. Though his sentiment in regard to the union between the states was that of his fellow-Northerners, Irving only a few weeks after South Carolina had passed its Ordinance of Nullification (declaring as not binding on the people of that state the tariff acts of 1832), did not at all hesitate to dine as the guest of Governor Hamilton at Columbia. He reached the capital of South Carolina, after having travelled by mail stage through all the southern states that lay between it and New Orleans. This still largely French town he visited after his weeks among the Indians were ended, on leaving the Mississippi steamboat that had brought him from Arkansas. Patrick Henry's brilliant nephew, William C. Preston, who so many years before had travelled with Washington and Peter in England and Scotland, and who now was a Senator from South Carolina, had taken him to Governor Hamilton's, an acquaintance of Irving's when both had been young men in New York. On leaving the Governor's house, and to Hamilton's cordial invitation to come soon again, "Oh, yes!" said Irving, with a smile: "I'll come with the first troops!"

Briefly thereafter, at the national capital, Irving was present at the discussions brought forward in the Senate when those two giants of intellect, Calhoun and Webster, met in combat concerning the question of whether a state was empowered to annul acts of Congress. He listened with close attention to every speech uttered in the legislative halls during those pregnant days that preceded Jackson's Nullification Proclamation in December, a proclamation ascribing to the advocates of nullification the object of disunion, and positing the contention that "disunion by armed force is treason." In the course of listening to these debates Irving, who had so recently come into close touch with the wilder regions and the wild life of the American continent, now gained an "acquaintance with the nature and operation of our institutions and the character and concerns of the various parts of the union that I could not have learned from books for years." But as between North and South, he himself took no radical position.

A few April weeks in New York, with so many social engagements that his "time and mind" were cut up "like chopped hay," and he was off again on another excursion, now to Virginia. The students at Jefferson University sought to arrange a public dinner for him, but he managed to escape it. He could not, however, when again in New York in June, avoid taking part in the reception to Andrew Jackson, and he accompanied the officials of New York City as far as Brunswick to meet the President. With his usual loyalty to old times and friends, he left Saratoga (where, in July, he was taking the waters), to visit old Herman Knickerbocker, at Schaghticoke. There he found that worthy old congressman with a houseful of children, and simultaneously exercising the functions of "judge, farmer, miller, manufacturer, politician, etc." To this same summer belongs also another excursion which (as its record is of flavour for the student of American history, and as this record is entirely absent from any biography of Irving) may at some length engage our attention.

On September 11th, 1833, "Leave Albany with Mr. Van Buren and John Van Buren for Kinderhook," Irving writes as the first entry in the little note-book entitled by him "Esopus and Dutch Tour." At Kinderhook, once the home of Irving's friend Judge Van Ness, and the asylum to which Irving had retreated during the two months following the death of Matilda Hoffman, Martin Van Buren was born some four months before the birth of Irving. The residence of Judge Van Ness was now Van Buren's home, and there Irving spent the night before leaving the next morning, with his friend the Vice-President, on the fortnight's journey that took them through the romantic country on the west side of the Hudson. There old Dutchmen could still be seen sitting under great sycamore trees and reading the "Dutch Bible in a chanting tone," and in the quaint little towns the Dutch language was still spoken by some of the villagers. It is possible that outside of this note-book of Irving's there may be found the first-hand record of an American man of letters testifying to the fact that half a century after America had become a nation the language of Holland still obtained in parts of New York State: but certainly this diary's description of old Dutch houses, "and the pomposity of Dutch dignitaries," and the joviality of some of the Dutchmen, has a unique interest from the pen of the author of "Knickerbocker's History," and the creator of that Rip Van Winkle through whose country Irving was now leisurely driving. There Irving found old treaties with the Indians, written in Dutch and English and tied with wampum belts, and other old documents call for his inspection. Among his treasure trove is the record of Hildegarde Van Steghenhorst, who "once kept a store—was summoned to appear in court—asked if ready for trial. Yes if Judge would swear and kiss the book that he would decide rightly between all parties— said he had sworn so when he had entered upon office—well, she thought he could have no objection to swearing again by way of refreshing his memory."

At Kingston (originally called "Esopus" after the Esopus Indians by the Dutch settlers in 1652 and changed to its present name six years after the English came into possession of it in 1663) Irving met a witch doctor and added to his stock of ghost stories. At Monroe he visited the headquarters of Claudius Smith, the leader in Revolutionary days of a gang of "Skinners," the nickname for the American marauders who pursued operations in what was neutral ground, beginning at Spuyten Duyvil and extending some forty miles in length during the British occupancy of New York. At Haverstraw he saw the house where André and Benedict Arnold had their interview, and whose owner, Smith by name, disguised André and rowed him to the east bank of the river, only a few hours prior to the capture near Tarrytown of the brave young English spy. At Nyack, Irving saw the hill where André was hanged. The Arnold-André episode was later to provide the material for one of the finest chapters in the Life of Washington, as, similarly, the legends of the Catskill region had furnished Irving wth the theme of the most famous of his stories. The Dutch tour that he made with Martin Van Buren is thus that of all the many excursions of our wanderer most interestingly related to the beginning and the end of his career as an author.

Irving, during the ten years separating his diplomatic appointments, was not quite as lazy as in the ten years following the publication of "Knickerbocker's History"; but in any case, sufficiently indolent. The Western travels; papers based on his sojourns at the homes of Scott and of Byron: and some legends of the Conquest of Spain made up the "Crayon Miscellany" pub-

lished in 1835. The next year, "Astoria, or Incidents of an
Enterprise Beyond the Rocky Mountains," was written at the
request of John Jacob Astor, but the main labour was by Pierre
M. Irving, Irving contenting himself with rounding it out in its
final form.   In 1837, Irving, after purchasing Captain Bonneville's manuscript record of Western experiences, expanded the
original manuscript into two volumes entitled "The Rocky
Mountains; or, Scenes, Incidents, and Adventures in the Far
West."   In 1840, the Life of Oliver Goldsmith was published, with selections from his writings; but Irving's biography
took up only some one hundred and seventy-five pages of the first
of the two volumes.   The next year he wrote a short biography,
introductory to the poems of the gifted Margaret Davidson,
whose too early death had greatly touched him; and the following year appeared a biographical sketch of Thomas Campbell
in "The Poetry and History of Wyoming."   Thus these ten
years brought forth a paucity of imaginative work, and, if we
strike an average, less than one hundred pages a year of descriptive or biographical writing.   Washington Irving Esquire is taking life easy.

   Although his interest in national politics was quickened by his
attendance at Congress in 1833 and by later visits to Washington, Irving continued in his early aloofness from political affairs.
His dislike for the grime of politics and his aversion from public
office led him to decline candidacy for Congress during the Jack-
sonian era; the nomination for the mayoralty of New York
City offered him by Tammany Hall in 1838; and, shortly thereafter, the appointment to the Secretaryship of the Navy under
his old friend, Van Buren.   Statesmen and fellow-citizens were
continually trying to honour him, and he was continually trying
to escape.   The record of these years is one of increasing enjoyment in domestic circles and among friends, with music, the
theatre, and occasional travelling as special pleasures.   In 1835
he bought ten acres at Tarrytown and the little Dutch stone
house, which, originally called by him "Wolfert's Roost"
("Roost," the Dutch word for "rest," and "Wolfert," one of

the characters in "Knickerbocker's History"), was later renamed "Sunnyside." By this name the cottage is known the world over; and it is the home where later generations of Irvings—including a young Washington Irving—still reside. Philip Hone, that Mayor of New York best remembered because of his diary, wrote of it as "a quaint Dutch looking tavern, with small rooms, inconvenient, and only one story high; but the admirers of the gentle Geoffrey think, no doubt, *one story* of his is worth more than a half dozen of other people's." The house has grown greatly in the ninety years since Irving began his career as a gentleman-farmer; but it still retains its flavour, and the old trees, the old lawns, the ivy from Abbotsford, are lovelier than ever. It was here that Peter joined Washington on his arrival from France in the springtime of 1836, twenty years after his departure for Europe; and here, too, brother Ebenezer came with his children, so that Irving's closing years were spent in the affectionate companionship of the many nieces, and, now and then, nephews, who were so welcome under his roof.

All was simplicity and happiness in that old Dutch cottage, its only note of mystery (unrecorded in any Life of Irving, but the theme for amusing comment by great-grand-nephews) being a secret doorway that led from his bedroom to a window into the garden. We shall, however, not suggest that the fifty-year old bachelor, who somewhat remodelled the little house in 1835, was the originator of this hidden passageway for any romantic purpose, but shall sedately assume that the mysterious staircase was built by an earlier owner.

Hone's diary makes numerous mention of Irving during these American years. "He talks a great deal and is in high spirits, a thing not usual with him, except in excitement as he is in this moment", Hone writes of their first meeting, after the return from England; and adds, a few days later: "The return of Geoffrey Crayon has made old times and the associations of early life the leading topics of conversation amongst his friends." Charles King, Ogden Hoffman, James Paulding, Henry Brevoort, Professor Renwick, Captain Nicholson, were among the

SUNNYSIDE

New Yorkers whom Irving frequently saw, and with one or another of them, he would visit the public institutions of New York, attend meetings of the St. Nicholas Society (to whose office of President he was elected), dine and wine on the occasions of his city visits, go to theatre and opera, or spend an evening in chat with old John Jacob Astor. It was Irving who suggested to Astor the creation of the Astor Library. He became its first President after the death, in 1848, of the famous merchant whose original capital had been a few musical instruments, and whose trade in fur, when shipped to China, brought him in return rich cargoes of silks and teas.

The minor grief of these ten years was the news that Gilbert Stuart Newton, the painter with whom Irving had been so intimate in London, and the nephew of the decidedly eccentric Gilbert Stuart, had gone insane. The major sorrow was the death in 1838 of Peter. "Every day, every hour," Washington writes to his sister Sarah, at Birmingham, "I feel how completely he and myself were intertwined together in the whole course of our existence . . . since our dear mother's death, I have had no one who could so patiently and tenderly bear with all my weaknesses and infirmities and throw over every error the mantle of affection. I have been so accustomed to talk over every plan with him and to think aloud when in his presence that I cannot open a book or take up a paper or recall a past vein of thought without having him instantly before me and finding myself completely overcome." Such affection and understanding between brothers as existed between Peter and Washington are indeed rare; and when, during a visit to Rouen in Irving's final years in Europe, he sat on the bench in the Cathedral garden where the invalid Peter had played with the little French children, the tears of Washington Irving were those of the idealist rather than of the sentimentalist, an honour to himself as well as to the brother who had died.

To become increasingly fond of Washington Irving it does not much matter what stage of his life is studied; but of that essential courtesy which manifested itself equally to beggar and king, to stranger and kinsman, there is one of the most outstanding illustrations in his act of literary and financial self-sacrifice in favour of William H. Prescott, in 1838. Irving had in Spain gathered together material for a history of the Conquest of Mexico, and losses from western land speculation during the year in which Peter died, made Washington eager to earn, despite his habitual indolence, a greater revenue from his pen. After he had drafted the first volume, he went to make further research at the Society Library, whose stately house, where Edgar Allan Poe delivered "Eureka," and Emerson lectured, still stands in University Place. There Irving happened to hear from Joseph G. Cogswell, first librarian of the Astor Library, that Prescott intended to write a history of the Conquest of Mexico. Although he was first in the field Irving immediately decided to abandon the theme to Prescott, whose history of Ferdinand and Isabella had, on its appearance a short time before, so evoked the admiration of historians and public. The courtesy with which Irving relinquished his claim to the subject constitutes an amenity of literature to which nothing recorded by Irving's old time friend the elder D'Israeli offers a parallel. Irving did not know Prescott personally, but he learned that the Boston writer had already made wide studies and had spent over fifteen hundred dollars in collecting material, and the thought that Prescott was the greater scholar of the two led Irving to write to him: "In at once yielding up the thing to you I feel I am but doing my duty in leaving one of the most magnificent themes in American history to be treated by one who will build up from it an enduring monument in the literature of our country."

It was not until after the appearance of Prescott's "History of the Conquest of Mexico," in whose preface the author acknowledged his obligation to Irving, that the latter disclosed in a letter to his nephew Pierre how really great was the generosity of his act. "I doubt whether Mr. Prescott was aware of the sacrifice I made. This was a favourite subject, which had de-

lighted my imagination ever since I was a boy. I had brought
home books from Spain to aid me in it, and looked upon it as the
pendant to my Columbus. When I gave it up to him, I, in a
manner, gave him up my bread, for I depended upon the profit of
it to recruit my waning finances. I had no other subject at hand
to supply its place. I was dismounted from my cheval de ba-
taille, and have never been completely mounted since. Had I
accomplished that work, my whole pecuniary situation would
have been altered . . . when I made the sacrifice, it was not
with a view to compliments or thanks, but from a warm and sudden impulse. I am not sorry for having made it. Mr. Prescott
has justified the opinion I expressed at the time, that he would
treat the subject with more close and ample research than I
should probably do, and would produce a work more thoroughly
worthy of the theme."

Whether or not Prescott fully understood how unselfishly
Irving had behaved towards him, this unusual episode led to a
lasting friendship between the two men. Among Prescott's
literary memoranda there is under May 7, 1842, the following
note: "Since last entry, paid two visits to New York—a marvelous event in my history! First, a visit, about three weeks
since, I paid to meet Washington Irving before his departure for
Spain. Spent half a day with him at Wainwright's;[1] indeed,
till twelve at night. Found him delightful and—what they say
is rare—wide awake. He promised to aid me in all my applica-
tions."

The talk on that occasion included, also, mention of Irving's
"Life of Washington," on which he was engaged during his
term as minister at Spain. Prescott, no doubt delighted at the
possibility of his requiting to some slight extent the obligation
under which he rested, volunteered to furnish Irving with such
material in the way of anecdotes concerning Washington and
facts regarding the Revolution as might be available for the
"Life." This he was peculiarly enabled to do as Prescott's

[1] Later Bishop of the Diocese of New York.

father had, at Harvard, been a classmate of Tobias Lear, Washington's secretary, and had been offered the position of private tutor in Washington's household prior to Lear's acceptance of the place. Prescott's grandfather had fought as a colonel at the Battle of Bunker Hill and had later received the public praise of Washington.

His promise Prescott fulfilled in a lengthy (and unpublished) letter in 1824 where he wrote to Irving, "With respect to the anecdotes, one was repeated to me by General Cobb, Washington's aid. He said he did not remember to have ever seen Washington laugh heartily but twice while he was with him. Once when, somewhere in Virginia, he was playing whist. The party consisted of Washington, Cobb, a Virginian doctor and a clergyman. The two latter were partners, and the clergyman played execrably. The consequence was the tricks were lost, and the doctor lost his temper. As he was much addicted to swearing, he gave vent to his vexation in repeated oaths. The parson much scandalized threw down the cards, and declared that he would not play with a man who indulged in such profanity. This brought the doctor to his senses. He protested he meant no offence to the cloth, and if his partner would overlook it this once he would not utter another oath in the room, let him play ever so badly. On this concession the parties again assumed their game. The clergyman played as ill as before. Trick after trick was lost, then the game, and finally the rubber. But no sooner was this catastrophe accomplished than the son of Esculapius, whose wrath had been bottled up till he was near bursting—ran to the empty chimney, and thrusting his head up, to the great consternation of the parson, poured forth such a volley of oaths as made ample amends for his long silence. The effect was irresistible, and Washington, concluded Cobb, threw himself back in his chair, and laughed till the tears ran down his face.

"The other anecdote shows the naturally strong passions of Washington and the promptness with which he could recover himself. As Colonel Preston,—of Virginia, I think—at any rate father of the present Senator from South Carolina,—was on a visit at Washington's home, he passed one morning along the piazza when his attention was caught by certain loud and angry tones in a room on the ground floor, by which he was walking. Casting his eyes toward the window he perceived his host with angry look and gesture, speaking to a man who was employed in doing some stucco work on the cornice of the apartment. The workman was mounted on a scaffolding laid across some barrels. Col. Preston had hardly caught a glance of the parties when he saw the scaffolding give way with a violent crash, and the man of stucco disappear amidst a cloud of dust and lime. The underpinning had been kicked away by the General in his wrath. Preston did not think it proper to remain a spectator of the comical scene, but continued his walk. The breakfast bell soon after sounded, and as he went into the house, he felt some curiosity as to the appearance which Washington would make, or, indeed, whether he would choose to appear at all immediately after this excitement. Washington, however, did not long keep them waiting, and the only trace of the storm was a certain nervous twitching of his ruffles or wristband, as he adjusted them while taking his seat at table. I have heard this story told by a friend of the present member of Congress, from whom, however, you could, doubtless, get a more accurate report of it."

"The Conquest of Mexico" having been given up by Irving to Prescott, and Irving having in mind no theme for another book, he agreed at the beginning of the year 1839, to contribute papers to the *Knickerbocker Magazine,* of which J. Gaylord Clark was the editor, papers that were many years later collected into the volume entitled "Wolfert's Roost." Some of the most charming of these little story-essays appeared briefly before the arrival of Charles Dickens in America, and it was Irving who, of all Americans, most attracted Dickens to the United States. "Everything you have written," Dickens tells Irving, "is in my thoughts and in my heart of hearts . . . Diedrich Knickerbocker I have worn to death in my pocket and yet I should show you his mutilated carcass with joy past all expression." Equally did Irving admire young Dickens, and when in February, 1842, a great dinner was given in New York to the visiting Englishman, Irving departed so far from his usual custom as to preside at the banquet, although he could not get away from his habit of breaking down in public speeches. The occasion is so noted in the literary annals of New York City that it is worth while to amplify its record by including here a letter found among Irving's papers and written to him by his friend, Charles A. Davis, a well-known merchant who was something of a man of letters, and who, as chairman of the committee on arrangements, gave Irving full instructions regarding his duties as toast-master.

NEW YORK, Thursday, 17 Feb. '42.

My dear Sir:

You will please be at the receiving room, City Hotel, as soon after Six of tomorrow evg as practicable as it is designed to bring Mr. Dickens there at that period and it will be easier to introduce people to him as they *come in*—than after the room is crowded. Do you understand that notice Sir?

The Committee of arrangements will see that a correct & well selected number of gentlemen will be requested to remain with young Mr. Dickens in the "receiving room" when the rest of the company are requested to go in the dining hall and take their places, which being done, then you, Mr. Dickens and these invited guests or persons thus selected to occupy the head and cross tables will enter the dining hall and go to your places. Each man's name will be found on his plate. The music will cease as soon as you & Mr. Dickens have reached your places, the company all standing. A blessing will then be asked, then all take their seats & go to work eating.

When the cloth is removed you will rise, make *that speech* & give *that toast,* which will be followed by music. Then Mr. Dickens responds and as soon as he has finished, then music &

after that you will call in rotation on the following gentlemen in the following order

1st Judge Betts
2 John Duer
3 Philip Hone
4 G. C. Verplanck
5 Jno A. King
6 J. Prescott Hall

and after that I shall be at your coat tail & will let you know what next will follow as to song, speech, etc. etc.

I don't want to have you surcharged with more to remember than is stated above and as the Chinese say, "A Special Edict obey and note."

Yr. Friend,
CHAS. A. DAVIS.

P.S. If you will let folks talk and propose as they will, but yet just follow the inclosed plan it will all go off as "regular as a tea party." You will call on nobody for toast or speech beyond the Vice President unless you know or are advised that they are ready & desirous—then all will feel easy.

But no chairman of a committee could give the shy Irving the necessary stamina for after-dinner oratory, and when he broke down all he could manage to do was to conclude with the toast, "Charles Dickens, the literary guest of the nation." Philip Hone includes in his diary—a note of special interest in our own days of woman suffrage—"An unusual feature in this festivity was the presence of a coterie of charming women who were at first stowed away in a small room adjoining the upper part of the hall and who edged by degrees into the room and finally got possession of the stage behind the President, to the discomfiture of certain pleasant old bachelors and ungallant dignitaries, but to the great delight of us who profess to have better taste in such matters."

Public speaker or no public speaker, Irving's qualities, the value of his character and his experience, and all his international charm were too well known to permit his continuance in the career most to his taste, that of private citizen. In the very week that he failed so sympathetically and delightfully at the Dickens dinner, he received from Daniel Webster, then Tyler's Secretary of State, notification of his nomination as Envoy Extraordinary and Minister Plenipotentiary to the Court of Madrid. On assuring Irving of the pleasure it gave him to have been instrumental in calling the author of "Columbus" to this distinguished post, Webster wrote: "If a gentleman of more merit and higher qualifications had presented himself, great as is my personal regard for you, I should have yielded it to higher considerations." Irving's confirmation by the Senate was unanimous, statesmen of all parties joining with enthusiasm. "Ah!" said Henry Clay, who knew Washington Irving personally, "this is a nomination everybody will concur in! If the President would send us such names as this, we should never have any difficulty."

Thus, as in 1832 he had returned to his country, the best beloved American among the English, in 1842 he again set sail for Europe, the most affectionately regarded among his own countrymen.

Chapter XIV

THE LETTERS TO MARTIN VAN BUREN

In the preceding chapter the sentence appears: "Although his interest in national politics was quickened by his attendance at Congress in 1833 and by later visits to Washington, Irving continued in his aloofness from political affairs." There were, however, some phases of politics, domestic and international, that engaged his attention to a degree hitherto unknown; and how potent a factor Washington Irving (characteristically in the background) may have been in leading to the avoidance of war between France and the United States is suggested by the following letters to Martin Van Buren. In neither any biography of Irving or Van Buren do these letters appear, and it is through the courtesy of the Library of Congress that they now find their way into print.

The earliest of these manuscripts, after showing Irving as coming loyally to the support of James K. Paulding, his old friend and his collaborator in the *Salmagundi* days, and after evidencing his interest in the careers of his nephews Edgar and Theodore Irving, closes with allusions to the tariff agitation of 1833, and—Irving had foreseen the advantage that must accrue to Van Buren from the Senate's rejection of him as Minister to England—to Van Buren's election to the Vice-Presidency under the "old general," Andrew Jackson. South Carolina's opposition to tariff legislation in 1832 had reached a point where at the time of Irving's letter (when he was "lingering" in Washington "to witness the 'outbreak' of the subject of the tariff"), an armed conflict between State and Federal authorities seemed imminent. Indeed, a fortnight later Jackson sent to Congress the "Force Bill," authorizing the President to use the army and navy in enforcing the laws of Congress; but civil war was avoided when, the next month, Henry Clay offered the compromise bill which took the place of the Verplanck Tariff Bill. The consequent reduction of the tariff mollified Calhoun and his followers, and South Carolina then agreed to the repeal of its Proclamation of Nullification.

WASHINGTON, Jany. 2d., 1833.

My Dear Friend:

Letters from my friends in New York mention a rumour existing there of an attempt to displace Mr. Paulding as Navy Agent in favour of a Mr. Vanderpool. I can find no grounds for such a rumour *here:* should there be any thing in it, and should any attempt be made to procure your influence in the matter I would caution you against it. Paulding is a public man, known throughout the nation by his writings, which have ever inculcated the most patriotic and truly republican sentiments. He is a staunch and sincere friend to the administration and to the old general. He is a most honourable high minded man whose character gives a dignity to office. He is widely connected by marriage etc., and his connexions are all strong friends to the administration. He is moreover prized and beloved by a wide circle of friends of a class and standing and character to have an influence on society by their opinions. Such a man is valuable to a party by the very respectability of his character and conduct, but I know Paulding to be a very useful man by his pen, which he exerts anonymously, and merely for his own gratification, in the newspapers, on the administrations side. I give these hints out of my friendship both for yourself and him—lest there should really be an attempt making to dislodge him, and your influence should be sought in the matter: but I have little doubt the whole is an idle rumour.

So much for the business concerns of others—now for my own. You were kind enough to interest yourself in behalf of my nephew Edgar Irving for a pursership. He has since abandoned all intention of continuing in the navy & has resigned his midshipman's warrant. I have substituted in his place, as candidate for the pursership his brother Theodore Irving and should feel greatly obliged by a good word from you in his favour. He served under me in the office of the Legation at London, and is in every respect a young gentleman that would not disgrace the appointment. I have spoken to Mr. Woodbury on the subject; but he is so cold and cautious that I cannot gather from him whether there is any chance or no of my nephew's success. Having asked this thing of the government as a favour to myself, and in so doing given up a point of pride about which I have been excessively tenacious I should be extremely mortified at being disappointed. I am aware however that I can give few reasons of policy in aid of my application, not being the kind of man whose good will is of any material importance to a political leader. You, however, will act in this matter I trust from motives of private friendship.

I am lingering here to witness the "outbreak" on the subject of the Tariff—after which I shall travel on slowly towards New York.

I had nearly forgotten to congratulate you on your election. Did I not prognosticate how it would be, at that memorable breakfast table where you read the news of your rejection?

Ever with the greatest regard
Yours
WASHINGTON IRVING.

A decidedly important manuscript is the next letter, showing how the Vice-President was privately consulting Irving at a critical juncture in our affairs with a European nation, and how wisely Irving could both prophesy and advise in international affairs. In his annual message of 1833 Andrew Jackson had taken up in violent fashion the question of the claims of the United States against France, claims arising from seizure of American property by Napoleon Bonaparte. In 1831 a treaty had been signed with France that provided for the payment to the American Republic of twenty-five million francs, but this sum had not yet been voted by the French Chambers. Jackson, wishing to force the vote, asked Congress to authorize the seizure of French property in the United States. As a result of this recommendation the French Minister at Washington was recalled by Louis Philippe, and, some time later, the American Minister withdrew from Paris. Throughout 1834 and 1835 public excitement in both countries was at high pitch, and war loomed ominously. Irving's comment concerning the references to France in Jackson's message of 1834, and his comments concerning the French themselves, must unquestionably have impressed Van Buren, then the most influential of Jackson's advisers. The surmise that this letter was shown to the President may well be considered.

Finally, it is amusing to note that in even so grave a letter Irving, in his reference to the speech of Richard Rush—the statesman who, in 1829, had been the Vice-Presidential candidate on the ticket headed by John Quincy Adams—indulges in a happy pun; while, further on, he alludes in similar good-humoured manner to South Carolina's famous proclamation, saying that he wishes that the part of Jackson's message which most deeply offended the French nation "had been *nullified*."

NEW YORK, Decr. 15th, 1834.

My Dear Sir:

I have to acknowledge the receipt of yours inclosing the message and the *Rush light*—may the latter shine far and wide, and the former kindle no flames. You ask me if I think Louis Philippe will be brought to do us Justice. I think there would have been more probability of such a result had the suggestions of letters of marque and reprisal been omitted; for, explain it as you may, it has the air of a menace, and as such will be considered by the French chambers. Flagrantly as the French are in the wrong, they could not long have persisted in such a course, but they will find it irksome and difficult to do that, under a menace, which otherwise their own sense of justice and good faith, would have led them to do with some appearance of cheerfulness. Even if we do compel them to execute the treaty, the threat that has been used will rankle in their minds and leave a scar on their pride that will mar the cordiality of our future intercourse. As to the menace of Letters of Marque & Reprisal —God defend us from it. We might do some damage to French commerce, but we should bring upon our own rich and widely extended trade the plunderers of every nation on the globe, who under French commission, the French Flag, would swarm the ocean with licensed pirates. However, I do not apprehend war. It is too wide from the interest of either party to get entangled in it: but I wish that part of the message had been *nullified*. I cannot think you were among the advisors of it. Excepting that point, I relish highly the tone in which the French affair is treated.

I have written to the Secretary of War on the subject of a nephew of mine Richard Dodge Frothingham, a lad between 15 & 16 years of age, for whom I wish to procure a cadetship at Westpoint. If you would have the kindness to speak a word in his favour you will oblige me greatly. He is a lad desirous of the situation from his own merits & capacity.

You went away from New York quite unexpectedly, to me at least, as I supposed you meant to stay ten days or a fortnight here. I was quite surprised, on enquiring, to find you gone.

Commend me to the Major if with you and believe me ever very truly

Yours,

WASHINGTON IRVING.

Hon. Martin Van Buren.

In his message of 1835 President Jackson was much more moderate—courteous even—in his tone toward France, and in the spring months of 1836, after England's mediation had paved the way, the embroilment came to an end with the initial payments of the debt to the United States. In the following letter to Van Buren, Irving again refers to the "unnecessarily harsh" language of Jackson's earlier message; advises wisely in regard to England's offer to mediate, and concludes with a phrase whose sentiment might well make appeal to the brave and fiery old soldier in the White House.

NEW YORK, Feb. 1st, 1836.

My Dear Sir:

I find by a letter received this morning from my nephew Edgar Irving at Baltimore, that he is urging an application made last summer for reinstatement in his commission of Lieutenant in the Marine Corps, and that he has written to you on the subject. This commission, you will recollect, was procured for him through your kindness. He hastily resigned it some time since, in consequence of some harsh measure on the part of his superior officer for a supposed neglect of duty. I do not recollect the circumstances of the case, but I know that there were palliating circumstances on the part of Edgar, who at the time was absent at Baltimore, on leave of absence, and a little engrossed by a young wife whom he had just married. A proper explanation at the time would have adjusted the whole affair; but to my extreme vexation he tendered his resignation and it was accepted. He has no doubt explained to you the grounds on which he hopes for the restoration of his commission, and if you think them sufficient you will do an essential kindness to his father and family as well as to myself if you will interest yourself in his behalf.

We are looking with deep interest to the result of the proposal of mediation by England. I hope it may be such as will suit the dignity of our government to accept, and can scarcely think it will be otherwise. I have always considered, as you know, the language of the message of 1834 in respect to France, unnecessarily harsh, and such as to render it difficult for her to act conscientiously without appearing to do so under a menace. If we are really desirous of settling this matter amicably, and of restoring the relations of the two countries to a cordial tone, we must beware of pushing our punctilio too far, and inflicting additional mortification. Through the mediation of England the whole matter may be so arranged as to permit the French to extricate themselves from their present awkward predicament without any further floundering; while we should come out of the affair with a vast accession of national character.

Much has been calculated on here from your moderation and discretion in this delicate matter, to temper the old general's "heady valour" into true magnanimity.

Believe me my dear Sir,

Very truly yours

WASHINGTON IRVING.

The Hon. Martin Van Buren.

In expressing his happiness at Jackson's "friendly and conciliatory" message Washington Irving, so essentially the broadminded and generous gentleman, voices in his next letter to Van Buren the hope that there shall nowhere be heard any "taunting exultations." We see him again in that light wherein we have so often rejoiced to consider him as the most important of our men of letters and one of the most important of our diplomats in striving towards good will between America and Europe.

To Van Buren Irving is inclined to give "great credit for the happy management of this matter," and no doubt the Vice-President, formerly Jackson's Secretary of State, had been largely instrumental in the solution of the difficulties. Yet, as Professor Bassett suggests in his "A Short History of the United States," the approach of the presidential campaign had something to do with the more amicable attitude of Jackson and his Cabinet.

NEW YORK, Feb. 24th, 1836.

My Dear Sir:

I have just read the President's message and the accompanying documents and cannot sufficiently express the delight I feel at the way in which this perplexed and momentous affair has been terminated; By heavens you have brought us nobly through this affair and placed the country in a high footing abroad. I have been much pleased with the manner in which all the messages this year have spoken on the subject. They have corresponded with the tone of some few observations which dropped from you in the course of one of our conversations at Washington, and on which I founded hopes of a magnanimous and pacific course of policy. I am delighted with the noble and generous tone in which both England and France are spoken of in this last message and the friendly and conciliatory expressions towards the latter. I hope all the papers on the side of government will take their tone from that of the government and that we shall have no taunting exultations, no back handed flings at France. Now that the cause of difference is at an end every effort should be taken to obliterate all scars.

I am inclined to give you great credit for the happy management of this matter, and for the able manner in which the *collisions* between the two countries have been prevented from striking fire. I am happy to read the same opinion is entertained even by those who are usually disposed to gainsay your merits and misrepresent your actions.

I scrawl this in great haste—it is merely to express my hearty feelings in this matter and to give you my warm congratulations.

Very truly yours,
WASHINGTON IRVING.

Van Buren was the President-elect when Irving's next letter reached him. He had been chosen by more than twice the electoral votes received by William Henry Harrison, more than ten times the votes received by Daniel Webster. Even so, Van Buren's was not a popular choice. For all his good qualities he was not the kind of man to arouse enthusiasm, and he had long had many bitter critics for acts both of omission and commission. In congratulating him upon his election, his old friend Washington Irving, where he counsels Van Buren not to think of temporary popularity, and to act (Irving underlines the words) *without caring about a re-election,* advises him in terms so frank that one must feel admiring astonishment at such courageous admonition from a private citizen to a President of the United States. But Irving, for all his gentleness, always knew when to be brave.

NEW YORK, Feby. 6th 1837.

My Dear Sir:

My niece Mrs. M. Grinnell sails tomorrow morning with her husband for St. Croix on account of her health. They are accompanied by a very worthy friend of theirs and of mine, Mr. William W. Swain of New Bedford. As they will remain two or three months at St. Croix, I am desirous of obtaining an introduction for them to the Governor (Van Sholten) with whom I understand you are on terms of friendship. May I ask, therefore, for a letter of introduction for them; the party is Mr. and Mrs. Moses Grinnell and Mr. William W. Swain. If you will enclose the letter in a cover addressed to Messrs. Grinnell, Minturn & Co. New York, it will be forwarded after them. I can assure you the party will not disgrace your introduction.

I have not written to you to congratulate you on your election; because I presumed you would be overwhelmed with congratulations. I hope some time or other to be at Washington, and to take a breakfast with you in commemoration of that memorable breakfast in London when you received news of your rejection; which I then considered the seal of your political advancement. You have now arrived at the most distinguished post in the world, at the head of the *great republic:* it depends upon yourself to make it the most honorable. There is but one true rule for your conduct: act according to the sound dictates of your head and the kind feelings of your heart, without thinking how your temporary popularity is to be affected by it, and *without caring about a re election.* You have it in your power to leave a most enviable name behind you, by a conscientious and benignant administration of the affairs of this vast and splendid country. I anticipate every thing from what I know of your qualities of head and heart; but I know you will have difficulties to contend

with which will require you to summon at times almost stern-
ness of resolve, somewhat at variance with your genial nature.
God bless and prosper you
Your friend
WASHINGTON IRVING.

The panic of 1837—its immediate cause a furious, nation-wide
speculation in public lands—was one of the worst financial crises
in our history. It seemed for a while as if the entire fabric of
American commerce and finance must crash down into irreme-
diable ruin. With sagacity and, what is more, with unflinching
courage, Van Buren refused to have the Chief Executive of the
nation made either the guardian or the administrator of financial institutions, well aware of the corruption that might swiftly
arise from such action. How greatly Irving's advice: *"Dare
to be unpopular rather than to do wrong"* influenced the President; whether the articles written by Peter Irving, and forwarded by his brother Washington to Van Buren, affected that
statesman's decisions; and, if so, to what degree, is left to conjecture. But in any case in this letter of August, 1837 there is
further evidence of a wise counsellor giving that kind of advice
which is superior to the exigencies of any one period or panic.

The other men who, in addition to Peter, are mentioned in
Irving's letter are Benjamin F. Butler, the Attorney General
in Van Buren's Cabinet and, in 1816, his law partner; Joel R.
Poinsett, the Secretary of War; and William C. Rives, who had
been the American Minister to France when Van Buren was
Secretary of State under Jackson.

TARRYTOWN, Aug. 22d, 1837.
My Dear Sir:
I send you four articles from the Journal of Commerce signed
Mercator. They are by my brother Peter, who is very much of
an invalid and a recluse; shut up among books and papers in
New York, and who occasionally amuses himself by such little
escapades of the pen. It was by mere accident that I discovered
252

political advancement. You have now arrived at the most distinguished post in the world, at the head of the great republic: it depends upon yourself to make it the most honorable. There is but one true rule for your conduct: act according to the sound dictates of your head and the kind feelings of your heart, without thinking how your temporary popularity is to be affected by it, and without caring about a re election. You have it in your power to leave a most enviable name behind you; by a conscientious and benignant administration of the affairs of this vast and splendid country. I anticipate every thing from what I know of your qualities of head and heart; but I know you will have difficulties to contend with which will require you to summon at times an almost sternness of resolve, somewhat at variance with your genial nature.

God bless and prosper you

Your friend

Washington Irving

IRVING LETTER TO MARTIN VAN BUREN

him to be the author as he is very shy and silent about such matters. You have the opinions of busy politicians, scheming finan-
ciers and aspiring partizans in abundance; it may be worth your
while occasionally to have those of one who has no interest to
win, and who is singularly placed aloof from the passions and
prejudices of party. My brother, as you may know is a man
of keen reflection and expression; he wishes well to you and
your administration but is entirely withdrawn from active life,
and is a mere looker on. The articles in question appear to me
to present a simple, concise and lucid view of the state and progress of our pecuniary difficulties, and to give some suggestions
worthy of consideration. They at any rate have the rare merit
of being honest and disinterested.

I had the pleasure a short time since of meeting with Mr. Butler on board of a New Haven steam boat, and of hearing of you
through him. I rejoice that you have so fine a being at your
elbow and one so thoroughly attached to you. I am gratified
also to find that you and Poinsett are on such cordial terms;
he is a man of worth and a gentleman in spirit. "Grapple such
men to you" with hooks of steel. I had hoped to see Rives in
your cabinet, having ever had a most favorable opinion of
him.

Your situation is an arduous one, but a good heart and a clear
head will I trust carry you safe through every trial. Never
think how any measure is to affect your political fortunes, and
dare to be unpopular rather than to do wrong, and your name
will eventually be one which history will perpetuate with applause.

> Ever my dear sir
> Most truly and heartily yours
> WASHINGTON IRVING.

Martin Van Buren
    President of the United States.

Van Buren was not alone grateful to Irving for advice during
the days in England and the subsequent period in America, but,

aware of how excellent this advice had been proved by events, was in a unique position to recognize Irving's qualifications as a statesman. In offering him the Secretaryship of the Navy Van Buren was thus acting from high public as well as happy private considerations. But from the "turmoils of public and political life at Washington" Irving shrank, feeling that he was "too sensitive to endure the bitter personal hostility" and those newspaper attacks which even to this day are the lot of our public officials. If things were otherwise we should have a greater number of honourable and able gentlemen in charge of our national affairs. Although in his letter refusing the President's offer Irving confesses to "weakness of spirit and a want of true philosophy," it might well seem that the fault was not his, but ours.

NEW YORK, April 30th, 1838.

My Dear Sir:

Your letter of the 23rd inst. being forwarded to me at Tarrytown, remained a day or two at the post office uncalled for; which I mention to account for my not having sent an earlier reply.

I cannot express to you how deeply I feel the proof of esteem and confidence which you have given me in offering me so honourable a post in your cabinet. It has indeed completely surprised and agitated me; and I have had to take a little time to recover that composure of mind necessary to give the subject a due consideration. Mature reflection and self examination have served to confirm my first impulse, which was to decline your most kind and flattering offer. It is not so much the duties of the office that I fear; for I take a delight in full occupation, and the concerns of the Navy department would be peculiarly interesting to me; but I shrink from the harsh cares and turmoils of public and political life at Washington, and feel that I am too sensitive to endure the bitter personal hostility, and the slanders and misrepresentations of the press, which beset high station in this country. This argues, I confess, a weakness of spirit and a want of true philosophy, but I speak of myself as I am, not as I ought to be. Perhaps, had my ambition led me to a higher career, and aimed at official distinction I might have become enured to the struggle; but it has laid in a different and more secluded path, and has nurtured in me habits of quiet, and a love of peace of mind that daily unfit me, more and more, for the collisions of the world. I really believe it would take but a short career of public life at Washington to render me mentally and physically a perfect wreck, and to hurry me prematurely into old age.

Permit me then most gratefully to decline the brilliant offer with which your partiality has tempted me; but to apprise you at the same time that it has served to rivet, more strongly, that friendship conceived for you, not from benefits conferred or expected, but from an intimate knowledge of your worth.

Ever, my dear Sir,
Most truly yours,
WASHINGTON IRVING.

Martin Van Buren
   President of the United States.

Although Irving did not always approve of Van Buren's public acts—and we may have already noted that the President on one occasion complained that Irving somewhat neglected him—the friendship between the two men was never broken. In the following letter of July, 1839 (written at Greenburgh, this being at the time the name of the township which included among its houses Irving's residence of "Sunnyside") the author, unable to get to New York to meet his friend, invites the statesman to the cottage on the Hudson where, according to the delectable hint given in the reference to the chicken, there will be reminiscences of the Dutch tour on which Irving and Van Buren had set out together. But most to our liking in this brief note is the closing phrase.

255

WASHINGTON IRVING ESQUIRE

GREENBURGH, July 2nd, 1839.

My Dear Sir:

I had intended to come to town to meet you, but I fear I shall be prevented, as I am suffering under the effects of a severe cold, attended with acute pain in the head. I wish you would drop me a line to let me know when I may expect you at my cottage, where I shall be most happy to receive you. I can only promise you plain country fare, but you shall have chicken dressed in the true Dutch style as we used to have them during our tour through the Dutch neighbourhoods of the Hudson. Above all, you shall have a hearty welcome given by one who has as honest a regard for you as if you were not in place and power.

Yours ever,

WASHINGTON IRVING.

Chapter XV

FAMOUS PEOPLE

ALTHOUGH Van Buren, after defeating William Henry Harrison for the Presidency, was unable to persuade Irving to become a member of his Cabinet, John Tyler, succeeding to the Presidency after the death of General Harrison (who had meanwhile defeated Van Buren), was more fortunate in enlisting the services of Irving. The offer came via Daniel Webster, another of Van Buren's unsuccessful opponents in the campaign of 1836, and now holding that office of Secretary of State which had been Van Buren's under Jackson. Statesmen of whatever parties had come to recognize not only the honourable deserts of the beloved man of letters but also the intelligence and the warm tact of the diplomat. And so when Joseph G. Cogswell, Irving's first choice as Secretary of the Legation to Spain, at the last moment declined the appointment, President Tyler was immediately willing to comply with Irving's second request in the matter, a request brought forward in the following hitherto unpublished letter.

NEW YORK, March 28, 1842.

My Dear Sir:

Mr. Cogswell having been induced by considerations of a substantial and satisfactory nature to decline the appointment of Secretary of the Legation to Spain, I take the liberty of recommending in his place Mr. Alexander Hamilton of New York, son of James Hamilton Esq. once District Attorney. He is a young gentleman of high moral worth, sterling talents and varied acquirements and promises fair at no distant period, to take an honourable and popular stand in public life. He is the author of a

257

series of articles that have recently appeared in the Courier and Enquirer in defence of Mr. Webster's position in the case of the Creole. His appointment would give great satisfaction to an extensive and influential connexion in this state, who were very efficient in the support of General Harrison and yourself in the last election, and who regard this young man with hope and pride.

Lastly I would ask his nomination as a *great personal favor to myself*. On my relations with the Secretary of Legation will depend in a great degree my comfort, and the prosperous conduct of my mission in a place like Madrid; so isolated, so apt to be distracted by factions and tumults, and where an American minister has none of his countrymen to rally round him and render him counsel and support in cases of emergency. Mr. Hamilton I know intimately: his family reside in my immediate neighbourhood in the country. We have been in habits of cordial intercourse for years and in having him by my side I shall feel as if I were taking a portion of my home with me.

With kindest regards to your family I remain
Dear Sir very respectfully truly
Your obliged friend and Servt.,
WASHINGTON IRVING.

John Tyler
President of the United States.

Irving sailed for Europe on the tenth of April, driving down to the Whitehall Ferry in a carriage with Abraham Schermerhorn. Accompanying him to the packet ship, *Independence,* which was to take him to Liverpool, were his sole surviving brother, Ebenezer, his nephews, Washington and John Treat Irving and Irving Paris, and his two old friends, Brevoort and Davis. Henry Lee of Boston and Hector Ames of New York, two young friends whom Irving had invited to become his attachés, set forth with him on the voyage.

Before his arrival at Madrid as the new American Minister Irving was to have more than three months of welcome and acclaim among many of the most distinguished personages of England and France.   The diary wherein he sets down the doings of those days seems entirely to have escaped the attention of Pierre M. Irving and has remained unknown to succeeding biographers.

On arriving at London on the first of May, Irving took lodgings at the Thomas Hotel in Berkley Square.   A few hours later —it was a Sunday—he was watching the notable parade of carriages in St. James' Park.   He felt "singularly low spirited," and "dreaded to be thrown once more into this turbulent stream of life to encounter the harrassing parade and dissipations of the great world."   Whether this mood was due wholly to a consciousness of the imminent break into the privacy which he so much cherished, or whether it was in part due to his now being, for the first time, in an England where Emily Foster was a married woman, there is no way to determine.   The dispirited mood continued throughout the next day when he called on Edward Everett, the American Minister to the Court of St. James, and his friend, Preston, the South Carolina statesman, and on Leslie, who was absent from home.   Tuesday, Everett took him to call on Lord Aberdeen.   Prior to going in the evening to the opera, Irving visited his old publisher, Murray.   "My heart was in my throat on finding myself in the drawing room, the scene of so many interesting literary meetings in the early period of my London career."

After this evidence of trepidation the diary records no further nervousness and Irving seems to accommodate himself with adequate ease to a succession of dinners and receptions and to meetings with a greater number of persons of distinction than in any previous period of his life.   With Samuel Rogers he went on May 4th to Lady Holland's—to her home in South Street where she "keeps up a kind of Holland House on a small scale," her larger establishment in Kensington having been the famous resort of statesmen and men of letters.   There he met "Lady Seymour, the Queen of Beauty," and Colonel Charles Fox, "grown stout and grey."   Two days later he accompanied Edward Everett to Queen Victoria's levée, where Sir Robert Peel, First Lord of the Treasury and England's most powerful statesman, welcomed him with cordiality. Irving was introduced by Everett to the entire diplomatic corps. Of Victoria and her consort he wrote: "The Queen is pleasing in her appearance and acquits herself with grace and ease; Prince Albert, tall and elegantly formed, bland and prepossessing in countenance and demeanour." He found Victoria "though not decidedly handsome, agreeable and intelligent," and impressed by the devotion of the young couple to one another, "it is rare," he wrote, "to see such a union of pure affection on a throne." A day or two with his sister Sarah, at Birmingham, and Irving was again in London where he took up his quarters with James Bandinel of the Foreign Office, a friend of former days. Bandinel, whom Irving describes as "a peculiar character, a capital scholar, a man variously and curiously informed, of great worth, kindness and hospitality," kept bachelor's hall in one of the inner buildings connected with Westminster Abbey. "His quarters in the old abbey," writes Irving, "are a perfect 'old curiosity shop,' furnished with all kinds of antiquities and curiosities." The entrance to this "singular and monkish nest" was through the vaulted passages and the long arcades of the cloisters," and Irving's sojourn deep in the "very heart of this old pile" was a realization of romantic dreams. Westminster Abbey had been a favourite haunt of his during, as he called them, "his scribbling days," and "the little cloisters" had for him much of the charm of the Alhambra.

Old Samuel Rogers was greatly affected on meeting Irving again. Irving's other friends were no less delighted, Thomas Moore in especial. At the anniversary dinner of the Literary Fund where Prince Albert presided, Sir Robert Inglis and G. P. R. James, the novelist, Lockhart, Lord Lansdowne and many other Englishmen of prominence joined heartily in the toast that was drunk to Washington Irving. Irving sat between Moore and Hallam, laughing with them at the maudlin speech that Thomas Campbell (having indulged too freely in wine), made in Hal-

260

lam's honour. The next day (May 13th), Irving breakfasted with Hallam, where he again met William Wordsworth to whom, a few days before, he had been introduced at a breakfast given by Miss Rogers. Wordsworth, at the age of seventy-three, was the next year to become Poet Laureate, after having arranged with Sir Robert Peel that no official verse should be required of him—a stipulation offering evidence that Words-worth was indeed a poet.

That evening at Samuel Rogers', Lord John and Lady Russell, Lord Prudhoc and the artist, Leslie, were among the guests. A fancy dress ball given by the Queen rounded off the night. It was a splendid affair, with some two thousand persons present, a general motif being provided for the costumes by making the ball a representation of Anne of Brittany's visit to the Court of Edward III. Prince Albert assumed the rôle of Edward, and Victoria that of Queen Philippa. "Here," Irving writes, "royalty represented royalty and nobility represented nobility. Many of the personages present played the parts of their own ancestors, their dresses being faithfully copied from old family paintings by Van Dyke and other celebrated persons." Observing that the young Queen found her crown of gold weighing too heavily on her brow ("She was continually raising her hand to move it slightly when it pressed"), Irving hopes and trusts "her real crown sits easier." Albert, handsome "as a Prince in fairy tales," came up to where Irving was standing and spoke to him at length.

Briefly thereafter Irving, having refused an invitation to accept a public dinner at Glasgow, made his escape from London in spite of "hosts of tempting invitations," and passed a few days of family life at the Van Wart's. This was followed by a visit to Sulgrave, the home of the Washington family, whence, in Cromwell's time, George Washington's great-grandfather, John, had emigrated to America. The old church where Washingtons of the sixteenth century lie buried, the old manor house (then much dilapidated but in our own day restored); the little garden with its low stone wall; the great rook-visited elms about the building—everything made Sulgrave "literally a piece of old England" for Irving. The hours that he spent there, talking with the country people and watching the country dances, were a lyric finale to the last considerable visit to England of the author whose fame so essentially belongs to the traditions of English literature.

Irving's predecessor at Madrid did not expect the new Envoy Extraordinary until some time in July, and Irving determined to spend the intervening weeks in France. After a day at Southampton, where he dined at the home of his old friend and former literary agent, the American Consul, Colonel Aspinwall, he arrived at Havre on the 23rd of June, and there he dined with another old friend, Mr. Beasley. His journey to Paris, via Rouen, was made by steamboat. He was met at Paris by Mr. Storrow, the husband of his favourite niece. General Lewis Cass, then the American Minister to France, and later Secretary of State under Buchanan, soon took Irving in hand. The first person of distinction to whom he was introduced by the General was François Guizot, scholar and historian, at that time the Minister of Foreign Affairs. A few days later Cass drove out with Irving to Neuilly, to present him to Louis Philippe. The King was decidedly cordial. In his conversation with Irving he "showed himself well informed of all the passing events in America." All the members of the royal family "took occasion to say something complimentary" about Irving's writings; the Queen, and the King's sister, Madame Adelaide, were most amiable, and in a good-natured and simple family circle Irving soon found himself quite at ease. Many members of the old aristocracy of the Faubourg St. Germain Irving met the next day when he dined at the Hotel Monaco, the great mansion in the Rue de Varenne of Colonel Herman Thorne, an exceedingly wealthy American whose entertainments were noted for their magnificence. The Prince de Béthune, head of the house of Sully, amused Irving as "a somewhat dandyish old gentleman"; he enjoyed talking to the Princess who struck him as "a woman of good sense, knowledge of the

262

world and excellent manners"; but the person in whom Irving took most interest in meeting at Colonel Thorne's was the Sardinian Ambassador, the Marquis Brignole. Thirty-seven years earlier when both were young fellows in Italy, Irving had "seen the young and elegant Brignole" taking the part of the hero in an amateur performance of Voltaire's "Zaïre." The American Minister and the Sardinian Ambassador exchanged reminiscences with more than usual pleasure concerning those far past days, when Irving was a guest at the country place of Brignole's mother, at Sestri Ponenti near Genoa.

During the succeeding weeks Irving met everybody in the great world of Paris. The Duchesse de Dino, who had married Talleyrand's nephew, Count Alexandre de Perigord, had him to dinner to meet Lady Rencliffe, whom he had not seen for sixteen years. And there with his unceasing liking for women he was equally gracious to old Lady Oldborough, "nearly ninety years of age, fashionably dressed, animated, and full of conversation," and to Mlle. de Noailles, the beautiful granddaughter of Lafayette. At Lord Cowley's the British Ambassador, he was welcomed into the distinguished English set at Paris, and at Colonel Charles Fox's, he talked with Alexander Dumas, already famous as a playwright, and already engaged in the collaboration with Auguste Magnet which, in 1844, was to result in that sheer masterpiece of romantic fiction, "The Three Musketeers." The previous evening, at Colonel Thorne's, Irving had discussed the works of James Fenimore Cooper with Eugene Sue, whose "Mysteries of Paris," a series of volumes then in course of publication, was in literary circles perhaps even more the talk of the day than the early novels of Dumas. Nor, of course, was Irving forgetful of old friends, and with the Greenes, the Storrows, and the Welleses (members of the American colony with which he was so intimate in 1825), we find him much at home. Baron de Rothschild (Jacob, the youngest of the five brothers), invites him to dine at Boulogne, where, although Prussian, Saxon and English diplomats were gathered (including, among the English, Sir Henry Lytton-Bulwer, brother of the novelist), and such members of the old French nobility as the Duke de Grammont, Irving was most interested in meeting Madame de Girardin, better known as Delphine Gay, the authoress of plays and romances, and the hostess of that brilliant drawing-room where Balzac and Gautier and Victor Hugo were among its stars.

The collocation in this chapter of so many names famous in spheres of genius, of aristocracy, statesmanship and finance emphasizes, in however superficial and glittering a manner, the success Irving had achieved since those far off days when he was a bankrupt young hardware merchant in Liverpool. But if we see him fêted among the great and the wealthy, let it again be recalled that he was equally welcome among all ranks, and that indeed he was throughout his life at his happiest when he was playing with children or when he was enjoying simple affectionate relationships with his own kith and kin. At Paris, in 1842, Irving was still the shy man, and to Helen Irving, wife of Pierre M. Irving, he writes that he has "no great relish for the pageantry of courts or the thronged saloons of fashionable life"; that he is "drawn into the vortex occasionally in spite of myself, so am kept in a half-drowned state, neither one thing nor t'other; neither enjoying repose or dissipation." He adds that he has been spoiled by the life at Sunnyside and that since his arrival in Europe, he has not had "one of those right-down frolicksome moods that I have enjoyed at the cottage; but, indeed, they would not be becoming in diplomatic life. I shall therefore put by all merriment until my return home and will endeavour in the meantime to be dignified and dull." No doubt all these dinners, these meetings with celebrities, were not greatly to his taste, but very certainly they formed a valuable step from the quiet loveliness of a country gentleman's life to the onerous position of American Minister at the court of the Queen of Spain.

Chapter XVI

THE ENVOY EXTRAORDINARY

JOURNEYING to Madrid Irving was accompanied by Alexander Hamilton, his Secretary of Legation, and by Henry Brevoort's son, Carson, his attaché. They broke their travels at Orléans, Tours, Poitiers, Angoulême, the architectural attractions and historical associations of these French towns appealing especially to Irving. At Bordeaux, he spent some four or five days with his old friends, the Guestiers, the Johnsons and the Bartons, who had been so kind to him during that period of dejection when he was slowly recovering from his disappointment at Emily Foster's refusal. With old Mrs. Johnson, who had been particularly devoted to Peter, Washington talked in the "most touching manner" about past times.

On arriving at Madrid on the 25th of July, Irving took possession of the habitation vacated by Mr. Vail, his predecessor in office. It was a wing forming half of the hotel of the Duke of San Lorenzo, the other half being occupied by the Brazilian minister, Mr. Albuquerque, whose wife, formerly a Miss Oakey of New York, was an especially pleasant neighbour for the three New Yorkers in the American Legation.

Irving's household had as its housekeeper the Spanish Juana, who had been Mrs. Vail's head maid. The cook was a Greek, Antonio by name, and "said to be excellent in his art." A mulatto, Benjamin Gowien, who spoke many of the European languages fluently, was the butler and managed the business affairs of the ménage. The footman or valet was a Spaniard named Lorenzo, while a nephew of his acted as page and general errand boy to Hamilton and Brevoort. These, with, of course, a coachman, completed Irving's establishment.

265

One of the first visitors in the home where Irving felt an initial strangeness in having "servants running at my call and bowing to me with profound respect," was the Duke de Gor, the nobleman to whom he had taken so great a liking during the Alhambra period. Irving, ever inclined to enjoy the flavour of the past more than the taste of the present, had from the Duke news of old friends in Granada. Mateo, his former guide and companion, was now, on the strength of Irving's writings, "quite the cicerone of Granada and the Alhambra."

The little Nicholas, who "had chased bats about the vaulted halls of the Alhambra," was grown into a fine young gentleman and had accompanied his father, the Duke de Gor, on this visit to his old playmate, Washington Irving.

The American Minister's first official act was to present to the Regent of Spain, Espartero, the letter of credence from the President to the Queen. In presenting it to the Regent, Irving was establishing a significant precedent. France had taken the position that her Ambassador, with his letter of credence from the King of France to the Queen of Spain, should deliver the document without the intermediation of the Regent—an attitude that had led to the withdrawal of the French Ambassador. President Tyler's communication was, of course, also to the Queen, but Irving, with his customary tact, used his discretion in immediately approaching Espartero. This made it easy for diplomats from South America to follow suit, avoiding the arrogant method that Louis Philippe so fruitlessly had attempted.

To understand the chaotic drama wherein Irving was soon to take an important and meliorating rôle, there is need to recall that the dissolute Queen-mother, Maria Christina, the niece of the French Queen, was then at Paris, plotting her return into power. The little Queen, not yet twelve years of age, "a mere effigy of royalty in the hands of statesmen," had, with her younger sister, very nearly been kidnapped the preceding October when the reactionary party made a midnight attack on the palace. Espartero, whom Irving describes as "a fine, manly, soldier-like fellow, with a frank deportment and a face full of

266

resolution and intelligence," was attempting to establish firmly that constitutional form of government which Don Carlos, the eldest brother of Ferdinand VII, had sought to overthrow. In 1839 the civil war had temporarily been brought to a close by the exile of Don Carlos from the Kingdom, but shortly thereafter Maria Christina, by signing an act making the appointees of all municipal offices subject to the choice of the Crown, so aroused popular indignation that she was forced to abdicate the regency, which then passed by election to Espartero. Her amour with Munoz, a low type Spaniard, caused the forfeiture of her guardianship of the royal children, who thereupon came under the charge of the Countess Mina, the widow of a patriot general. This practically orphaned situation of the two little girls more and more touched Irving's heart. The insurrection that had taken place in the North of Spain in October, 1841, when Maria Christina was proclaimed Queen Regent again, was disavowed by her after its failure; but that she had a share in the conspiracy and that the French Government stood behind her there seems no reason to doubt. "Louis Philippe," writes Irving, "in manifesting such hostility to the constitutional forms of the government, and such disposition to discountenance Espartero seems singularly to have forgotten the history of his own elevation." A little later, in the hope of extending the influence of France over Spain, Louis Philippe entered, with Maria Christina, into one of the scurviest stratagems in the records of royal courts. The French King wished to have his son, the Duke de Montpensier, marry the little queen, but England was opposed to this. When the question of the Spanish marriage was discussed between Queen Victoria and Louis Philippe, the decision was reached that Isabella might make her own choice, the English sentiment being that the young Queen of Spain might well marry one of the Spanish rather than one of the French Bourbons. Thereupon Queen Christina, who had been restored to the Regency in 1843, brought her influence to bear on her young daughter and arranged, in connivance with Louis Philippe, the marriage of the Infanta, Louise-Fernanda, to the Duke de Montpensier, and the marriage of the young Queen herself to the Spanish Bourbon prince, her cousin Don Francisco de Assisi, a man so diseased that there could be no expectation of Isabella's having children by him. The offspring of Louis Philippe's son would thus, they thought, be heir to the throne of Spain.

When Isabella, after her marriage to Don Francisco, came into knowledge of this contemptible stratagem, she determined that she herself, husband or no husband, would provide a wholly Spanish child to succeed her; and when, in later years, the amours upon which she had so immediately entered became the scandal of the kingdom, Washington Irving doubtless remembered with sympathy and understanding the cause that had first led into a life of shamelessness the little Queen who had been so gracious to him in the days of her girlhood.

In September, 1842, Irving changed his residence and took the principal apartment in the magnificent house belonging to the Marquis de Mos. The windows of "his range of salons" looked into a little garden where goldfish swam in an old marble fountain. His bedroom was a curious octagonal room crowned by a little cupola. One window of his study overlooked the garden of an old convent; and altogether his new home was far quieter and more picturesque than the residence he had abandoned. Here he found his "brooding spells of homesickness gradually wearing away," and here he gave his first official dinner, a small party, as he had "to play the Ambassador on a cautious scale."

Irving's intimacies, as he writes in a letter to Prince Dolgorouki (then the Russian Envoy at Naples), were "generally few and cherished." During this second sojourn in Spain, although he became much liked at court and in the diplomatic corps, he formed none of those closer friendships which now were the half-sad, half-happy memories of the earlier years. Recalling the hospitable home where he had first met Dolgorouki, and where Antoinette Bolvillier had resided, Irving writes: "What would I not give to have that house of the D'Oubrils once more inhabited by its former tenants, just as they were when I was

268

here in 1826. I long for such a resort; I long for beings in whom I can take interest and feel delight." Irving needed the sympathetic companionship of women, and though Hamilton and Brevoort were intelligent and attentive young fellows, his bachelor household accentuated his sense of loneliness. To his sister Mrs. Paris, to his nieces, and to his nephew Pierre, he writes frequently for details concerning the home life at Tarrytown, and in turn sends them such frank accounts of Spanish affairs that he hopes they will not "get to Mr. Webster's ears." He confides such innocent information as his conversation with the young Queen, when "with a smile and a little flirt of her fan" she complimented him on the excellence of his Spanish after he had regretted his want of fluency in that language; but he also discusses freely with his family the character and the not always worthy actions of many of the protagonists in the drama going on before his eyes.

In November, 1842, an insurrection took place in Barcelona. Espartero left Madrid to quell it. As the Regent rode down the "troop-flanked Prado a solitary raven came sailing down the course of the public promenade, passed immediately above him and over the whole line of troops and so flitted heavily out of sight." This was considered a bad omen, but Irving suggests that the raven may have been "let loose just at this opportune moment by some of the politicians inimical to Espartero." The explanation, characteristic of Irving's attitude towards incidents affecting superstitions, is plausible; yet not so very many months thereafter, Espartero fell from power and was driven out of Spain.

The insurrection culminating in the Regent's overthrow in July, 1843, was preceded by the siege of Madrid, insurgent armies having marched upon it from various directions. Streets were deserted, shops closed, and the city was lighted up at night. (These were the days before bombing aeroplanes.) Thousands of Espartero's soldiers were waiting for the invaders who might at any time succeed in breaking through the gates and barricades. Irving was advised not to leave his residence, as "one may get involved in tumults in such times." But the gentle, non-militant country gentleman paid no attention to this advice, and on the day when Narvaez, the insurgent general, was, with his troops, only a few miles from Madrid, Irving drove forth as usual, at times alighting and walking among the soldiers. From gate to gate he drove, his carriage being one of the only three in the usually crowded thoroughfares of the city. He wrote to his niece Mrs. Storrow that he "could not resist the desire to see something of a city in the state of siege. I sallied forth with as much eagerness as, when a boy, I used to break bounds and sally forth at midnight to see a fire." But may one not assume that the real reason, modestly withheld, was quite different? No doubt it seemed to Irving that in a time of danger the American Envoy should not refrain from following his usual custom; and when he alone, of all the foreign diplomats at Madrid, sauntered forth among the soldiers, he laid another stone in that structure of admiration wherein to this day his name is preserved by the people of Spain.

Irving's quiet courage was more importantly shown in the suggestion that he made at this crisis to his fellow members of the diplomatic corps. His was the suggestion that the envoys of the various countries send a note to the Government, urging that the safety of the Queen and the Infanta should receive "the most scrupulous attention." They further offered "to repair in a body to the palace and remain there during the time of peril." While this offer was declined (the Spanish ministry deciding that the Queen's safety was "sufficiently secured by the devotion of the inhabitants of Madrid"), Irving gladly acceded to the request to provide his house as a refuge for a young bride, a member of the Rothschild family who had recently arrived from England, "and whose residence was in the main street leading from the gate that would be attacked." Happily, when the insurgent army succeeded in entering Madrid, a moderate policy was adopted, and the excitement died away with the exile of Espartero. It was again characteristic of Irving that when he paid visits of ceremony to the new ministers who had been brought into power by the change of government attending the Regent's overthrow, he made it a point to call also upon Espartero's wife, the Duchess of Victoria, whom he had always esteemed and whom he admired more than ever "since her great reverses of fortune." He records how when the two chiefs of the new government, Serrano, Minister of War, and Narvaez, the Commander-in-Chief, sent her offers of an escort to conduct her to France, she accepted the courtesy of Narvaez because "he has always been an avowed enemy of my husband, but an open and frank one, who practiced nothing but what he professed." As to the Cabinet Minister, "he professed to be my husband's friend; he rose by his friendship and favours and he proved faithless to him. I will accept nothing at his hand and beg his name may not again be mentioned to me."

The strain of the responsibilities of the summer months of 1843, together with a severe attack of his old trouble, inflammation of the ankles, led Irving, in September, to entrust Alexander Hamilton with the affairs of the Legation, when the American Minister set forth on an excursion into France. Of course he stopped off for a few days at Bordeaux, to visit his old friends the Guestiers and the Johnsons, and then went on to Versailles, where his niece Sarah Storrow had her home. There the sixty-year old diplomat had most delightful hours with the two-year old Kate. The "babe" was his playmate, with a thousand winning and amusing ways. "We now understand each other perfectly and have a great many jokes together. She relishes my jokes greatly and enters into the spirit of them completely, which makes me think she has great perception of wit and humor." Almost a fortnight Irving passed with the Storrow family, reviving his youth with the "dear, darling, restless little thing." Then came several weeks in Paris where he ran into his friend, Samuel Rogers, who, now eighty years old, was on "one of his yearly Epicurean visits to Paris." For hours at a time Irving and Rogers would sit together over breakfast while the remarkable old Englishman related anecdotes of "all the conspicuous persons who had figured within the last sixty years." Among them was the story of Lord Aberdeen who, "very much against his will, or at least his stomach," had to attend the little Queen Victoria on the nautical excursions in which she so delighted, and who had declared that "if Her Majesty persisted in her cruisings he would have to resign."

In returning in December to his post Irving, without waiting for the considerable escort that he had been advised to take with him on the road from Bayonne to Madrid (a mail coach having recently been robbed and "the passengers extremely maltreated"), pressed on with only two musketeers to guard his carriage. As they passed by night through the region most infested by robbers, the guards on either side of Irving were asleep. There is charming simplicity in Irving's own conduct. He writes: "As I did not care to keep watch myself and alarm myself with shadows, I arranged myself comfortably and fell asleep likewise and continued napping through all the dangerous part of the road."

Madrid was indulging in public rejoicing at Isabella's succession to the throne when Irving arrived. The Cortez had declared her of age and she had taken the constitutional oath. Her brilliant court was now filled with the old aristocracy. Tapestries hung from the balconies of decorated houses; parades, public dances, and illuminations, with all the people in holiday attire, made the city festive; the fountains ran with milk and wine. But the bayonets of soldiers still flashed the message of those critical times through which Spain had not wholly passed. By the following February an insurrection again broke out and the entire kingdom was placed under martial law. "Plot and counter plot rule the country." In March the Queen Mother, Maria Christina, returned from France and resumed command of the government. The citizens who four years ago were "almost in arms against her now received her with fêtes and rejoicings." Maria Christina again became guardian of her daughters whose care had so long been in the charge of the patriot Arguelles. With his customary admiration for the finer qualities of even a debased human nature—that tendency to

272

ISABELLA II, QUEEN OF SPAIN

look for the good in people which had made him an admirer
of Byron—Irving records an incident casting credit on the none
too admirable Neapolitan Princess who again shaped the policies
of Spain. "When the Queen Mother was entering Madrid in
state, in company with the little Queen and her sister, an official
courtier rode up to the carriage and announced to her with congratulations the death of her enemy, Arguelles. 'Hush!' said
the Queen Mother: 'Do not let the children hear, for they
loved the old man!'"

Illness obliged Irving to refrain from attending many of the
festivities and ceremonies in honour of the return of the Queen
Mother, but he was present at the first Besamanos when all
the grandees, court dignitaries and foreign diplomats kissed the
hands of the two Queens. Under a velvet canopy and on a
raised platform stood the chairs of state for Isabella and Maria
Christina, and a little lower down the chair of the Infanta. In
the great Hall of the Ambassadors there was no other seat, as
one does not sit down in the presence of royalty. Not knowing
how long it would be before the two Queens would enter, Irving,
with his poor legs, feared a "severe trial." But the Chevalier
de Arana, whose function it was to introduce the foreign envoys, suggested to Irving that he seat himself on the low ped-
estal of a statue at the end of the hall. There he indulged himself "in a quiet survey of the scene before me, and in meditations
on the various scenes of the kind I had witnessed in this hall
in the time of Ferdinand VII." "What rapid vicissitudes had
occurred," even within his limited experience, "in the gilded and
anxious throngs which, each in their turn, have glittered about
this hall. How brief has been their butterfly existence! How
sudden and desolate their reverses!"

Irving loved to describe dresses, having, as he said, "a knack
at it." So he tells of the white satin dresses richly trimmed with
lace, worn by the little Queen and her sister, and of their trains
of lilac silk and of the wreaths of diamonds on their heads.
"The Queen Mother had a train of azure blue, her favorite
color." Handsome women of the old nobility were so gor-

geous in their silks and plumes and laces and jewels that Irving doubts "whether even the lilies of the field though better arrayed than King Solomon in all his glory could have stood comparison with them." Parenthetically in a letter to his sister Mrs. Paris he adds: "I hope it is not wicked to so say."

Irving's mood was much more cheerful in these April days, as the baths that he had been taking had caused a great improvement in his health, and he could again walk about fairly freely for the first time in well over a year. To his niece Helen he writes: "I do not figure about yet in streets on foot lest people should think me proud. . . . But one cannot help being puffed up a little on having the use of one's legs." His good spirits were further increased by favourable news from his nephew Pierre, concerning his American investments, and he gave a series of diplomatic dinners, being "terribly afraid my purse will get ahead of me and I shall grow rich and stingy." When Pierre writes that General George P. Morris desired permission to include in a magazine of which he was the owner Irving's story of "The Wife," from "The Sketch Book," "Give my regards to General Morris," answers Irving, "and tell him he is quite welcome to my 'Wife,' which is more than most of his friends could say."

But when Alexander Hamilton in the following month resigned from the Legation (young Brevoort having previously departed), Irving's great mansion took on an "inexplicable loneliness," and though he found enjoyment in strolling through the green alleys of the retiro in the "companionship of nightingales," he became "more and more wearied of the wretched politics of this country" which had shown him "so much of the dark side of human nature that I begin to have painful doubts of my fellowmen, and look back with regret to the confiding period of my literary career, when, poor as a rat, but rich in dreams, I beheld the world through the medium of my imagination and was apt to believe men as good as I wished them to be."

Irving became more cheerful again when young Jasper Livingston, son of a Judge of the Supreme Court of the United

States, arrived at Madrid to succeed Alexander Hamilton as the Secretary of Legation. A further diversion in July was the visit to Barcelona where the Queen now held her court and whither Irving carried letters to her from President Tyler, one of congratulation on Isabella's attaining her majority, and the other of condolence on the death of a member of the royal family. On June 15th, Irving writes to Mrs. Paris that the deceased royalty was an uncle, and on July 5th, that it was an aunt. An Almanac de Gotha could easily settle the question, but as it does not seem to have made much difference to Irving, we shall not pretend to greater interest. It is more important that Irving was delighted with Barcelona, where, instead of baking in the "naked desert which surrounds Madrid," he revelled in the "gardens and groves and in the soft voluptuous climate of this lovely city," whose splendid Italian opera added so decidedly to the pleasure of the sojourn.

Irving never cared for money-making and had, as we have noticed, largely refrained from the task of authorship whenever his purse was sufficiently full to carry him on for a while. Now that some speculative stock, long considered defunct, had turned out to be quite valuable, he felt all the more eager to set forth on a vacation in France, where he wished to consult the physician who had helped him the previous year. The "unlooked-for influx of wealth" made it, he writes to Pierre, "indispensable for me to hurry to Paris to prevent a plethora of the purse. Jupiter! How I will burn the candle at both ends when I get there. Don't tell your aunt, though, for I see she thinks I'm a wild, expensive young dog." The aunt was now the seventy-year old Mrs. Paris, the "Kitty" with whom John Anderson had been in love almost half a century earlier. Irving, past sixty, was, in her eyes, still the somewhat harum-scarum, improvident young brother.

After instructing Livingston to have his old carriage, "vamped up and varnished," and a taller cockade put in the hat of his coachman (these being the splendid initial extravagances), Irving boarded a steamer during the last days of July

275

and set forth from Barcelona to Marseilles. The voyage had a touch of innocent romance indicative of Irving's life-long susceptibility to the attractions of women. While he was writing at a table in the ship's salon, he became "sensible of the power of a pair of splendid Spanish eyes which are occasionally flashed upon me, and which almost seem to throw light upon the paper." Their owner was a young woman in the twenties, with a Grecian nose, large and beaming dark eyes, long eyelashes, "lips full and rosy red yet finely chiselled," and teeth of dazzling whiteness; nor had Irving ever seen a female hand more exquisite, nor black locks more clustering. So often did Irving interrupt his writing to look at this vision of beauty, that finally the young woman said, with a smile: "Really, Señor, one would think you were a painter taking my likeness!" Thereupon the young-old diplomat paid her so charming a compliment that "the lady's cheek mantled with the rose." But she was married, and her husband was on board, and the episode did not progress further than what Irving called a "very tolerable touch of romance for a gentleman of my years."

Irving's August weeks in France were spent mainly at Paris; at Versailles, where he was again with the Storrows; and at Havre, the home of his friend, the American Consul, Beasley. Another visit to Louis Philippe in his palace at St. Cloud was the sole notable event of the French sojourn, Irving being intent on escaping, as far as possible, social festivities in general. Similarly desiring to pass through England without an influx of invitations, he had all letters forwarded to him from France sent in an envelope addressed to his brother-in-law, Henry Van Wart, at whose home in Birmingham he spent a few quiet weeks before the final stay in France that preceded his return to Spain.

The welcome Irving received from his Spanish household shows (if further evidence is necessary), how decidedly Irving was the kind of man who is loved in all circles. Only a brief time ago the French King had engaged him in a long conversation of a more intimate and jovial nature than was even his good-humoured custom. Now it was Juana, Irving's housekeeper, who threw her arms around Irving's neck, while old Pedro, the coachman, "cut a most uncouth caper" in his joy at his master's return; and Irving had "much ado to avoid the embraces of the cook's aid-de-camp and the footboy." The Envoy Extraordinary and Minister Plenipotentiary from the President of the United States to the Queen of Spain was first of all dear old Washington Irving to the servants who adored him.

This was in November, 1844. The most powerful person in Spain was now General Narvaez, and at a ball given at his palace Irving had enjoyment in watching the young Queen get into almost a convulsion of laughter at the old-fashioned and decidedly queer dancing of the Portuguese Minister. Isabella herself danced with numerous members of the diplomatic corps, and Irving was repeatedly invited to join the royal quadrille; but he made his lameness an excuse, not knowing whether his "years would have been a sufficient apology where royalty was in question." A few days later, at a banquet, his partner was the Queen Mother, but he was growing, he writes, "too old or too wise" for any thrill at mingling in the life of courts. At many of these festivities he would wander away from the titled company and loiter about the great halls, "musing, and weaving fancies" as he looked at the paintings of royalties now silent in the Court of all-puissant Death.

During the winter of 1845, dissension as to constitutional reform arose between the Queen Mother and General Narvaez, and the country was soon again in the arena of revolution. Irving, tired of Spanish politics and without any really dear friends at Madrid (the former English Ambassador, Aston, the best of Irving's friends among the diplomats, was no longer there), kept more and more to himself. The opera; watching the children playing in the Prado; and reveries concerning old days were, aside from a little literary occupation, his favourite recourses, but of these reverie was the chief. "When I was young, my imagination was always in the advance, picturing out the future, and building castles in the air; now, memory comes in the place of imagination, and I look back over the region I have travelled. Thank God! the same plastic feeling that used to deck all the future with the hues of fairyland, throws a soft coloring on the past, until the very roughest places through which I struggled with many a heartache, lose all their asperity in the distance." But even so, Irving writes on his sixty-second birthday: "Oh days of my youth! How much younger and greener the world then was than now. And the women!—the world is full of old women now; they were all young in those times!"

The heat of autumn again drove Irving to France. On the way to Bordeaux he made a détour to visit Tonneins, the little town where, travelling as a boy of twenty-one with the eccentric and joke-loving Dr. Henry, he had masqueraded as an English prisoner of war. At Paris he stayed quite a while and then went on to England, largely, of course, to see his sister Sarah, and largely also because his old chief, McLane, American Minister at the Court of St. James, wished to consult him concerning the Oregon question. The controversy concerning the 49th parallel had aroused considerable excitement in England, and the two nations were very near the verge of war. Settlement of this vexed question came after some confidential talks between McLane and Lord Aberdeen. Though it is not generally known, it was Washington Irving, whom both these statesmen held in great affection, who brought these American and English ministers into "frank and confiding intercourse." In Irving's entire career, the only instance of self-commendation is to be found in a letter to his nephew Pierre, where he writes he has reason to congratulate himself that, in a "quiet way," he was thus enabled to facilitate the settlement of the Oregon dispute; and when Washington Irving states "I have reason to congratulate myself" one may feel well assured that his services were momentous.

While escaping war with England, the United States became involved in war with Mexico during Irving's closing months at Madrid. After the early engagements at Palo Alto and Resaca de la Palma, the news reached Irving in June of the "gallant manner in which Taylor and his little army had acquitted themselves, and the generous manner in which they had treated their vanquished enemies" brought the tears to Irving's eyes and took a load from his heart. With the wide generosity that was always so essential an element in his patriotism, he hoped that "this brilliant victory will be followed by magnanimous feeling on the part of our government and that the war may be brought to a speedy close on fair and honorable terms."

A few weeks after Irving wrote these lines, General Saunders, his successor at the Court of Isabella, arrived. Irving had his farewell audience with the Queen and delivered the speech that he had prepared in Spanish. In her reply, the Queen, departing from the "cold, commonplace style of diplomacy," told Irving: "You may take with you into private life the intimate conviction that your frank and loyal conduct has contributed to draw closer the amicable relations which exist between North America and the Spanish nation, and that your distinguished personal merits have gained in my heart the appreciation which you merit by more than one title."

The often difficult, the often delicate labour that Irving carried through successfully at Madrid can best be studied in the voluminous unpublished Irving papers, more than one hundred thousand words in extent, deposited in the files of the State Department. To use all this material were manifestly to overweight the present biography. The publication of these manuscripts in their entirety may more advisedly be left to a future and separate volume on Irving the Statesman. Even so, this chapter may readily be enriched by the inclusion of at least some of the notable and illuminating dispatches sent by Irving to the American Government. Our earliest famous man of letters is for the first time clearly revealed as a diplomat by these hitherto unpublished missives. Those that follow deal with various of the events that have been touched upon in the preceding pages; nor, in view of the general outline of Spanish affairs that has already been given, does it seem necessary to add any explanatory note, beyond the statement that the two letters to merely "The Hon. The Secretary of State" were so addressed because Irving had not yet learned that John C. Calhoun had been appointed Secretary of State after the death of Hugh S. Legare. Irving's vagaries in matters of spelling, punctuation and capitals are not interfered with, in these manuscripts.

LEGATION OF THE UNITED STATES.
MADRID, August 27th, 1842.

No. 3

THE HON. DANIEL WEBSTER,
  Secretary of State of the U. States. Washington.
    Sir,

I understand that Mr. Pablo Anguera who is at present acting as our Consular Agent at Barcelona, has made application for the Consulship of that Port; This office is virtually vacant, Mr. Leonard who was appointed to it more than two years since having never presented himself to be installed. I take the liberty therefore of recommending Mr. Anguera as a Person extremely well fitted for the place. I have had opportunities of knowing his character and course of Conduct for many years past; he having had extensive commercial transactions with some of my relatives who have confided largely in his honor, intelligence, and punctuality in business, and have never found him wanting. He holds a most respectable Station in public opinion in Barcelona and my predecessor, Mr. Vail, who is now at that city on his way to France, speaks highly of his amiable and obliging deportment and pronounces him "in all respects a fit depositary for the Consular honors"—It would give me much satisfaction therefore should my representations have any effect in procuring him the Appointment.

I have but little news to offer of a Political nature. The Government relieved from its immediate fears of Foreign machinations and internal Conspiracies seems to have a breathing Spell. Still it is obliged to keep up a powerful army, which is at once its Strength and its weakness: for that army must be punctually paid to keep it in goodfaith and goodhumour; so that, while it rallies round the Government, it exhausts the Treasury.

The finances are indeed in a lamentable condition. The high duties, which were expected, while they protected Domestic Manufactures, to produce a large revenue have given rise to a system of smuggling which overspreads and demoralizes the Country, and defrauds the Government of the anticipated revenue: It is impossible however to get a reduction of those duties; Whenever it is attempted the Cry is raised, That it would ruin the Manufacturies and that 30,000 Manufacturers would be turned destitute upon Society to become "facciosos" and ladrones. Attempts are making however to cut up the contraband System. To this end the armed force employed to scour the Country in pursuit of Smugglers, and which has generally played booty with them, is now to receive a military organization, to be subjected to Courts Martial and all the other regulations observed in the Army. Thus they are lopping at the branches, instead of cutting at the root of this evil which overshadows the land. Still the measure as far as it goes, will be very beneficial.

Efforts have been making also to trample out the smould-'ring sparks of sedition which exist in various parts of the Country, in the shape of prowling bands of what they term latrofacciosos, that is to say robber-factionists; who have been partizans during the rebellion and are public marauders, robbing villages and laying travellers under contribution. It has hitherto been found impossible to extirpate them, having so many friends among the people, and being able to evade or corrupt the slow process of law. A kind of Lynch law however has lately been put in force against these ruffians by General Zurbano, who commands in Catalonia where they most abound. Wherever he has detected them he caused them to be instantly shot, without waiting for the forms of law: he has adopted the same treatment with those guilty of harbouring or abetting them, and has even threatened like punishment to captured travellers who should ransom themselves from the hands of robbers; who

were making this an important branch of their nefarious ma-
raudings.

His measures have been exclaimed against in Spain and else-
where as sanguinary and atrocious; and the Ministry has been
assailed for authorizing them—but they have been efficacious—
Robberies are at an end in Catalonia: those persons who had
been carried off in hopes of extracting a ransom, have been
suffered to return home and the roads are travelled in safety.
The good effects of these measures begin to be acknowledged,
and it is thought they will be adopted in other parts of the
Country which are still infested by robbers. Spain is a Country
accustomed to violent remedies and seems now and then to require a political Sangrado.

The Country, however, notwithstanding the long Civil War,
through which it has struggled is really in a much better condition than I had expected to find it. There is a general air of
Improvement in its Cities; industry and enterprize are reviving; the People seem better off—indeed it is the Government
chiefly that is poor. The reforms that have taken place during the late political revolutions have benefitted the great masses
of society. They have got rid of a standing army of monks
and are relieved from the oppressive imposition of tithes. The
sales of the Convent and Church lands though they have mainly
enriched the Capitalists have also been of general benefit.
There are more small Proprietors than formerly; The cutting
down of the "Mayorazgos" or entails also, though its effects
will be more slow, is already breaking down the overgrown
estates of the Nobility and tending to equalize Conditions.
The People at large who are quick witted and Sagacious, per-
ceive the advantages they are enjoying, are becoming more and
more attached to their constitutional form of Government, and
anxious for a continuance of peace, that it may be confirmed
and Strengthened: One Thing the Government has to guard
against is the zeal of some of its own adherents, Men who, it
is true, desire nothing but salutary reform but who are for
pushing it forward too rapidly: eager to accomplish every thing

during the two years minority of the Queen, while they have the power of reform in their hands, lest, when she comes to the Throne, still immature in Judgment, she should be operated on by adverse influences.

Then there has been some talk of late of the dissolution of the present Cortes; and of changes in the Cabinet. Meetings are held by the Coalition, which ejected the late Ministers, to organize opposition to their Successors. The leaders of that Coalition were disappointed at not being chosen to seats in the Cabinet, and represent the present Incumbents as deficient in the political science, energy of action, and above all the financial talent requisite for the management of affairs of State during the present crisis. A great part of the Members of the Coalition, however, are satisfied of the honesty, patriotism and good intentions of the present Ministers, and are disposed to give them a fair trial. With these differences of opinion in its ranks, The Coalition may be considered at present neutralized, and the present Cortes is likely to continue, and the Ministers to keep their places, at least until the next meeting of the Chambers.

The Department has already, I believe been informed by Mr. Vail, that the Papers and Public Documents forwarded by way of Cadiz, do not in general reach the Legation until after two or three months delay, and even then at a great expense. Permit me, therefore, to suggest, that for the future they should be sent by the Havre Packets, to the care of our Consul at that Port, or the Legation of the United States at Paris.—A copy of the Census and returns recently published by order of Congress and particularly the documents relating to our Commerce, would be of great service, should an opening present itself for the formation of a commercial arrangement, in relation to our intercourse with the Spanish West India Islands.

I am Sir, very respectfully
Your obdt. Servt.
(s) WASHINGTON IRVING.

283

WASHINGTON IRVING ESQUIRE

LEGATION OF THE UNITED STATES
MADRID, November 5th 1842

No. 5

THE HON. DANIEL WEBSTER
Secretary of State of the U. States.   Washington

Sir,

I had the honor to receive, on the 28th ult. despatches No. 6 & 7 from the Department of State, the former enclosing the commissions of Mr. P. Pon and Mr. John R. Cooke, as Consuls for Barcelona in Spain, and Xebara in Cuba, and the latter enclosing a copy of the treaty lately concluded with Lord Ashburton.   The enclosed copy of my application to the Minister of State will shew that I have complied with the instructions relative to the consular commissions.

I enclose likewise a note from Count Almodovar, received in reply to my application in favour of the claim of Michael Drausin Harang, a reply which, according to the slow process of Spanish investigations, does not promise a speedy decision of the question.

I have received and forwarded, via New York, the Exequatur of Thomas M. Rodney, Consul for Matanzas in the Island of Cuba.

Political affairs here are rising to fever heat, as the time for the opening of the Cortes approaches, and powerful preparations are making to displace the present Cabinet.   You may recollect, that the actual Ministers came into office uncalled for by any party; being selected by the Regent, with one exception, from the Senate, much to the disappointment of the ultra exaltados, and of certain active leaders in the Cortes, who had contributed to unseat their predecessors, in the hopes of being chosen in their stead.   The consequence has been, that the actual Ministry has not hitherto had the support of any party, and at present it is the object of attack from all quarters.   The constitutional party itself has long been broken up into divisions of conservatives, progressives, and republicans, with intermediate shades in favour of particular men or measure; while the

284

moderados, or absolutists, take advantage of these feuds in the constitutional ranks, to attack the Regency itself and the whole scheme of the existing government. All these discontented elements have recently been formed into a formidable coalition against the present administration, but threatening the very basis of the public tranquility. The pretext has been a commission appointed by the government to revise the laws respecting the press, and to prepare some plan to be submitted to the Cortes, for correcting the licentiousness in which it has recently indulged. This has been denounced as a high handed attempt to check the freedom of opinion and annihilate the liberty of the press. The *Eco del Comercio,* a paper hitherto of the Progressive Party, but recently gained over to the interests of the Infante Don Francisco, has sounded the alarm and proposed a coalition of all parties to resist this flagrant invasion of their rights. All the public papers excepting three which are in the employ of government, have responded to the call, and a kind of manifesto has been published in which they pledge themselves, however they may differ on minor questions, to stand by each other in defending the sanctity of the press and resisting every infringement of the Constitution. In all this, there is a vast deal of solemn farce, but it will have its effects on the nation; while under cover of it a thousand petty plots and interests are at work. It would be difficult and indeed unprofitable to unravel the complicated web of intrigues and cross purposes, woven over the whole surface of public affairs in this country and impeding every effort for the general good; a few of the principal, however, are worth noting.

The minority of the Queen is made a fruitful source of political agitation. The absolutists are anxious to abridge it as much as possible, to get her from under the guardianship and tutelage of Arguelles and the other champions of constitutional government; the exaltados would fain prolong it until her mind should be matured, her education advanced, her habits and opinions formed in consonance with the existing institutions of the country, and until those institutions should have had time to take root and be completed. With these views, attempts have been made and are still making in various parts of the country, and especially at Barcelona, to set on foot a movement in favor of restoring the Constitution of 1812; according to which the minority of the Queen would only be completed with her eighteenth year.

These attempts are clamorously denounced by the absolutists, who make no scruple of attributing them to the underhand management of Espartero himself, in the design of prolonging his regency, if not of ultimately possessing himself of the Sovereign Power. It is in vain the government have publicly and indignantly repelled such insinuations, and declared the determination of the regent and the ministry to maintain the constitution of 1837 and the limits of the royal minority thereby defined. The enemies of Espartero persist in asserting that whatever may be his public professions, his secret wishes are such as have been represented. He has suddenly, say they, been elevated from the ordinary ranks of life into the dazzling proximity of the throne; he has drunk deep of the intoxicating draught of almost regal power; it is impossible that he can look forward with complacency to descending after two short years, from his brilliant elevation, and retiring to the modest, and monotonous, obscurity of Logrono.

Whether Espartero is really visited by any of these flutterings of ambition I have not had opportunities from personal observation of forming an opinion. Those who know him intimately assure me that he is sincere in his professions and honest in his intentions: little skilled in intrigue; more of the soldier than the Statesman, and indebted to his bravery and good fortune, rather than to artful management, for his political elevation. Prone to sink into apathy on ordinary occasions, to let things take their course; and to appear less in intellect than those about him; but to be roused to action by questions of exigency or danger, and then to show all the fearless energies of a man worthy to command. I rather apprehend that at such moments of sallying energy, the prompt soldier now and then needs the warning voice of the wary statesman, to keep him from trampling involuntarily over the boundaries of the constitution.

The marriage of the youthful Queen is another topic of political perplexity, prematurely agitated and kept in a state of agitation both at home and abroad; certain reverend crowned heads and grey diplomatists, in neighbouring countries, being wonderfully anxious to provide a suitable match for this child, scarce entered in her teens. The better thinking of the Spanish nation would fain keep the mind of the youthful Sovereign unagitated by a theme so unsuited to her years; and they claim the right of judging for themselves what alliance would be best for the interests of the nation: recalling, moreover, what Spain has experienced of the fruits of powerful matrimonial alliances in the disastrous ascendencies of the houses of Hapsburg and Bourbon. They are not suffered, however, to rest in quiet on this subject; various young princes of different lines being spoken of from time to time as being agreed upon by foreign powers: and one at this moment being said to be on the point of visiting this Court *incog,* like a prince in fairy tale.

In the meantime a native candidate is started, near at home, but one, for various reasons equally unwelcome to the government. This is the Duke of Cadiz, Son of the Infanta Don Francisco de Paula: a youth of about twenty years of age. His mother, the Princess Luisa Carlota, sister of Maria Cristina is a woman of an ambitious, intrepid and designing character. She has long endeavoured in various ways to gain power into her immediate branch of the family; such as to have her husband appointed guardian to the Queen, or advanced to the regency. Her favourite project now is to bring about a marriage between her son and the young Queen. The government, however, is wary of her, and her political intrigues when in Madrid last summer produced an intimation from high quarters that it would be advisable for the health of Don Francisco and his family that they should pass the hot season at some watering place. They have accordingly passed some of the recent months in the northern parts of Spain, courting popularity, and really gaining favour, the people being pleased with the unusual sight of some of the Royal family circulating familiarly among them. Don Francisco, especially, has pleased the lower classes, being a man of easy temper, familiar habits, somewhat plebeian appearance, and a great amateur of bullfights and other gross amusements in which the populace delight. His wife, meantime, carries on her scheme among people of higher intellect and pretension, and takes care to bring forward her son conspicuously as a native born Spanish Prince, devoted to the country and the nation. The reception they have met with at Saragossa, that ancient & important strong-hold of Aragon, has encouraged the Princess to develope her project more boldly. Crowds have assembled under the balconies of the Princely residence, serenading the family; hailing the Duke of Cadiz as one of the hopes of the nation, and coupling his name with that of the youthful Queen, in songs and acclamations. These have been carefully reechoed throughout the Kingdom in gazettes under the pay or influence of Don Francisco, and are represented as the enthusiastic expressions of public feeling. The consequence has been another intimation from head quarters that it is expedient for Don Francisco and his family to leave Saragossa; and that their intended return to Madrid for the winter will be dispensed with.

All this would be mere diplomatic gossip, of little interest, did not everything connected with the minority and marriage of the young Queen bear upon the vital politics of the nation and affect the future destinies of Spain; and were not the whole policy of the country a game of trick and hazard. Among various charges of arbitrary and unconstitutional conduct, brought against the administration, is the kind of Lynch law exercised by General Zurbano towards the *latro-facciosos,* or seditious robbers of Catalonia. It is probable that, in the exigencies of the case, knowing the province to be menaced with irruptions of refugees and robbers from the french frontiers, the general has been clothed by the government with those old fashioned discretionary powers, usual under the ancient regime; for the Spaniards have not yet become accustomed to the somewhat

288

slow operations of constitutional machinery, and are apt, in moments of emergency, to push the machine aside and resort to the rough but prompt measures of despotic rule. The apologists of General Zurbano, however, declare, that many of the charges against him are false, and others exaggerated; and that his rough exercise of power has been honestly directed and productive of the most beneficial effects. A recent act of the General has brought the government into somewhat of a dilemma. He is charged with having ejected a worthy old Frenchman named Lefevre, from a convent in which he had established a manufactory; with having taken possession of the same, as quarters for his troops, and with having accompanied the ejection of the occupant with personal violence. The french government have seized upon this as a matter of national import; being irritably disposed in the present state of their diplomatic relations with this government, and well inclined to make the most of any subject of complaint, against a country towards which they have been so much in the wrong. Strong letters I am told have been passed to the Spanish government, by the french diplomatic agent at this Court, demanding explanation or redress for this outrage on the rights and person of a french subject; but as yet no reply has been given. The Spanish government require time to examine thoroughly into the circumstances of the case. The friends of General Zurbano alledge in his defence that when Lefevre hired the convent of the public authorities it was with the understanding that he should vacate it on receiving timely notice of its being wanted for public purposes. That he received four months notice that it would be wanted for General Zurbano's troops. That he neglected to attend to such notification. That General Zurbano finding him still in possession gave him some further days of grace, but on his failing to avail himself of them, ordered the edefice to be cleared of his effects:—that thereupon the gallic spirit of the occupant being roused, vented itself in such terms as to provoke a sudden movement of the General, before which Lefevre found it prudent to retreat with some precipitation. It is added that the general utterly denies having touched the respectable person of the worthy but vociferous gaul, but claims no merit of forbearance, as it was only, he says, in consequence of his retreating so rapidly as to be out of the reach of his foot.

Such is one of the petty subjects recently woven into the serio-comic tissue of diplomatic cross purposes between this country and France, and to which, if public papers and private rumors may be believed, the latter is inclined to attach serious importance. In the meantime General Zurbano, instead of being disgraced is clothed with new trusts, being appointed Inspector of the Custom houses of Catalonia; under the late provisions for the detection & suppression of abuses and frauds in the collection of the revenue. This gives him complete control, for the time being, of every Custom house that he may visit; with powers to examine books, papers, and individuals. He is said to be not much versed in accounts, but it is hinted that in the various phases of his fortune he had had some practical experience in contraband, and knows where to look for delinquencies; it is added that he will in all probability, look into the accounts with a pen over his ear but a sabre under his arm.

The policy of the government with respect to this man appears to be one of mere expediency. To retain him in Catalonia during the present feverish time, where the terror of his name and the promptness of his hand may keep that restive and seditious province in check; and it is probable all decision as to his alledged misdeeds will be avoided, and he will be continued there until the present crisis is past, and the "cotton question" which is again coming up, has been disposed of.

I have thus ventured to give a rough sketch of some of the political affairs of this country as far as I can make them out, being as yet but new to the ground and surrounded by mystery and ledgerdemain. If I have not treated some of them with the gravity they may be thought to deserve, it is because it is impossible always to look on with solemnity where so much of the petty is mixed up with the grand; where princes are playing such a paltry game, and where the patriotism that has sprung up with the constitution is overlaid by the oldfashioned trickery of the days of Gil Blas.

The administration is now bracing itself up and preparing with dubious heart for the tempest that awaits it in the coming Cortes. Its great reliance is upon Calatrava the Minister of Finance, who is prepared to lay before the Cortes at the opening of the session a scheme of finance, which, if adopted, will, he feels assured, relieve the nation from its present exigency and gradually extricate it from all its difficulties. Affairs, he says, have arrived at a crisis. The expenditures are three years in anticipation of the resources of the country and yet the treasury is empty. *There is a mere alternative between a financial and a social revolution.* His scheme contemplates the former, and among other important measures will include a reduction of the tariff and a more liberal policy generally in respect to commerce; should his scheme be rejected he will resign; though it is added, that should ministers meet with the same opposition that they experienced in the last session, the Cortes will be dissolved.

In my interviews with members of the present Cabinet I had forborne to touch upon our commercial relations thinking the time unpropitious after the defeat of the cotton question in the last Cortes; and the Ministers too likely to be transient in office. Understanding however, the liberal policy in commerce about to be recommended, I have recently brought up our own claim to participate in the benefits of the contemplated reform. I have spoken generally on the course of our trade both with the Colonies and the mother country, as burthened and impeded by prohibitions, differential duties and countervailing regulations, and as capable of great augmentation under proper laws; but I have particularly adverted to the tobacco monopoly, knowing it to have come under the consideration of recent Cabinets, and to be a fruitful cause of that contraband system which is the bane of the Peninsula, and which the government at present, seems so anxious to put down. It is needless to repeat here the facts and arguments used on this subject, and which have been used so repeatedly with former Cabinets. I have found them generally admitted by those with whom I have conversed; and Count Almodovar has recently assured me that a free trade in tobacco was one of the measures under consideration with Mr. Calatrava, in the financial scheme which he was preparing.

I shall look to the opening of the budget with some solicitude. Should the scheme of Mr. Calatrava be such as has been represented, and should it be favorably received by the Cortes, I shall entertain a sanguine hope that our Commercial relations with Spain may eventually be put upon the footing so long desired by our government. I fear, however, the present Ministry is not sufficiently strong to carry out any plan of reform, however salutary, especially one to which so many interests, legitimate and illegitimate are opposed, but that they will fall, under the tempest of opposition conjured up against them with the consolation of falling in the support of a great question, for which the world will give them credit.

I am Sir, very respectfully,
Your obt. Servant
(s) WASHINGTON IRVING.

LEGATION OF THE UNITED STATES.
MADRID December 10th 1842

No. 11
THE HON. DANIEL WEBSTER
  Secretary of State of the United States—Washington.
  Sir,
I have the honor to enclose copies of official notes between Count Almodovar and myself on the subject of the submission of Barcelona to the Government.

The City held out longer than was suspected, and only yielded at last to a severe bombardment. This destructive measure though repeatedly threatened, and the time notified was deferred from day to day and hour to hour, until the forbearance of the

Regent was made a matter of taunting scoff and ridicule by the Coalition prints of Madrid. The same papers are now loud and foul mouthed in their abuse of him for the harsh measures he felt ultimately compelled to adopt; but indeed there is a licentiousness of language indulged here by the opposition press in speaking of the Government that far exceeds the excesses of our free press in the United States. It is lamentable to see also how all patriotic feeling is lost in the violence of parties, and how opposite factions coalesce in their efforts to fan a partial flame into a general conflagration.

In the present instance the hopes and wishes of the Agitators have been disappointed. The Insurrection has been confined to Barcelona, and though slight attempts were made to get up agitations in other parts of the Country, they were promptly checked, and the general tranquility of the Kingdom maintained. This shews that the present Government rests upon a firmer basis than its enemies had supposed, and that the nation at large is desirous of order and repose.

Great efforts will be made to cast odium upon Espartero for the bombardment of Barcelona, and for the rigorous punishments with which the Insurgents are menaced; but the Catalans are not favourite throughout Spain, and their turbulent Capital has so often troubled the tranquility of the Nation by its seditions that the public seem disposed to acquiesce in the policy of a castigation that may serve as a warning to it in future. Beside, the Spanish Public is exceedingly tolerant of strong measures and accustomed to those severe remedies, incident to what may be called a national state of intermittent revolution. It is thought, therefore, by some of the connoisseurs in Spanish politics, that this abortive insurrection, and the prompt and vigorous manner in which it has been quelled will tend to strengthen the hands of Government.

How the affair of Barcelona will operate upon the Cotton Question is yet to be seen. The influence of England with the Government certainly increases on recurrence of these national

293

outbreaks from the friendly countenance and efficient aid it ever seems disposed to render to those in power: and it has shewn strong sympathy with the Government in the present instance; having ordered ships of war round from Gibraltar with provisions for the Garrison of Monjuich.

What it gains with the Government, however, it is likely to lose with the people. The Spanish public ever quick to imbibe the most absurd suspicions with respect to Strangers, have been assured that English Intrigues in favor of the cotton trade and hostile to Spanish Manufacturers are at the bottom of the troubles and disasters in Catalonia; rumors have been circulated that at the time of the bombardment, the British Ships of War fired upon the town, and an opposition paper insidiously remarks, that the same day on which news arrived at Madrid of the batteries of Monjuich being opened upon this rich and *manufacturing* Capital of Catalonia, intelligence was received that a treaty of Commerce between Spain and England had been signed in London!

A strong representation has recently been made to the Cortes by the municipality of Malaga on the subject of the necessity of more liberal commercial arrangements with other countries and especially with the United States: instancing the decline of our trade with that place in consequence of high duties and restrictive measures. This comes opportunely though I much doubt of anything beneficial being done at present with respect to our relations. On the Contrary I am sorry to find our tobacco trade likely to suffer from the disposition of the Spanish Government to foster the growth of tobacco in Manilla. The tobacco of that Island, which was formerly introduced without success on account of its inferior quality, has been much improved in cultivation and is now found to answer extremely well for popular use when wrapped in the low priced Havana tobacco, called "Vuelta de arriba." A partner of a British House at Madrid, therefore, which has for several years past taken contracts of the Spanish Government to furnish its fabrics with tobacco of the United States, informs me that they have been unable to get a contract for the present year; the Government having determined to supply itself with tobacco the growth of Manilla.

I remain Sir
very respectfully
Your obt Sevt
(s) WASHINGTON IRVING.

LEGATION OF THE UNITED STATES
MADRID April 1st 1843

No. 18

THE HON. DANIEL WEBSTER
  Secretary of State of the United States—Washington
    Sir,

I have the honor to enclose a copy of a note passed to the Spanish Government on the 28th ultimo on the subject of the outrageous treatment of the Barque Empress of New York by the Intendente of the Port of Malaga. Within two days, I received a reply from Count Almodovar, stating that my communication had been referred to the "Ministro de Hacienda" to whose department it belonged. It now appears by the Official Gazette of this morning that a decree was made by the Regent on the 30th of March, appointing the Intendente of Alicante to the post of this delinquent officer, previously removed from Office. This remarquable and very unusual promptness on the part of this Government, whether due to my official note or springing from their own sense of duty, indicates a friendly disposition towards us, which I shall consider it my duty to acknowledge properly as soon as it is officially made known to me.

The Cortes will be opened with great state on Monday next: as far as I can learn there will be a majority in the Chamber for the Constitutional Government, but not for the actual Ministry. In the last Cortes, a Coalition of parties expelled from power the Gonzalez Cabinet; but their leader having declined to form a new Ministry upon the invitation of the Regent, he selected for his Ministers, Moderate men of different parties.

In the present Congress there are supposed to be 103 members opposed to the former coalition, 61 in their favor, and 18 doubtful: The greater part of the members opposed to the Coalition are understood to be in favor of Espartero, as the representative of a Constitutional Government, against the efforts of other factions, but not the present Cabinet which will probably be dissolved; indeed a Courier has already been despatched to General Sancho, the Spanish Ambassador in London, inviting him to return and form a new ministry.

There will be violent opposition and strong discussion in the house: The Infante Don Francisco who had been kept aloof from Madrid, has managed to get himself returned as a Deputy from Saragossa, and entered the City two days ago in great style. He himself, however possesses very little energy or character, but his wife Louisa Carlotta is a scheming, ambitious, intrepid woman, anxious to bring about a marriage between her son and the little Queen; and there is an unprincipled, dangerous man Count Parsent, who is always with them, supposed to be the paramour of the Princess, and who has great influence with the lower orders: This arrival will complicate still more the difficult question of the Queen's Marriage, which will probably be one of the agitating topics before the Chambers, and thus Madrid is likely to be a scene of new intrigues from that quarter.

Jerome Napoleon, a son of the Ex-King of Westphalia has been here for some time past: he was favorably received by the Regent, and has had a private audience of the Queen: It is thought that he is a new candidate, and one that would not be unacceptable to the Government—He is about twenty two years of age; bears a strong resemblance to his Uncle the late Emperor, and is well spoken of as to his moral and intellectual qualities.

I am still confined to the house by indisposition but am slowly recovering; I am so reduced however by this long confinement, that I may find it necessary to visit some watering place, or make some journey to recover my health. I shall not do so, unless compelled by circumstances: In case, I have to absent myself from my post, I will have the satisfaction of knowing that in leaving it in charge of Mr. Hamilton, I confide it to a person, who by his intelligence, and apt and prompt discharge of business, is fully competent to carry on the affairs of the Legation.

I have the honor to acknowledge the receipt of Despatch No. 12, from the Department, enclosing the documents of Madame de Viar, whose claim, I shall in compliance with your instructions urge upon the favorable consideration of the Spanish Government.

Since my last communication, the Exequaturs of Messrs. Campbell, and Pon, Consuls at Havana and Barcelona, have been received and forwarded to with the original commissions to these gentlemen respectively.

I transmit also to the Department in order that it may be more surely conveyed to her, the enclosed letter to Mrs. M. Cloud, containing the result of an application made in her behalf in relation to a claim against a Spanish Citizen.

I am, Sir,

Very respectfully

Your Obdt Servt

(s) WASHINGTON IRVING.

LEGATION OF THE UNITED STATES

MADRID July 22 1843

No. 25

THE HON. HUGH S. LEGARE

   Secretary of State

     &c &c &c

Sir,

Since the date of my last despatch Madrid has been in a state of Siege. The insurgent troops from Leon and Old Castile under General Aspiroz took a position on one side while a superior force under General Narvaez, who had managed to out manoeuvre or out march the regent's generals, invested it on the other. They had brought no artillery and evidently calculated on a cooperation from within, expecting that a *pro-*

nunciamento would take place, and the gates be thrown open to them; or, at least, that the City being defended merely by the National Guards, would soon surrender. In this expectation they were disappointed. The Militia behaved admirably. Martial law was proclaimed on the 10th instant. On the 12th the whole population seemed under arms, and twenty thousand men, well equipped, were at the orders of the Captain General of Madrid. The gates were barricaded, batteries planted commanding the approaches to the city, trenches digged and breastworks thrown up in the principal streets; troops stationed in the houses on each side, to fire from the upper windows and every preparation made to defend the city street by street and step by step; and to make the last stand at the palace.

For three days and nights the siege continued; with much skirmishing about the Gates; the city holding out in the hope of relief from troops under Generals Soane, Zurbano and Iriarte which were known to be on the march for the capital. Aware of their approach the besiegers repeated their summons to surrender, with threats of a general attack and of rigorous terms in case the place were carried by storm. Their summons and threats had no effect.

Apprehensive that, should the city be carried by storm the lives of the Youthful Queen and her sister might be endangered by the defense being pushed to an extremity, and the palace used as a citadel; the Diplomatic Corps addressed a note [1] to the Government, urging the utmost caution with respect to the royal children, and offering to repair in person to the palace and be near the Queen at any moment their presence might be deemed useful. This offer was respectfully declined.

Two days since the besieging troops, finding the advancing forces of the regency were near at hand, drew off to a distance of two or three leagues, where they took up a position. General Iriarte has since reached Madrid with about three thousand men, but sallied forth this morning to cooperate with Generals

[1] *With his usual modesty, Irving does not inform the Secretary of State that he himself had suggested this kindly and courageous diplomatic message.*

Soane and Zurbano, who, with a large force and considerable train of artillery are close upon the army of Narvaez and are confident of success. Tidings are incessantly expected of a battle decisive of the fate of the capital.

July 23d. The question is decided. The armies met yesterday morning; a few shots were exchanged when a general embracing took place between the soldiery, and the troops of the regency joined the insurgents. General Soane and a son of Zurbano were taken prisoners; as to Zurbano himself, he contrived to escape and arrived in Madrid in the evening attended merely by three aids de camp. The city was overwhelmed with astonishment. The members of the cabinet resigned their functions excepting Mandizabel; the municipal authorities have taken the management of affairs and have sent out deputations last evening and this morning to treat for terms. The last deputation has not yet returned. The main point of difficulty is the demand of Narvaez that the whole National Guard shall be disarmed. This may occasion some trouble; and some scenes of violence. Narvaez, however, has the power at present to impose his own terms, but will doubtless be influenced by leading men of his party within the City, who will be cautious not to exasperate the populace.

I consider this blow as decisive of the political fortunes of the Regent. Other troops from various points are marching upon the capital; where the insurgents will soon concentrate a force of between thirty and forty thousand men. The insurrection is too wide and general to be quelled by any troops the Regent can collect. He is at present in Andalusia; seeking it is said to bring that rich province into obedience. Others think he is desirous of making his way to Cadiz; from whence, in case of extremity, he may embark and save himself by sea. On hearing of the signal defection of the army and the capture of the Capital it is thought he will either resign, or endeavor to leave the Kingdom.

I shall keep this despatch open until the last moment, to give any further tidings that may arrive.

299

WASHINGTON IRVING ESQUIRE

A tardy pardon has at length been granted by this government to Captain Love Straw, a prisoner in Havana for having embezzled money on board of his own vessel, and for whom intercession was made, according to instructions from the Government of the United States nearly three years since. The pardon is on condition that the party or parties aggrieved approve of the same. I have requested that, to save time, the pardon be forwarded to the Audiencia at Havana, to take effect on the approbation of the aggrieved party being properly authenticated. It will be necessary to obtain such approbation; have it authenticated according to legal forms, and forwarded to our Consul at Havana, to be laid before the Audiencia.

I am, Sir,

Very respectfully

Your Obt Servt

(s) WASHINGTON IRVING

LEGATION OF THE UNITED STATES

MADRID July 25th 1843

No. 26

THE HON. HUGH S. LEGARE

&c &c &c

Sir,

My last despatch was sent off the day before yesterday; since then the city has surrendered, and has been taken possession of by the invading armies, which have arrived from various points, and have entered, to the number of between forty and fifty thousand men. The national guard has been disarmed; and troops are stationed in every part of the city. The revolutionary Government, now styling itself the Government of the Nation, and acting in the name of the Queen Isabella II has entered upon its functions. It is chiefly composed of the Lopez Cabinet; formed by a decree of the Regent dated the 9th of May last. The brief time allowed me before the departure of the courier by which this despatch will be forwarded, does not permit me to enter into particulars.

300

The different members of the Diplomatic Corps have received notes from Don Joaquin de Frias, Minister of Marine and (ad interim) of Foreign affaires one, informing them of his reentering on the discharge of the duties of those departments, as confided to him by the decree of the 9th of May last; another giving them a brief account of the origin and intentions of the Actual Government. Some of the Diplomatic Corps have determined to abstain from opening regular communications with the Government until they can receive instructions from their respective Governments. I have felt my situation to be different from theirs; partly on account of the distance I am placed from my Government, and the time that must elapse before I could receive instructions, and partly from the general policy observed in our diplomatic concerns; to treat always with the Government *de facto,* without enquiring into its political history or origin. I have consulted however with one of the Corps Diplomatic, whose position is in many respects similar to mine, and who is a person of great judgement, and integrity, I mean Mr. Valdevielso, the Mexican minister. He agrees with me in considering the government of the Regent as virtually at an end; and the Government just established at Madrid, so powerful in its armed force; so extensively acknowledged and obeyed throughout most parts of the Kingdom, and above all, possessing such a tower of Strength in the person of the Queen, that it may be fairly esteemed the Government *de facto.* We have, therefore, replied to the notes of Senor Frias opening communications with him as the Minister of the departments of which he has charge.

I have the honor to enclose a copy of the second note of Senor Frias, before alluded to, illustrative of the political state of the country and of the origin and views of this Government.

I have the Honor to remain
Very respectfully
Your Obt Servt
(s) WASHINGTON IRVING

WASHINGTON IRVING ESQUIRE

LEGATION OF THE UNITED STATES.
MADRID Aug. 3d 1843

No. 27
THE HON

The Secretary of State of the United States—Washington
Sir,

Intelligence through the public papers which will reach you at least as soon as this Despatch, will give you particulars of the catastrophe of Espartero's regency. The intelligence of the reverses at Madrid reached his camp while pressing the Siege and bombardment of Seville. A dissolution of his army seems almost immediately to have taken place. He hastily raised the siege and retreated toward Cadiz, but, being deserted by most of his troops, and finding he was likely to be headed by a force under General Concha, he made for the little port of St. Marys, nearly opposite Cadiz, from whence he with the chief part of his suit, was conveyed by a Spanish steamer on board of a British Ship of War; the yards of which were manned and a salute of twenty one guns fired on his entering on board. From thence he will probably issue some manifesto to the Spanish Nation.

The closing campaign of Espartero's career has certainly been unfortunate. An ambiguity has hung about his movements; which has perplexed his best friends; an inactivity in times of gathering peril; an apparent want of decision and an absence of concerted plan. The bombardment of Seville, too, is exclaimed against as an act of barbarism, particularly as it was continued after intelligence of the loss of the Capital had time to reach his camp and to shew him that his cause was helpless.

His friends explain all the ambiguities and cross purposes in his military movements by alledged treachery on the part of General Soane, on whom he depended as upon a second self, and who they affirm, was false to him from the very outset of the campaign, disconcerting all his plans, and who finally gave up his army and betrayed the Capital into the hands of Narvaez.

As to the bombardment of Seville, say they, it was undertaken while Madrid was considered secure; and was justified by the exigencies of the case, the prompt reduction of Seville being important to the subjugation of Andalusia. It was protracted longer than it would have been had the Regent received news of the reverses of Madrid in due time; but the despatches sent to him were all intercepted, and the tidings reached his camp circuitously and by chance, two days later than they ought to have done. These explanations, however, will have little effect, for some time at least, in obviating the load of calumny and execration his enemies are heaping upon his name; nor will he now have any opportunity of proving the sincerity of his reiterated declarations of his intention to uphold the constitution and the throne of the Youthful Queen, and to surrender the reins of government into her hands on the 10th of October, 1844. It is one of the singular reverses and transitions characteristic of the political affairs of this country that its legitimate ruler, at one moment a popular idol, and the favourite of the army; is at the next by a successful rebellion, and by the desertion of his troops obliged to fly for his life; driven an exile from its shores; his justifiable defense of the constitution and the throne committed to his charge, construed into a crime against the nation, and that he should be branded as a traitor and a rebel by those who have successfully rebelled against him!

It remains to be seen how the coalition which has risen to power upon his downfall, will cohere; now that the object of common hostility is removed. Most heartily do I wish, for the sake of Spain, that a government may be formed capable of carrying on the affairs of the nation in a durable and prosperous manner, but I fear there are too many elements of discord in a state of fermentation to permit such an event. There are already three rival generals in the Capital each watching with jealousy the honors accorded to the others. There are opposite factions each claiming the merit of the recent victory and grasping at the lions share of the spoils. The Country is in a general state of disorganization; every provincial junta arrogates to itself almost sovereign powers; some already begin to dictate to the Capital and to question the authority of the provisional government. Barcelona, that political volcano is again heaving and murmuring with internal fires; the army is demoralized; it is broken up into seperate legions having provincial interests and prejudices, and provincial leaders; the dismembered troops of the regency also are roving about and will soon fill the country with robbers and *facciosos*. A stern discontent and silent uneasiness prevail in the Capital; the inhabitants see with humiliation and chagrin bands of rough soldiery, and Catalan guerrillas, who look like demi savages, roaming about their streets with triumphant air, while their National Guards, the legitimate defenders of the City are disarmed. There is a "fearful looking out" for future feuds and bloody dissensions; and many who have been great sticklers for National independence begin to talk of an armed intervention from abroad, as the only means of rescuing the country from a state of anarchy and maintaining it in tranquility.

There is a strong party in favor of immediately declaring the Queen of age; others, desirous of respecting in some small degree the forms of the Constitution, propose the creation of a provisional regency to continue until the 10th of October 1844; or, at least the postponement of all action in the premises until the Cortes can be convoked.

An assembly of the Cortes for the ensuing 15th of October has been called by the Government, when, beside the question of the Queen's majority, that of her marriage will probably come under discussion. This is in fact the European question of Spain, in which the various powers will take more or less interest, but which will be a matter of jealous rivalship between France and England. The latter power has certainly been outmanaged of late by her great rival, in the struggle for ascendency in the peninsula, and having been represented as the adviser and protector of Espartero, will feel mortified by his downfall. She will therefore have a watchful and angry eye on every future movement of France toward Spain and it will need the profoundest skill of Louis Philippe to carry his favorite scheme into execution, without an open rupture with his irritated neighbor.

I have the honor to enclose a note recently received from the Spanish Government announcing and explaining the Resignation of Don Augustus Arguelles of the post of tutor to the Queen and Princess, and the provisional nomination in his place, of the Venerable General Castanor the Duke of Bailin.

I have just received Despatch No. 14 dated the 20th of April last, announcing the change in the diplomatic banking house to take place on the 1st of July last. I have already drawn for the quarters salary due on that day, on the house of the Rothschilds, but trust my draft will be protected by the Barings. The despatch in question came in the centre of a bundle of news papers, sent via Cadiz, and was of course three months and a half in reaching me. I would again suggest that despatches might always be sent by mail, either by way of England or through our consulate at Havre.

I remain Sir
Very respectfully
Your obt S
(s) WASHINGTON IRVING

LEGATION OF THE UNITED STATES
MADRID Aug. 19 1843

No. 28
THE HON
  The Secretary of State
    Washington
Sir,

In my last I mentioned that there was a strong disposition on the part of some of the ruling party immediately to declare the Youthful Queen of Age. This was particularly the wish of Narvaez, Captain General of this district, and in fact the military head of the Government; a man strongly inclined to exercise military sway. Indeed he had determined that the declaration should take place on the 7th inst. and be celebrated

305

in military style, having arranged a review of the whole army to pass under the balconies of the royal palace and hail the youthful Isabella as Queen. This measure was objected to by Mr. Lopez and others of the Cabinet as unconstitutional, the Cortes alone having the power to make such a declaration and to receive from the Queen the necessary oaths. A warm dispute ensued which was with difficulty settled by compromise, and the adoption of a half way measure. According to this the review was postponed till the 8th on which day in presence of all the public authorities the state functionaries and the diplomatic corps, assembled at the palace the Queen was addressed by the Cabinet ministers, announcing to her that it was the wish of the nation she should be declared of age by the next Cortes; before which body she would take the necessary oaths, until which time they would conduct the government in her name.

The Queen having in a short reply signified her concurrence; received the homage of the Spaniards present; and afterwards was hailed as Queen, by the troops as they passed in review before the palace. This half way measure however, has proved very unsatisfactory to those of the ruling party who are for prompt and vigorous action in the Government.

The Great political question however is the marriage of the Queen; It is already producing discussion in the Cabinet and the "league." A grand division is said to be taking place. On one side report marshalls Serrano, Minister of War, Narvaez the Military chieftain; all the moderados, together with the influence of Maria Christina and of the Tuilleries. On the other side are arrayed Lopez, Caballero and Aillon of the Cabinet; the republicans, many of the progresistas; with the influence of Don Francisco. This last division counts upon the discontented in Catalonia, Aragon and the Basque provinces; and will probably be joined by the Ayacuchos or partizans of the late Regent. This party will be for reforms in the Constitution; modifying if not entirely abolishing the Senate, which is decried as, by its subservient intervention enabling the government to defeat the intentions of Congress. It will likewise be for abridging the royal power, especially in regard to the frequent dissolution of the Cortes. The great aim of this party at present however, is the marriage of the Queen; which it is urged should be settled by the next Cortes. Their candidate is the Duke of Cadiz the son of the Infante Don Francisco; whom they hold up as most likely to sustain the Independence and promote the prosperity of the Country being a native born Spaniard and a liberal.

The other party, having other interests, and a foreign alliance in view, are desirous of postponing the question of the marriage, ostensibly on account of the extreme youth of the Queen but probably to gain time for the maturity of their plans.

In the mean time there is a growing jealousy and sensitiveness on this subject; as is apparent from the reports and alarms, which begin to be circulated with respect to the movements of the Queen and the designs of those about her. She and her sister, have been taken within a day or two to La Granja one of the Royal Sitios or country residences, for the benefit of air and exercise. It has been whispered that she has been taken there to have private interviews with some emissary from her Mother, Maria Christina relative to an alliance with one of the Sons of Louis Philippe. Another report inserted in one of the papers, was, that she was to be spirited away to the Basque provinces, out of the reach and control of the people of Madrid, and within the influence of French policy. The last rumor which I heard from the mouth of an ex-Minister was that on the 25th instant, Narvaez was going to have her proclaimed of Age *by the Army* at La Granja having detached five thousand troops there for that purpose. She was then to form a new Cabinet and to be affianced to a prince of her mother's choice.

Such are some of the reports which abound in this idle and gossiping Capital; and which serve to shew the feverish state of the public mind. In fact the Capital and the whole country are in an anxious and detracted state, and ready for new commotions. Secret societies are forming among the discontented and the factions military, emissaries are despatched by them to

307

all parts of the Kingdom, to foment new disturbances and to take the lead in any new outbreak; and great efforts will be made to get up a counter revolution.

At present the youthful Queen is the only rallying point of national feeling and she will continue to be so, as long as she continues politically unbiased and insignificant; but the moment her minority ends, and, as queen, she favors either party, that moment she will become an object of hostility, and her very throne may be shaken in the violent convulsions which are likely to arise. Already in one of the public meetings in which the abridgement of the royal powers was discussed it was observed by one of the ultras, that he would be content with the taking away of the royal veto, but he would be much better pleased with the taking away of the Queen. I dwell on this subject because on it hinge the destinies of the country for a long time to come. The judicious and satisfactory espousals of the Queen are important to the tranquility of the country; Thus it is to be hoped this agitating question may be disposed of amicably in the next Cortes; but between this and the 15th of October next is a critical space of time in this country of events and revisions and many apprehend that there will be outbreaks in various provinces sufficient to prevent an election.

I am Sir
very respectfully
Your obt Servt
(s) WASHINGTON IRVING

LEGATION OF THE UNITED STATES.
BARCELONA, July 3d 1844

No. 47
THE HON. JOHN C. CALHOUN
    Secretary of State.   Washington
Sir,

Agreeable to the intention expressed in my despatch No. 45 I left Madrid at day break, on the 25th Ult, for Barcelona, via Saragossa. I travelled in the Dilligence in company with the

Brazilian Minister and the Danish Charge d'affairs, and, after three days and a half of almost unremitting travel, rendered excessively fatiguing by heat and dust and rugged mountainous road, I arrived in this city on the evening of the 30th.

I have since had an audience of the Queen and have delivered to her the two letters from the President. She has a much more healthful aspect than when she left Madrid, and indeed, is in every way improved in personal appearance. She acquires more and more a womanly deportment, and acquits herself with a dignity and self possession hardly to be expected at her years.

I also had an audience of the Queen Mother, who received me with her characteristic grace and amiability, and expressed her friendly hope that I had favorable accounts from the United States and that all our affairs were prosperous.

The Ministerial crisis from which so much was apprehended, or predicted, has ended in the resignation of the Marquis de Viluma. The main point of policy on which he is said to have separated from his colleagues was the immediate dissolution of the present Cortes and the convocation of a new one; a measure which he considered as calculated to prolong the agitations of the country, and to defer indefinitely the organic reforms so loudly called for; his idea apparently being to continue to legislate by decrees until the desired reforms were actually carried into operation. He is a man of elevated and honorable character, and of open and courteous deportment; with whom it would have been a pleasure to transact business; it is to be regretted, therefore, that his political views would not allow him to continue in the cabinet. He has retired with grace and dignity, and his resignation has been accepted with great reluctance. He will be succeeded by Gen. Narvaez, who will continue to be president of the council. No official notice has yet been given of the appointment of the latter, but it is stated as certain. Gen. Mazarredo, it is said, will again have the department of War. As he is the great friend and adherent of Gen. Narvaez, the latter may be considered as having both civil and military sway; his position, therefore, becomes of great importance and he has the power of doing a vast deal of good and evil.

I have spoken in a former letter of the independent stand which he took with regard to foreign influence and interference, when he had to form a Cabinet; I have not yet had an opportunity of judging whether during the recent crisis he has continued to adhere to this creditable line of conduct. I am pleased to find that he has declared in favor of a strictly constitutional course of policy, a contrary course having been apprehended from him. He will no doubt administer the government with vigor, and with somewhat of a military spirit; but, as long as he does so within the limits of the constitution, his energy will be beneficial in the present state of Spanish affairs. I shall look with great interest to his course of conduct and hope he may have the capacity to act up to his situation, and the true ambition to gain for himself that honorable fame which is now within his reach.

I am Sir, very respectfully
Your Obt St
(s) WASHINGTON IRVING.

LEGATION OF THE UNITED STATES.
MADRID 7th December 1844

No. 56
THE HBLE. JOHN C. CALHOUN
  Secretary of State
    Sir,
I returned to this city a short time since much recruited in health and nearly freed from the malady which has so long harassed me. Since my return I have received your Excellency's Despatch No. 37 enclosing the commission of Patrick I. Divine. In applying for the Royal Exequatur I have taken occasion to follow your instructions in protesting against the tax levied by this Government on similar documents. I enclose a copy of such part of my note as relates to the subject and shall follow up my written remonstrance by personal representations.

THE ENVOY EXTRAORDINARY

You will have seen by the public papers that the late revolutionary attempts in various parts of the peninsula have been promptly quelled and rigorously punished. They do not seem to have been sympathised in by people at large, who in fact, are tired and exhausted by past agitations and troubles and are desirous of peace at any price. The party in power rules with a strong hand and having the army at its command and having disarmed the national militia, feels confident of retaining its stern domination. Having managed the elections so as to ensure the almost unanimous vote in the parliamentary bodies, the measures of reform are nearly completed and will leave the Constitution so modified as vastly to increase the power of the Throne and to render the matrimonial question almost independent of the will of Cortes. By the way, I have just received private information which if true will cause new perplexities as to this all important question. It is said that an arrangement formed under the auspices of the Queen Mother had nearly been completed for the marriage of the young Queen with her uncle the Count Trapani; that the Pope had with much difficulty had been propitiated and was about to grant the necessary dispensation (the parties being within the forbidden bounds of kindred), when the Austrian Ambassador suddenly interposed and, in the name of his Sovereign "forbade the bans." The tidings of this untoward event, it is said, have completely disconcerted the plans of the Palace. The chances of Trapani are at an end: indeed I am told, they had never received the countenance of Narvaez. It is added that a new candidate for the hand of the Queen will be brought forward in the person of the Archduke Frederick, nephew of the Emperor of Austria, who is said to be about twenty seven years of age, well educated and accomplished, of manly character and who has distinguished himself before Beyrout. His pretensions, it is said, will receive the support of England. If this be true it will bring the diplomacy of France and England in arduous competition at this Court. From some recent symptoms the french influence would seem to be endangered with the ruling party. Spanish pride has been

311

ruffled by certain articles in the french semi-ministerial paper the *Journal des Debats* strongly animadverting on the recent measures of the Spanish Government. Recriminations have appeared in the Ministerial journals of Madrid. The *Heraldo* particularly resents the remarks of the *Journal des Debats* on the military execution of the son and brother in law of Zurbano and observes: "The Spanish Government ought to investigate whether the journal countenanced by the French Government speaks from its own inspirations or under the inspirations of others. If the first contempt is all that is merited by language dictated by the most petulant arrogance or the grossest ignorance; if the second; this incident will serve to make our Government regulate its conduct according to the proofs of amity shewn it. For our own part we are not accustomed to mingle with passion or acrimony in the affairs of our neighbors; we respect ourselves too much to repay, in the same money, the good offices of the *Journal des Debats;* but we feel assured that if the *Spanish Press* should meddle in so strange a manner in the acts of the French Government and *should reveal certain transactions* (hechos) and should be less circumspect and generous; in such case the damage received by our neighbors would be more serious than any that could be caused to us by the shots of the *Journal des Debats. If decidedly they throw us the gauntlet, they may be assured we will not suffer it to be left on the ground."* The passages which I have underlined in the above extract are extremely significant, especially as they are said to have been written under the dictation of Genl. Narvaez. They do not speak well for the cordial understanding between the two Governments. As far as our own interests are concerned it may perhaps be more to our advantage that the influence of France should predominate over that of England in the peninsula; especially as it regards colonial questions; though it is much to be desired that Spain could be free from all foreign influences and have the independent management of her own affairs. Genl. Narvaez continues to be the master spirit of the present Government. He is prompt, sagacious daring and domineering. Under his military rule Justice is more apt to make use of her sword than of her balance; the latter being considered too tedious of adjustment for the exigency of the times. The vigor with which he acts, however, and the severity with which he punishes political offences have created for him many deadly enemies among those opposed to him in politics; while the eclat with which he moves, lavish ostentation with which he lives and the degrees of state with which he surrounds himself, create rankling jealousy and envy among military rivals in his own party. He is, therefore, in continual danger from secret perfidy more than from open violence. His life has been repeatedly attempted and most miraculously preserved, while his death would be likely to throw all things here into confusion.

Various capitalists in Madrid interested in the prosperity of Cuba are attempting to arouse the attention of Government and of the public to the State of Affairs in that Island and of the Colonial Affairs in Spain in general. A weekly page of the Ministerial paper, the *Heraldo,* has been secured for the purpose; in which articles will appear calculated to set the statistics of Colonial Trade in a proper light. I have conversed with a gentleman who takes a leading part in the measure, and, who, having resided for some years in the United States is well affected to our country and well acquainted with the nature and extent of its intercourse with the Spanish Colonies. I have promised to furnish him with any information on the subject which I might meet with in American newspapers, and public documents. I am in hopes that this may prove a favorable channel for conveying facts to the Spanish Government and people calculated to give them a right understanding of our commercial relations, to convince them of the loyalty of our intentions towards their Colonial possessions and to put them upon their guard against the invidious policy of any other power.

I am respectfully your obedient servant
(s)   WASHINGTON IRVING.

Legation of the United States.
Madrid, May 25th, 1845

No. 66
The Hon. James Buchanan,
   Secretary of State of the United States,
      Washington.

Sir,

I have the honor to acknowledge the receipt of your letter of March 10th informing me of your appointment to the department of State and of your having entered upon the discharge of its duties.

I enclose a copy of a rejoinder of the Spanish minister of State to my note of the 3rd instant relative to the affair of the *Zulette.* From attentively considering the case I am satisfied that no wanton outrage on our flag was intended; the darkness of the night preventing the garrison from knowing to what nation the vessel belonged. Neither does the shot appear to have been fired wantonly. The suspicions of the garrison had been awakened by the appearance of a number of vessels, probably smugglers, hovering at a distance during the day and approaching under convoy of what seemed to be a frigate at nightfall; and this at a time when rumors were prevalent of conspiracies hatching among Spanish exiles at Gibraltar, partizans of Espartero; of intended descents upon the Spanish coast, and even of a projected attempt to surprise this very fortress of Tarifa. In firing upon the vessels, therefore, on their neglecting to shew lights in reply to their signal guns, the Commander of Tarifa appears to be justified by the circumstances of the case and by the general usages of fortified posts. With this view of the affair, which there is nothing in the meagre log book minutes of the master of the *Zulette* to disprove, I have deemed it inexpedient to press the matter further; lest it should assume a querulous, litigious aspect, quite at variance with the feelings of our Government towards Spain, and with that magnanimous spirit which should accompany the consciousness of power.

I enclose a note from the Spanish Minister of State inquiring whether the Government of the United States intends to make reductions in the "enormous" duties levied on Spanish sugars; as the Minister of Finance, who has the commercial intercourse of the two nations under consideration, is disposed to regulate his measures accordingly. I am inclined to think this inquiry has been suggested by the late urgent remonstrances made against the excessive duties on American flour in the ports of Cuba. I enclose my reply, which, of course could be anything but explicit.

The session of the Cortes was closed by the Queen in person on the 23d instant. I enclose a copy of her speech, and a copy also of the reformed constitution which was promulgated on the same day. The latter is scoffed at by both absolutists and progresistas; it is an instrument, they say, which gives satisfaction to nobody; for its very devisers consider it a compromise between their conscience and their interests, with which they vainly hope to beguile the people.

I have forborne of late to attempt to trace the tortuous course of Spanish politics where every thing is perplexed with mystery and intrigue; and where even those in power, who have good intentions, find themselves over ruled or undermined by adverse influences. The recent diplomatic transactions, with the Court of Rome for instance, have taken even the cabinet by Surprize and nearly produced a convulsion at head quarters. Narvaez suspected that he had been out generaled by the Queen Mother, and that she had given secret instructions to the Spanish Minister at the Papal Court (late her private secretary) by which the Cabinet has been grievously compromised. A scene, it is said, ensued between Narvaez and the Queen Mother, and an open rupture was expected; but neither was prepared for such an event, which would have thrown every thing into confusion. A truce took place between them; matters were arranged by compromise; the document sent on from the papal Court in lieu of the anticipated and much trumpeted concordat, was returned as inadmissable but the supple minister who is suspected of negotiating under double instructions, is continued in the post from which, in the first moments of wrath, he had been threatened to be hurled with disgrace. It remains to be seen whether, in this diplomatic game, the woman and the priest will not be an over match for the soldier, bold and wary as he is. In fact the whole position of this Government is forced and false, and has no true foundation in the opinions and affections of the people; it is, therefore, liable to further revolutions.

The Queen, accompanied by her mother and sister, departed yesterday for Barcelona. They will be followed immediately by General Narvaez and others of the Cabinet Ministers.

I am Sir very respectfully
Your obt servt
(s) WASHINGTON IRVING.

LEGATION OF THE UNITED STATES
MADRID, July 10th, 1845

No. 69
THE HON. JAMES BUCHANAN
     Secretary of State
          Washington
Sir,

I have recently received Dispatches Nos. 44 and 45, containing the Consular Commissions of Simeon M. Johnson for Matanzas and Nicholas B. Boyle for Port Mahon in Minorca, and have made application for the Royal Exequaturs.

I have received no reply as yet to my note to the Minister of State claiming restitution for duties wrongfully imposed on American Merchandize shipped to Cuba, under the "duty free" decree. Indeed, the absence of part of the Cabinet with the court at Barcelona interrupts the whole course of business. I have forborne to follow the Court to Barcelona this year having received no instructions from Government on the Subject, and there being a probability that the royal sojourn in that city would be very short: Should the absence of the Court from the Capital be prolonged, I may find it expedient to pay it a brief visit to prevent being thought wanting in respect.

316

It is now decided that the Queen will depar'
toward the latter part of this month, but will v
Provinces before her return to Madrid, and will i
Coast for the benefit of sea bathing.   This measure
strongly opposed by the Ministers, and disapproved ι.
Press generally, who have thought it extremely important
have the Court, and Cabinet concentrated at Madrid, at the
present critical juncture.   The Queen Mother however had resolved upon the expedition to the Basque Provinces and she has
carried her point.   It is probable that she is actuated merely by
a mother's solicitude for a daughter's health; the physical condition of the Queen, and the critical point of life at which she
has arrived, calling for the most careful, and assiduous treatment.   The public, however, consider the Queen Mother a
great manœuvrer, and suspect a covert design in every movement.   They consider the projected journey into the Basque
Provinces as having some connexion with her matrimonial
schemes for her royal daughters.   Maria Christina has long
been desirous that her daughter Isabella II should marry the
Count de Trapani, and Louis Philippe had at length consented
to it, finding that he could not secure the hand of the Queen for
one of his own Sons.   The shrewd Monarch is said to have consented, on condition that his son the Duke of Montpensier
should have the hand of the Queen's sister the Infanta.   In
this he has shewn his usual forecast.   The constitutional infirmities of Queen Isabella make it not unlikely that she will
die early, and without progeny; in such a case her sister would
succeed to the throne.   The royal journey into the Basque
Provinces therefore is thought to be projected by the Queen
Mother to bring about a meeting between her daughters, and
the French princes, who are about to visit the Pyrenees.

With respect to the marriage of the Queen, there is a continual plot and counterplot, so that the game is perpetually
changing.   It is now said that the Trapani match is given up
by the Court of Naples; being found to be so generally unpopular in Spain.   A *Coburg* Prince is now talked of.   There

317

have been diplomatic conferences on the subject, it is said, at Paris, between Mr. Bulwer, the British Minister at this Court, and Mr. Guizot. It will have the English interest in its support, and Louis Philippe in his growing spirit of accomodation to the views of England is said to incline in favor of it; provided always that the Duke of Montpensier have the hand of the Infanta.

In the mean time, another candidate is suddenly brought into the field, supported by Narvaez, and the Cabinet; and likely to be popular with the nation. This is the Infante Dn. Enrique, Duke of Seville, and second son of the Infante Dn. Francisco. He is about twenty years of age, a Captain in the Navy, and in command of a Brig of War. Report speaks favorably of him; he has acquitted himself well in the studies, and duties of his profession and this implies intelligence, instruction, and manly qualities. Narvaez managed that he should visit Barcelona in his vessel of war during the sojourn of the young Queen at that Port. Here he was received with great distinction; Narvaez gave him a grand dinner; as did Martinez de la Rosa; he was feted by the local authorities, dined at court, and the young Queen visited his vessel in some degree of state. He is now the theme of eulogium in most of the ministerial papers; nor is it likely he will meet with opposition from the others, as he is a Spaniard by birth, and of the Branch of the royal family which has been inclined to liberal principles. A newspaper is about to be set up in Madrid, under the auspices of the Ministers to enforce his pretensions. Dn. Francisco, also, and his family, who have hitherto been half overlooked by royalty, have suddenly been invited to repair to S. Sebastian, during the Royal sojourn there: Dn. Enrique of course is included in the invitation. This also has probably been managed by Narvaez as a check to the Queen Mother. The latter now finding the Trapani match likely to be entirely defeated is anxious to postpone the marriage of her daughter, until she shall have arrived at a more mature age; until her health is established, and her constitution developed and confirmed. In this she is certainly right. The marriage of the Queen at her present immature age might be productive of domestic, and public evils, which it is needless to enumerate. All these, however, may be set at defiance by politicians; who are only actuated by present expediency, so that to settle this matrimonial question, which is so fruitful of difficulties and dangers, the poor young Queen may be hurried into an early marriage, which may hurry her into an early grave.

From the foregoing statement it will be perceived that a variance still exists between Narvaez and the Queen Mother: indeed there has been a contest for supremacy between them almost ever since the return of Maria Christina to Spain, and in nothing have they been more completely opposite than in respect to the Trapani match.

In bringing forward the Infante Enrique, however, Narvaez has something more in view, than mere dislike to Trapani, and opposition to Queen Christina. He feels the necessity of strengthening his own position, and the position of his Cabinet, and hopes, by supporting a member of the liberal branch of the royal family to conciliate the progresista party. He feels that he has completely lost favor with that party since he came into power. He engaged in the insurrection of 1843, as the leader of a section of that party, under the pretext of freeing the ultra liberals from the supposed, or rather the pretended, oppression of Esparerto, and with a prospect of carrying out a "juste milieu" in Spain as Louis Phillipe had in France. Since his elevation to power, however, the impetuosity of his temper, and his disposition to domineer has at times caused him to trample on constitutional forms, and privileges, and to be guilty of acts of the sheerest despotism. Such for instance was the arrest of two writers for a public journal, who were hurried away under military guard to Cadiz to be transported to the Phillipine Islands; a despotic act which has resounded throughout the Peninsula. Now Narvaez is an enemy to Despotism, excepting when practised by himself, and in this instance only gave way to a paroxysm of his ungovernable temper. His friends have attempted to palliate his conduct by insinuating that the persons arrested had been suspected of conspiring against the Government; but it is well known that the real offence was a wound inflicted upon the General's vanity. They had given a burlesque account of his pomp and style on a public occasion, with some ludicrous allusions to his person and his *wig*. This was not to be tolerated by a man arrived at a *certain age,* yet still a general gallant, and particularly ambitious of the smiles of the ladies.

Vanity in fact is Narvaez' besetting weakness. It overlays his bolder, and better qualities, and by its indirect operations has contributed greatly to lessen his stand in public opinion. He is prodigal and ostentatious in his style of living. Has his palaces, and state equipages; gives princely fetes, and entertainments at which royalty is sometimes present, and lives far beyond his income or his ostensible means. It is true his past services were rewarded by the Queen Mother, under the advice of the French Ambassador, with the round sum of $100,000 but this was insufficient to cope with his vainglorious prodigality. Among other equivocal modes of replenishing his coffers he has leagued himself with certain of the principal stock brokers of Madrid, and has engaged in some of those speculations in the funds, which have shaken society to its centre. These gambling operations have become matters of notoriety, and have injured him with the public. They have injured him too, with his main dependence, the Army, who detest every thing in a commander which may appear sordid or mercenary. Unfortunately for the general he has too many dangerous enemies in that army, disappointed rivals, who gladly trumpet forth, and exaggerate anything, which may destroy the military prestige of his name.

Thus vanity has contributed indirectly, but greatly, to diminish the general's individual weight with the public, and his moral force in the government. He feels therefore the necessity of some expedient to sustain his political eminence, and to enable him to keep the Queen Mother in check, who has the advantage of him in being permanent in her position.

But indeed, it is not the General alone, the whole Narvaez Cabinet needs propping. It occupies a mere isthmus between the absolutists (including the Carlists) on the one side, and the Progresistas on the other. This isthmus is continually narrowing. It has been shored up by the army, but even the army of late has ceased to be altogether a certain dependence, many of the officers being Carlists, and whole regiments of doubtful loyalty. Under these circumstances the bringing forward, and supporting a progresista candidate for the Royal hand is certainly an expedient of the Narvaez Cabinet to prop its tottering fortunes.

The negotiations with the Court of Rome continue enveloped in doubt, and mystery, and are a source of humiliation to the Cabinet, and the Nation. The cross purposes in this quarter are attributed to the secret manœuvres of the Queen Mother, and add to her unpopularity; though she may have been actuated in her intermeddlings by conscientious motives, anxiety for the papal recognition of her daughter, as Queen of Spain, and a desire to expiate her own sins, and weaknesses by zealous promotion of the interests of the Church. The public say she is conscience stricken, and conscience bound, and that the Pope takes advantage of it.

It seems there are two parties in the Sacred College of Cardinals, one called the Political, which is disposed to keep pace with the age and to render the yoke of the church easy to her somewhat restive children: the other the theocratic party, intent upon reinstating the chair of St. Peters in all the sway, religious, political and fiscal, which it exercised in the days of Gregory VII. Unfortunately the cause of liberal principles has sustained a great loss in the recent death of the Cardinal Cappacini, who was head of the Political party, and might have inclined the Pope to a liberal line of policy; his death leaves full scope for the councils of Cardinal Lambuschini, who, beside being Secretary of State, is head of the theocratic party. This party is guided in its policy towards Spain by an intriguing knot of Carlist prelates, priests and laymen, Spanish emigrants, who came to Rome under the banner of the late Bishop of Leon; and who represent their native country as the most promising theatre for the great theocratic plan of retrocession.

It is unfortunate that at such a juncture, the Spanish Government should have sent out Mr. Castillo y Ayense as their envoy to the Papal Court, a man of limited capacity, and completely subservient to Maria Christina. The consequence is that he has played a double part, openly acting in conformity to Cabinet instructions, and secretly, at the behest of the Queen Mother, subscribing to all the requisitions of Cardinal Lambuschini. The negotiation has thus been rendered of very difficult arrangement, nor would it be surprising if Rome, in case of persisting in her imprudent exactions, should lose altogether her supremacy in Spain.

The financial affairs of the Peninsula continue in a most embarrassed state. Mon, the Minister of Finance, bears an unimpeachable character for integrity, though many of his opponents pronounce him an empyric; as physicians, however, skillful, are apt to be pronounced, who have to deal with desperate cases, and rotten Constitutions. He has undertaken to reduce to order the immense chaos of national debts, and administrative abuses; but has set to work with scanty funds, slender public credit, and the distant hope of a loan; which may be deferred, if not defeated by the vicissitudes of political events, and of the government itself. He has the marriage question, with all its perplexities to contend with, and the still more dangerous task of levying about twenty millions of dollars of new taxes by a new process. He certainly deserves high credit for the attempt; perhaps in other and more settled times, it might have been attended with success; that it will be so now is more than problematical.

Having alluded to the Madrid Stock exchange, which at present has such an immense influence on the morals and fortunes of Society, I would observe that it is not governed by the ordinary rules of such institutions. Political events have comparatively small influence upon its fluctuations. Its supporters are not, as in other countries, holders of Stock as a permanent investment to derive their income from the interest. They are solely and purely gamblers, with more or less Capital. They combine among themselves, occasionally to play for a rise, or a fall, and are pretty sure to effect their purpose. When no combination of the kind exists, the funds are stagnant, or at a low price. It will take some years of tranquility and good administration to induce people to invest Capital in Spanish Stock as a source of regular income. Gambling will go on in the mean time creating and destroying mushroom fortunes. It is the mania of the day.

A better spirit of enterprize however is awakening in the country. During the late breathing spell of comparative tranquility, a disposition has been evinced to explore and develope the immense internal resources of the Peninsula, and to introduce those improvements prevalent in other parts of the world. The home capital which for a long time has remained dormant, is becoming active; foreign Capital is pouring into the Country, the ancient mines are being reopened, others sought for; rail road companies are forming; in a word it needs but a few years of peace, and tolerable government to effect a total change in the Peninsula; to restore external credit, and internal prosperity, and to elevate the nation to a level with the rest of Europe. The country, say certain of the old political augurs, has been long in a state of transition, moral, material, religious, and political. It is now undergoing its vital crisis, and one year more may solve the riddle of its future fortunes.

I must apologize for the long and rambling disquisition into which I have unconsciously been betrayed. I had intended merely to touch briefly upon the main points of Spanish politics, but the whole is a complicated web, into which it is difficult to venture, without getting completely entangled; one in which one is obliged at times to be prolix in order to be explicit.

I am, Sir, very respectfully Yr. Obt. St.

(s) WASHINGTON IRVING.

WASHINGTON IRVING ESQUIRE

PARIS Dec. 12th 1845

THE HON. JAMES BUCHANAN,
Secretary of State Washington
Sir,

The time having elapsed which I allotted to myself to remain abroad when I accepted the mission of Envoy Extraordinary and Minister Plenipotentiary to the Court of Spain, I now most respectfully tender to the President of the United States my resignation of that post.

The unexpected manner in which I was called to this high trust from the retirement of private life, without reference to any political considerations; and the cordial manner in which I was welcomed to it by my countrymen of all political creeds, have ever made me regard it as the crowning honor of my life. I have endeavoured to discharge its duties to the best of my abilities, though I regret to say my endeavors have occasionally been counteracted by the derangement of my health.   In now offering my resignation I am actuated by no party feeling, nor any indisposition to aid in carrying out the foreign policy of the present administration; but solely by an earnest desire to return to my country and my friends.

Communications, which I have had with Mr. King and Mr. McLane, have induced me to protract my sojourn in this city, and may carry me to London, in the idea that I may be able to render some service in the present crisis of our affairs with England.   I will indulge, however, in no idle delay; but, should I find my continuance in these parts of no utility, will return forthwith to Madrid, there to await the arrival of my successor.

I remain, Sir, very respectfully,
Your Obt. Servt.
(s)   WASHINGTON IRVING.

324

"What! Irving? thrice welcome, warm heart and fine brain,
You bring back the happiest spirit from Spain,
And the gravest sweet humor, that ever were there
Since Cervantes met death in his gentle despair;
Nay, don't be embarrassed, nor look so beseeching,
I shan't run directly against my own preaching,
And, having just laughed at their Raphaels and Dantes,
Go to setting you up beside matchless Cervantes;
But allow me to speak what I honestly feel,—
To a true poet-heart add the fun of Dick Steele,
Throw in all of Addison, *minus* the chill,
With the whole of that partnership's stock and good-will,
Mix well, and while stirring, hum o'er, as a spell,
The fine *old* English Gentleman, simmer it well,
Sweeten just to your own private liking, then strain,
That only the finest and clearest remain,
Let it stand out of doors till a soul it receives
From the warm lazy sun loitering down through green leaves,
And you'll find a choice nature, not wholly deserving
A name either English, or Yankee,—just Irving."

THRICE welcome, indeed, was Washington Irving on his final
return to the land of his birth. The verses of Lowell expressed
the attitude of all Americans towards the man of whom and to
whom William C. Preston, in the final year of both their lives,
wrote: "I do not believe that any man in any country has ever
had a more affectionate admiration for him than that given
to you in America. I believe that we have had but one man
who is so much in the popular heart."
- The record of Irving's closing years is largely idyllic, with

much of the "warm lazy sun" and the "green leaves" that the phrases from the "Fable for Critics" offered for the distillation that was Irving's soul. The quaint old cottage and the lovely grounds at Sunnyside became for Irving the lyric setting from which he seldom departed, and there, building an addition to the cottage, cutting down and transplanting trees, improving the farmyard, erecting out-houses and, later, a cottage for his gardener, pruning trees, so that a clear view might be had of the Tappan Zee and the hills on the other side of the Hudson, the old bachelor, kept young by his nieces and grand-nieces, and companioned, until death separated them, by his only surviving brother, Ebenezer, lives the life of a country gentleman. Of course he indulges in some improvements which turn out to be unprofitable, at times spending so much that he is unwilling for the moment to build even a wren coop, "for the slightest job seems to swell into a toilsome and expensive operation"; and he reflects that a "pretty country retreat is like a pretty wife—one is always throwing away money in decorating it." But how pleasurable it is in the more indolent hours to drowse and dream under the old trees, or in his old Voltaire chair! Aware, as he wrote his niece, Mrs. Storrow, that as "a man grows old he must take care not to grow rusty, or fusty, or crusty," he keeps his youth through the memories of youth; through associations with his few still living friends of youth; through his keen interest in the doings of the young in his own family; and by playing with little children. The cordiality with which New York society received Irving on his occasional visits to the metropolis was another source of rejuvenation; and music, to him "the sweetener of existence," continued to stir those sentiments and emotions which were so intrinsic a part of his nature.

"Life," said Emerson, "lies behind us and is the quarry from whence we cut the tiles for the masonry of to-day." I remember how Lord Dunsany (at that time Captain Dunsany of the British Army) said to me as we were driving together, during the armistice period, past a cemetery in Burgundy where French soldiers lay buried, that the difficulty in building one's life after the experience of the Great War was that the war was a brick greater than the building. In drawing from the rich quarry of bygone years, Washington Irving had no such baffling problem of adjustment, and we find him in his sixty-fourth year, the year of his return to America, and until he died at the age of seventy-six, using for the masonry of that period the choicest tiles that his nature and his philosophy had won from the past.

Irving's association with royalty deposed, wealth discomfited, genius ending in insanity, had for him given sharp point to Martial's epigram that "fortune gives too much to many and to none enough." His own experiences of disappointment in love, and of the hardship of penury, were circumstances intimately emphasizing the bitterness in the cup of life. Yet in old age as in youth he adhered to the fundamental belief that a "kind heart is a fountain of gladness making everything in its vicinity to freshen into smiles, and that happiness is reflective like the light of Heaven." He set himself, therefore, to the grateful task of giving happiness to his kinsfolk, and when he mingled with his friends he spread that good humour which was for him "the oil and wine for a merry meeting." Good nature, the acceptance of life without the rebellion of acrimony, he looked upon as "the most precious gift of Heaven, spreading itself like oil over the troubled sea of thought and keeping the mind smooth and equable in the roughest weather."

The sense of humour (which is philosophically equivalent to the sense of proportion) was manifested by Irving not only in the larger approach to life but also in the lesser realm of sheer fun. He was still in some ways the boy, as, for instance, on the occasion when he left the Astor Library, "chuckling at the idea" that he had, contrary to the rules of the institution whereof he was the President, escaped with a book that he was using for the biography of Washington and had thus "circumvented his friend, Cogswell," the librarian. He liked to relate the anecdote of how, after he had joked with a woman who had accosted him long ago on the streets of London, it had cost him a guinea for "having laughed at his own joke," as the woman had replied to his humour with: "Ah! God bless your merry face! Surely you're not the man who will refuse a poor woman sixpence," and the smallest coin that he had in his pocket was the guinea that he accordingly gave her. He enjoyed puns, and to old Mr. Grey of Baltimore, the father-in-law of his friend, John P. Kennedy, Irving, in thanking him for a delicious ham, wrote: "If I had the ordering of things, I should have all the pigs sent to Maryland to be *cured,* as they send patients to southern climates." Even when he was in ill health, suffering from that asthma which was the oppression of his final years, he could say on receiving a long letter from some unknown admirer who desired to pay him a visit: "Oh, if he could only give me his long wind, he would be most welcome." And once when his nervous suffering was intense Irving remarked that though his nephew could not lessen his discomfort he could yet be "like the sot who said to his brother sot in the gutter that he could not help him up but that he could lie down beside him."

Irving's love for little children that had ever been so predominant a trait—a quality which some may regard as surely the wisest as it is the happiest of traits—is instanced throughout the closing years. He would make merry with them on meeting little boys and girls in the city streets or country lanes. Once, in a railway car, he noticed that two restless children were giving some trouble to their mother. So he took both little boy and little girl on his lap and so effectively entertained them that "Ah! Sir," said the mother, "one can see that you are the kind father of a big family!" To his grand-niece in Paris, the Kate Storrow who "used to take possession of him and oblige him to put away his book and entertain her for the hundredth time with the story of little Miss Muss and Hempen House," he writes to tell her how happy he is to hear about her new little sister, and instructs her to take the baby, when it is old enough, to the garden of the Tuileries and "show her to the little fish that used to give good little Betsey Posy a silver dish,"—Betsey Posy being Irving's pet name for little Kate.

IRVING AND HIS AMERICAN LITERARY CONTEMPORARIES

Julia, the new baby of the Storrow family, was later to acquire a literary reputation when, under the pen name of "Julien Gordon" she wrote "A Diplomat's Diary," "Marionettes," and other works of fiction; while, as the wife of Colonel Van Rensselaer Cruger, she maintained a position in American society with such aristocracy of bearing that—I have the anecdote from my old teacher, Brander Matthews—she was spoken of in the intimate circle as "the grand damnedest grande dame in New York."—But to go back to Irving himself: At Saratoga, in 1852, Irving, now sixty-nine years of age, is present at a children's party where he is so attentive to "two or three little belles from six to ten years of age" that he is received "with smiles that might have made me vain had I been fifty or sixty years younger."

Irving's kind nature flowed forth of course in warm current also towards his fellows of the pen. When Edgar Allan Poe sought permission for the use of something that Irving had written as the material for a story of his own, the request was immediately granted, although the acquaintance between Poe and Irving was of the slightest. Whether Poe ever wrote this story, and what was the theme of Irving's that he may have adapted, remain interesting subjects for special research. It is already known that Irving admired "The Raven," a poem of "strange weird interest" for our lover of legends. To Hawthorne, also, Irving was courteous, and from Hawthorne, whose "Scarlet Letter" and "House of Seven Gables" Irving wrote of as "two of the best works of fiction that have issued from the American press," he received words of appreciation and of the deepest regard. Donald G. Mitchell, whose "Reveries of a Bachelor" ("a very beautiful work," Irving calls it) was dedicated to him, Irving encouraged in many ways; Ticknor, Holmes, Willis, Motley, Longfellow, Bancroft, Curtis,—these are only a few of the many writers of note who found in the dean of American literature a sympathetic brother-in-letters.

As to Irving's own writings, he began, immediately after his return in 1846, the revision of earlier works for a complete edition, and the next year he gave George P. Putnam the exclusive rights of publishing the set. This arrangement called for payment to Irving, over a course of years, of eighty-five hundred dollars. The issue sold on a large scale, and both Irving and Putnam proved fortunate in having entered upon the arrangement suggested by the honourable and enterprising publisher. When, during the panic of 1857, the Putnam firm became financially embarrassed, Irving bought back the plates from the publishers, but continued Putnam in the capacity of his agent, glad in this manner to be able to show his appreciation for the confidence that Putnam had previously displayed in the continued appeal of Irving's writings.

The most delightful of Irving's biographical works belongs to the year 1849. Oliver Goldsmith, whom Irving had already approached in a biographical introduction to two volumes of selections from Goldsmith's writings, was, in his generousness, his whimsicality, his point of view towards human nature and in his sentimentality, very much the lovable kind of being that we find Irving to have been. Though the American was the steadier and the wiser of the two, even in their faults of indolence and of improvidence, they were akin. As authors, also, they were alike in charm and simplicity of style, and in their appeal of genial humour, and in the mellowness of their rarer phases of melancholy. The writer who is inherently in sympathy with his subject has the most essential equipment of the biographer; small wonder, then, that Irving's Life of Oliver Goldsmith (the most quickly written of all his works), though it brings forward little that is new concerning the author of the "Vicar of Wakefield," is by far the most enjoyable of Irving's biographies. "Mahomet and his Successors" (published in 1849–1850) was an accomplishment involving much more research, and the extensive Life of Washington that so engrossed Irving during his last five years entailed an amount of labour that made it, in one sense at least, Irving's *magnum opus;* but neither the prophet of Islam, nor the chief founder of the

American republic was so near to Irving's heart as the simple-minded Irishman of whom Samuel Johnson said: "Let not his frailties be remembered; he was a very great man."

"Wolfert's Roost, and Other Papers now First Collected," was the only volume of non-biographical writing belonging to the final period of Irving's life. The vines in the garden of his imagination had little sap left in them, and he could no longer force their growth. He had said to George Sumner, one day when they were together in Madrid: "The best things of an author are spontaneous—the first pressing of the grape, the after squeezings not so rich." Even a compendium like the Life of Washington was no easy task, and Irving went on with it through days of asthmatic suffering and after nights of insomnia, with the ever more shaking hand of a man well over seventy, yet with that quiet courage on which he had so often successfully relied. Writing at a period when Prescott and Bancroft, historians whom he considered his superiors, were in the public eye, and ever modest about his own qualifications, Irving had many doubts concerning his biography of the great statesman who had patted his head, some three quarters of a century earlier, at Lizzie's request. When the fifth and final volume was issued only a few months before Irving's death, he wrote to his friend Kennedy: "Thank Heaven! Henceforth I give up all further tasking with the pen." He had feared that he would never bring the work to completion. "Whimsical as it may seem I was haunted occasionally by one of my own early pleasantries. My mock admonition to Diedrich Knickerbocker not to idle in his historic wayfaring, rose in judgment against me: 'Is not Time, relentless Time, shaking with palsied hand his almost exhausted hour glass before thee? Hasten, then, to pursue thy weary task lest the sands be run ere thou finish thy History of the Manhattoes.'"

Irving's Life of Washington was widely read in its day; and deserves Prescott's encomium: "Instead of a cold marble statue of a demigod, you have made him a being of flesh and blood like ourselves" and Bancroft's praise concerning the candour, unbiased judgment, the felicity of selection, and the "happy magic" of scenic descriptions.

Irving had, in 1848, paid a long visit to New York where he lived a part of the time with his nephew, John Treat Irving, and a part as the guest of John Jacob Astor, then eighty-four years of age. He would write in the morning, and enjoy society and the opera or theatre at night. He failed in persuading Astor to found a library immediately, but when, in the following year, the old multi-millionaire died, Irving's proposal had borne fruit in the will, and the great New York Public Library of to-day is the developed result of the suggestion of Irving who was both one of the executors of Astor's will and the first President of the Astor Library. But after this visit of many months to his native town, seldom save in summer did he absent himself for more than a day or two at a time from the little cottage which had become so endeared to him. An exception was due to his desire to hunt among the archives of the Capitol for new material for the Life of Washington. It was at the invitation of Kennedy, at that time Secretary of the Navy, that, in January, 1853, he left for Washington. On the Cortland Street ferry, Irving ran into Thackeray, bound for Philadelphia, and the two famous humorists had a delightful talk, continued a few weeks later in Washington where Irving records that he found Thackeray "very pleasant company."

Stopping off at Mr. Grey's home in Baltimore Irving was received with exuberant delight by the old negro servant Phil, who "rather values himself on our intimacy," and who treated him, in spite of his three score years and ten, as the "favorite child of the house." "Phil is my guardian spirit—though rather a black one." When, a few days later, Irving went with Kennedy to the levée of President Fillmore, the same joy evinced at his arrival at private homes was shown in his reception at the President's mansion where he "had to shake hands with man, woman and child who besought me on all sides until I felt as if it was becoming absurd and struggled out of the throng." With

332

Washington Irving

IRVING AND HIS DOG, GINGER

the President, Irving visits the *Ericson,* and with President-Elect Pierce he immediately gets on friendly terms, taking a liking to him when he hears that Pierce intends to provide for Nathaniel Hawthorne, the President-Elect's fellow student at Bowdoin. Hawthorne's surveyorship of the Custom-house at Salem was the issue of this decision. But Presidents as Presidents meant little to Irving, who was never over-impressed by wealth or position; and, indeed, when his friend Martin Van Buren was the Chief Executive of the nation, he on one occasion complained that Irving seemed to pay very little attention to him any more. In 1854 when Irving was invited to accompany Fillmore and Kennedy on a tour through the southern states, he declined on the score that he did not enjoy travelling with "political notables," although he was "always ready to clatter off on Douce Davie into the woods with the gentle Horseshoe"—Horseshoe being Irving's name for Kennedy, who had written a book entitled "Horse-Shoe Robinson, a Tale of the Tory Ascendancy."

A welcome similar to that given Irving by his Spanish household when he returned from Paris to Madrid, awaited the dear old man when the Washington sojourn, continued until after the inauguration of Pierce, came to an end. All at Sunnyside greeted him "with kissing and laughing and crying." When he went out to "inspect his domain," he was accompanied not only by his nieces, but by his "prime minister, Robert," "his master of horses, Thomas," and his "keeper of poultry yard, William." Irving's saddle horse "laid his head on his shoulder and would have nibbled his ear if permitted," and his "little terrier slut, Ginger," who had added five members to the Irving household during his absence, was "almost crazy with delight."

The summer of 1853 (after a brief visit to George Washington Lewis's home in the Shenandoah Valley for the study of manuscripts relating to Washington) Irving spent in part at Berkley Springs, where his chief amusement was bowling; in part at Saratoga; and in part on the St. Lawrence River, among the Thousand Islands, and thence to Niagara Falls. Arriving in New York late in September, he went to the Irving House, intending to stay there over night. The clerk, not recognizing him, told the visitor that there was little chance of getting a room; whereupon Irving recalled the advice that his niece Sarah Storrow gave him in Europe, and wrote out his name not as "W. Irving," but at full length in the hotel register. The quiet, modest stranger was the great man after whom the hostelry had been called! He was led at once to a "sumptuous apartment," where "everyone was enormously attentive," including the chambermaid. "If she had been pretty, I absolutely should have kissed her," wrote Irving, "and henceforth I abjure all modesty with hotelkeepers and will get as much for my name as it will fetch."

A few months later the little village south of Tarrytown, at the petition of all its inhabitants and by order of the Postmaster General, changed its name from Dearman to Irvington, in honour of its best loved townsman. This was but one in a long list of personal tributes during the closing years of his life. They varied from gifts for his garden, in the way of cuttings of figs and grapes, and gifts for his house, as the table for his study that Putnam sent him (and on which, it is pleasant to recall, some of the notes for this biography were written); to dedications of books by writers young and old; and to such more official tribute as the vote of the Board of Visitors in session at the United States Military Academy at West Point to pay in a body a call of homage on "so distinguished an American." But this visit, with his inevitable modesty and shyness, Irving refused, pleading ill health as an excuse. And though he was always accepting invitations to be the guest of honour at the "Irving Literary Union," a society formed by a group of young New York fellows in 1852, somehow or other he never turned up, although he wrote when the society was first formed: "As my long and desultory career is drawing to a close, I regard such demonstrations on the part of my young fellowmen as a soothing assurance that with all my shortcomings and however imperfectly I may have performed my part, I have not lived entirely in vain."

To old friends, however, his door was always open, and he would, from time to time, go on brief visits to Gouverneur Kemble, to James K. Paulding, to John P. Kennedy, and once to the home of Nathaniel Parker Willis, that now almost forgotten writer who was the prototype of later semi-literary journalists, and who, in his early years, had met many of the well-known English men and women among whom Irving had been such a favourite. The name of Thomas Moore, who had died after his mental faculties had broken down, came up in a talk between Irving and Willis, and Irving, with his old loyalty for old friends, insisted on the high-mindedness and liberality and generosity of the Irish poet. During this same talk Irving accepted with good nature Willis's teasing remarks concerning Irving's Beau Brummeldom during the London days, when Thomas Moore "insisted on being introduced to Irving's tailor."

Irving delighted in reminiscences. His conversation and his letters of later life are full of them. In 1851, on hearing from the schoolmaster, Jesse Merwin (Ichabod Crane's prototype, so it is said), whom he had met long ago at the Kinderhook home of Judge Van Ness, Irving recalls a fishing expedition in which Merwin, Congressman Van Alen and he had taken part. "Do you remember our piratical prank when we made up for our lack of luck in fishing by plundering John Moore's canoe of its fish when we found it adrift? And do you remember how John Moore came splashing along the marsh on the opposite border of the lake, roaring at us; and how we finished our frolic by driving off and leaving the Congressman to John Moore's mercy, tickling ourselves with the idea of his being scalped at least? Ah! well-a-day, friend Merwin, these were the days of our youth and folly!" Irving adds that this same John Moore, and the anecdotes Merwin had told of the old fisherman, gave him the idea of the vagabond character of Dirck Schuyler in "Knickerbocker's History" on which Irving was then engaged.

The "days of youth and folly" were, in the domain of memory, most happily renewed for Irving as he sympathetically watched the doings of the young people at Sunnyside. In a

335

letter to Sarah Storrow he writes concerning two grandnieces, Hattie, and "sweet little Nellie" (daughters of Pierre Paris Irving), who, with their young friends, are sailing by moonlight on the Hudson. "It puts me in mind of the water parties in former days in *The Dream,* with the Hoffmans, Brevoorts, etc., when the old chorus used to be chanted,

> We wont go home till morning,
> Till daylight doth appear."

With Sarah Storrow also, he reminisces concerning the days in France. The coup d'étât which set Louis Napoleon on the imperial throne brings up thoughts of the strangeness of destiny. "Louis Napoleon and Eugenie Montijo, Emperor and Empress of France! one of whom I have had as a guest in my cottage on the Hudson, the other of whom when a child I have had on my knee at Granada!" Strange indeed that the granddaughter of a minor American official—Kirkpatrick, Consul at Malaga— was now the consort of an emperor.

Irving's memory as an old man must have been unusually good for it carried him back almost to infancy. Once when he spoke of children who did not believe in Santa Claus as "too wise to be happy," he added that when he was a child his belief continued until "they ['they,' no doubt, being his elder brothers] put snow balls in my stocking." He remembers following Genet down Wall Street. The ten year old Washington, walking behind the first Minister from the French Republic, envied "a little boy who had a feather stuck in the side of his hat." In a letter to Mrs. Storrow in 1856, he recalls and explains why he never visited Florence during his travels in Italy in 1805. "A malignant fever had led a cordon of troops to be drawn around Tuscany." But though he regrets having failed to see Venice, he does not, we are amused to note, explain that this omission was due to the desire of Cabell and himself to get as quickly as possible to the gaieties of Paris. Doubtless the old gentleman did not wish the children of the Storrow family to know too much concerning their once rather gay uncle; and perhaps Sarah

Storrow was already aware of the circumstance. A more interesting bit of information in the same letter has to do with the Duchess of Duras, at whose castle Washington and Peter had received such delightful hospitality. The Duchess, Irving states he had later learned, "had hoped I might be excited to write something about the old chateau in the style of Bracebridge Hall; and it would indeed have been a fine subject."

Recollections of Scotland—"Scott stumping along in brown pantaloons, greenish frock coat, white hat and stick, and mumbling to himself in gruff tones some bit of old minstrelry"; of Spain, with Irving's first intense zest in bull fights that later he seldom attended—"the cruelty in my nature had been worn out"; of England, and of the performances at Covent Garden where Mrs. Siddons, Kemble and Cooke thrilled their audiences; of the Rhine country, and the dungeon under the old castle at Baden-Baden, where the "Vehm Gericht," the "mysterious and tremendous association that once held such sway over Germany," had its secret sessions;—of all these and much besides Irving reminisces in letters or in talks; but the most precious of his European recollections (as shown in a letter written in July, 1856, when he was seventy-three years old) have to do with the Dresden days. In writing to the Englishwoman—the English girl that he had loved—he refers to the miniature copy of the head of Herodotus she painted at Dresden and which he still treasures: "Farewell, my dear Mrs. Fuller," the letter ends; "if any of those of your family whom I ever knew and valued are at hand, assure them that I ever retain them in cordial remembrance; and believe me, ever, my dear Emily Foster, your affectionate friend, Washington Irving."

The past was renewed for Irving also by reminiscences penned by correspondents on both sides of the ocean. Notable among such letters are those of Preston concerning their early travels together; and of Robert C. Winthrop of Boston, who brought up Spain when he wrote to Irving of the sketch that David Wilkie had made of Irving when he was studying the archives at Cordova, a picture that now formed the frontispiece of the

Wilkie volume dedicated to Lord Lansdowne. Then, too, there
is the letter from Charles Dickens wherein Irving reads a pathetic story of Samuel Rogers in his advanced age. His memory gone, the old banker-poet was seated at breakfast between
Mrs. Proctor and Mrs. Carlyle and both these brilliant women
were eager to entertain the old man. But when Jane Carlyle had
done her brilliant best, "Who is *she?*" asked Rogers. So Mrs.
Proctor told him and spoke at length of the writings of Carlyle
himself. "All of which," writes Dickens to Irving, "he heard
staring in the dreariest silence, and then said, indignantly as
before: 'And who are *you?*'

Rogers, Newton and Moore, with dimmed or extinguished
faculties, these old friends of his had passed away. In 1848,
Henry Brevoort, the best of all Irving's friends, had died.
Death itself Irving did not in the least fear. He was "always
ready to lay down this remnant of existence," thankful that his
"erratic and precarious career has been drawn to so serene a
close." The thought of possibly becoming a charge on his relatives, of not going down "with all sails set," was the sole fear,
as it was indeed the fact, of the final months. Towards the
very end asthma and insomnia brought about a state of nervousness which frequently made him afraid to be alone at night, and
sometimes he would reach a stage of excitement where he would
become "horror-ridden" by some fantasy of the mind. But all
in all (despite depression and nervousness) unselfishness, kindliness and humour continued to give forth their warmth even at
the end of the path.

And to the end also Irving kept up his enjoyment of art and
literature, and of music and the drama. To the pages of
Shakespeare he had frequent recourse. As late as the autumn
of 1858 he went to New York to see young Joseph Jefferson
take the part of Goldfinch in Holcroft's comedy of "The Road
to Ruin." Young Jefferson, who was later to become for our
own generation so lovable a Rip Van Winkle, had, as a boy,
appeared in that play, in support of the elder Hackett, Jefferson's father also being on the program. James Henry Hackett

was the original Rip Van Winkle, and in a letter to me by his son, Mr. James K. Hackett, there is, among many interesting paragraphs, the following: "Washington Irving was a warm personal friend of my father, as were also most of the prominent literary men and men of culture of his time; and while I cannot put my hands upon the letter this moment, nor perhaps without great searching and trouble, there is among my papers a letter from Washington Irving to my father in which he says—this is not a quotation but the pith:—'My dear Hackett: I am astounded and surprised and amazed that you could have made such a wonderful play out of such scanty material as my sketch of Rip Van Winkle'; and he also said that my father was, to his mind, the embodiment of the character which he drew." The elder Hackett had made his début in London, at Covent Garden, in 1827, and it was shortly thereafter that his Rip Van Winkle secured for this American actor high recognition in Great Britain. Ninety-three years later, in "Macbeth," the younger Hackett made *his* début in London. "This," as he writes, "seems incredible, but it is true."

The thirteen years that intervened between Irving's return from the post he had resigned as Minister to Spain and his death in 1859, have been called a period largely idyllic. The joys of friendship, of family life, of his country place; the pleasure of opera and plays; of authorship and of reading; mild horseback rides, until too many falls ended these; occasional games of whist, chess and backgammon; correspondence whose chief charm lay in the reminiscences there involved; playing with children; a little church-going towards the end;—these attest the quiet tenor of the life that along paths of simplicity and in surroundings of natural beauty approached its gentle termination. In the sphere of public events there is nothing more important to record than Irving's participation, with William Cullen Bryant and Daniel Webster, in the trio that presided at the exercises in commemoration of James Fenimore Cooper. In civic celebrations perhaps the most important episode was associated with the laying of the Atlantic cable in 1858, which, as Irving wrote, "caused a day to be set apart for everyone throughout the union to go crazy on the subject." However valuable an influence he may have been, and was, in affecting the American world of letters, the former diplomat played no part in political events or in social movements during this period. In Woman's Rights, free trade, temperance societies, States Rights, and the abolition of slavery he seemed curiously uninterested. The year of his return from Spain, the Wilmot Proviso, with its plan to exclude slavery in the territory acquired in the war with Mexico, had, although it met with defeat, started anew those embers which the Clay Compromise of 1850 could not extinguish and which (when South Carolina seceded from the Union) were to burst forth into flames of civil war so very soon after Irving's death. Throughout that critical period when Daniel Webster, as a matter of principle, was trying, at all costs, to preserve the Union, and John Brown, equally as a matter of principle, was intent, at all costs, on freeing the slaves, the most generally, the most generously loved of American writers employed neither his pen nor voice in the sphere of public controversy. That he was an old man eager to enjoy repose, is not the explanation; nor that Preston, the Senator from South Carolina, and Henry Clay, the Senator from Kentucky, and men of all parties had been his friends from youth; nor that he did not love the Union; nor that he was not opposed to any system of human slavery. The cause of Washington Irving's abstention from the controversy which shook the foundations of this country is too deep for any surface explanation. He had, as a young man, become even at the risk of the severance of friendships, even at the cost of being misinterpreted by indignant fellow-countrymen, firmly convinced that an author best serves the world by adhering to the employment of those talents as an author which are peculiarly his natural gifts. A Washington Irving who would take sides in public argument with Calhoun or with Garrison, or, somewhere between the two, with Clay or Webster, was, in Irving's opinion, less serviceable than a Washington Irving who would portray for the American people and for all peoples the

illuminating life of George Washington, or the endearing qualities of Oliver Goldsmith.   Of course if his had been a different
nature, with the inherited traditions of a Whittier, a Lowell, a
Higginson, he must have entered the arena.   But with his temperament, and with the philosophy of life that he had with much
bravery maintained, there was neither the intellectual nor the
moral urge to cause him to deviate from his point of view.   He
believed in self-development, but not greatly in the reform of
others; in the sunshine of Nazareth rather than in the lightning
of Sinai.   He was the patriarchal embodiment of good-will
towards men, and it is much to be questioned whether his value
to America would have been greater had he, in those pre-Civil
War days, swerved from that beneficent symbolization.   Some
comments that he had made in connection with George Washington's Will, freeing his slaves, had called forth from a Southern
newspaper a casual gibe.   But, by and large, Washington Irving
was loved in all the states of the Union.   Indeed, it is not too
much to say that of all Americans during their lifetime he was
the most unqualifiedly endeared to his countrymen.   Benjamin
Franklin may have been his peer in this regard, but neither the
immensely popular Henry Clay, nor the intensely admired Daniel
Webster, nor Washington, nor Lincoln, was loved in such un-
partisan manner.

The glorious sunset, by whose beauty Irving had been captured
only a few hours before he died in the night of November 28th,
1859, glows forth with double significance as the mellow radi-
ance before the impending dark.   Irving's rôle, as man,
as writer, as statesman, was to meliorate, to reconcile, to give
pleasure, to refine.   We may leave to the literary historian the
evaluation of his achievement purely from the point of view of
belles lettres; to the recorder of unusual facts we may suggest
in passing that no other man has given a nickname to a great
city, a nickname to its inhabitants, so that even to-day, as in the
day of *Salmagundi,* we New Yorkers are "Gothamites" (Gotham
being that English town whose wise men could be depended upon
to speak nonsense) and New York is "Father Knickerbocker."

341

But in concluding, we must with emphasis recur to the thought that it was Irving, more than any other man, who brought into accord the English-speaking peoples; that it was Irving who through his legends and his descriptions developed in his countrymen local sentiment and pride in the natural grandeur of their land.   A fate not wholly kind to this kind and winning gentleman showed a fitting courtesy in bringing him to his simple grave at Sleepy Hollow before his brothers of the North and of the South faced one another, with vindictive eyes, on the however imperative, yet intellectually humiliating and ever tragical, field of war.

INDEX

INDEX

Aberdeen, George Hamilton Gordon, Earl of, 220, 259, 272, 278.
"Abu Hassan," see Irving, Writings of.
Adams, Agnes, 90.
Adams, John, 3.
Adams, John Quincy, 206, 246.
Addison, Joseph, 325.
Adelaide, Madame, sister of Louis Philippe, 262.
Adelaide, Queen, 220.
Albert, Prince, 260, 261.
Alfieri, 187.
Alico, Cardinal Pedro, 204.
Allston, Washington, 34, 35, 92.
Almodovar, Count, 284.
Amelia, Princess of Bavaria, 139.
Amelia, Princess of Saxony, 139.
American Civil War, 25.
American Indians, 15, 83, 84.
Ames, Hector, 258.
Analectic Magazine, The, 66, 82.
Ancient & Honourable Order, The, 69.
Anderson, Alexander, 17, 18.
Anderson, John, 17, 18, 275.
André, Major, 232.
Angelina, 26.
Antoine, Prince of Saxony, 139.
Antonio, Irving's guide in Spain, 210.
Arethusa, Fountain of, 30.
Arguelles, Don Augustus, 273, 305.
Arnold, Benedict, 232.
Aspinwall, Colonel Thomas, 199, 204, 262.
Aspinwalls, The, 181.
Aspiroz, General, 297.
Assisi, Don Francisco, de, 268, 285, 296, 307, 318.
Aston, Sir Arthur Ingram, 277.
Astor, John Jacob, 15, 76, 235, 332.
"Astoria," see Irving, Writings of.
Astor Library, 76.

Bailey, Joanna, 85.
Baker, Wadsworth, 24.
Balloon mania, 22.

Balzac, 264.
Bancroft, George, 118, 328.
Bandinel, James, 260.
Barbauld, Mrs., 85.
Barberini Palace, 32.
Basle, 36.
Bassett, Prof. J. S., 249.
Bath, 44.
Bavaria, King of, 141.
Beasley, Ruben, 262.
Beaumarchais, Eugene, 129, 132.
Beethoven, 131.
Belleforte, 40.
Belzoni, G. B., 109.
Bergh, Madame de, 55, 56, 138.
Berstatt, Baron de, 127.
Besborough, Count of, 109.
Béthune, Prince and Princesse de, 262.
Betts, Judge, 241.
Betty, William, 116.
Bianca and the Locket, 60.
Bibliophile Society, 54, 149.
Bird, Mrs., wife of English Consul at Genoa, 25.
Black Hawk, 226.
Blanchard, 22.
Blessington, Countess of, 120, 174.
Blessington, Earl of, 174.
Blucher, Field-Marshal, 123.
Boabdil, 193.
Boccaccio, 173.
Boileau, 173.
Bolvillier, Antoinette, 58, 63, 64, 195, 201, 268.
Bonaparte Family, 35.
Bonaparte, Joseph, 190.
Bonaparte, Napoleon (See Napoleon).
Bonneville, Captain, 233.
Bordeaux, 22.
Bordeaux Journal, 20.
Borgo, Pozzo di, 173.
Boynton, Henry W., 49.
"Bracebridge Hall," see Irving, Writings of.
Bradish, Mrs., 94.

345

INDEX

Brevoort, Carson, 77, 269.
Brevoort, Henry, 15, 52, 53, 70, 71, 73, 74, 77, 83, 84, 95, 221, 234, 258, 338.
Brevoort, Henry Sr., 78, 80.
Brevoort, Margaret, 78, 81.
Brignole, Marquis, 263.
Bristol, 43, 44.
"Broken Heart, The," see Irving, Writings of.
Brown, John, 340.
Bruce, Robert, 11.
Brussells, 42.
Bryant, William C., 20, 165, 200, 223, 339.
Brydges, Sir Edgerton, 173.
Buchanan, H. M., 100.
Buchanan, James, 262, 316, 324.
Bunyan, 14.
Burns, Robert, 11, 51, 52.
Burr, Aaron, 48, 71, 84, 170, 208.
Butler, Benjamin F., 252.
Byron, Lord, 62, 174, 232.
Byron, Lord and Lady, 179.

Cabell, James Branch, 34.
Cabell, Joseph Carrington, 33, 34, 35, 36, 37, 336.
Cadiz, Duke of, 288, 307.
Calatrava, José Maria, 291.
Calderon, 166, 173.
Calhoun, John C., 230, 280, 308, 310.
Calliopean Society, 16.
Campbell, Thomas, 66, 85, 94, 100, 109, 233, 260.
Campbell, Mrs. Thomas, 94.
Canova, 35.
Cappacini, Cardinal, 321.
Cargill, Lieutenant, 24.
Carhampton, Earl of, 54.
Carlyle, Jane, 338.
Carlyle, Thomas, 140, 338.
Caroline, Queen, 118.
Carson, Laura, 101.
Carter, Mary, 34.
Carters of Virginia, The, 184.
Cass, Lewis, 262.
Cassaro, Prince of, 194.
Castanor, General, 305.
"Castle of Otranto, The," 28.
Cervantes, 325.

"Charles II or the Merry Monarch," see Irving, Writings of.
Charles V, 130.
Charles IX, 173.
Charles X, 181, 216, 217.
Chatterton, Thomas, 92.
Chaworth, Mary, 176.
Choiseul, Duc de, 33.
Chouteau, Pierre, 229.
"Christopher North," 85.
"Citizen of the World, A," 39.
Clark, J. Gaylord, 239.
Clay, Henry, 101, 222, 242, 244, 340, 341.
Cobb, General, 237.
Cockburn, John, 138, 143.
Cockloft Hall, 69.
Cogswell, J. G., 236, 257, 327.
Coleman, William, 106.
Coleridge, S. T., 35.
Columbia College, 8, 53, 94, 216.
Concha, General, 302.
Conicoff, General, 138, 139.
Constable, Archibald, 174.
Constitutional Gazette, The, 18.
Cooke, George Frederick, 43, 76, 337.
Cooper, James Fenimore, 263, 339.
Cooper, Thomas A., 80.
Cowley, Lord Henry Wellesley, 263.
Cranford, Maria, 58.
"Crayon"—See Geoffrey Crayon.
"Crayon Miscellany, The," see Irving, Writings of.
Crebillon, P. J. de, 200.
Curran, J. P., 48.
Curtis, George William, 328.

D'Alvay, Mademoiselle, 197.
Dante, 187.
D'Arblay, Madame, 85.
D'Auvergne, De La Tour, 123.
Davidson, Margaret, 233.
Davis, Charles A., 240, 241, 258.
De Camp, Miss, 43.
Decatur, Stephen, 87, 170.
Depons, F., 65.
De Quincey, Thomas, 93.
Dercier, Sebastian, 161.
"Der Freischütz," 54.
Devonshire, Duke of, 220.
Diana, 30.

INDEX

INDEX

Russell, Lord and Lady John, 261.
Ryans, The, 198.
Ryckman, Mrs., 77.

St. John the Baptist, 29.
St. Peter's, 35.
Salar, Marquis of, 192.
"Salmagundi," 15, 17, 36, 58, 68, 109.
Sancho, General, 296.
Santa Cruz, Marchioness, 197.
Saunders, Romulus M., 279.
Saxony, Queen of, 141.
Schermerhorn, Abraham, 258.
Schiller, 125.
Scott, Sir Walter, 12, 29, 32, 53, 58, 77, 84, 85, 99, 100, 106, 118, 199, 214, 221, 232, 337.
"Sentimental Journey, The," 30, 39.
Serrano, Spanish Minister of War, 271, 306.
Sestri, 26.
Seymour, Lady, 259.
Shakespeare, 14, 89, 117, 338.
Shelley, 40, 61.
Shelley, Mary, 58, 61, 62.
Siddons, Mrs., 43, 85, 337.
"Sindbad the Sailor," 14.
"Sketch Book, The," see Irving, Writings of.
Slidell, A. S., 198, 221.
Smith, Claudius, 232.
Smith, John Adam, 198.
Sneyd, Ralph, 209, 211, 213.
Soane, General, 298, 302.
Somerset, Duke of, 220.
Sontag, Henrietta, 135.
Sorbonne, The, 36.
Southey, Robert, 109.
Spanish Diaries of Irving, 63, and passim.
"Sparkle, Sophie," 58.
"Spectator, The," 68.
Spencer, Lord and Lady, 107.
Steele, Richard, 325.
Sterne, Laurence, 31, 32, 36, 213.
Stevenson, Robert Louis, 5, 35, 48, 166.
Stroffregen, Secretary of Russian Embassy at Madrid, 200.
Storm, Hall, 26, 60.
Storrow, Julia, 328.
Storrow, Mrs. Sarah, 173, 270, 326, 334, 336.

Storrows, The, 262, 263, 271.
Stuart, Gilbert, 235.
Suchet, Louis Gabrielle, Duc d'Albufera, 212.
Sue, Eugene, 263.
Sumner, George, 331.
Sunnyside, 19, and passim.
Supernatural beliefs, Irving's attitude towards, 30.
Sussex, Duke of, 219.
Swain, William W., 251.
Switzerland, 36.
Syracuse, 29, 30.

"Tales of a Traveller," see Irving, Writings of.
Talleyrand, 217, 218.
Talma, 117, 173.
Tarfe, Moorish warrior, the, 192.
Taylor, Bayard, 27.
Taylor, Zachary, 279.
Thackeray, Zachary M., 34, 127, 332.
Thoreau, Henry D., 20, 84.
Thorne, Colonel Herman, 262.
"Three Weeks after Marriage," 55.
Tia, 207.
Ticknor, George, 328.
Tompkins, Daniel D., 85.
Tontine Coffee House, 9.
Toulouse, 28.
"Traits of Indian Character," see Irving, Writings of.
Trapani, Count, 311.
Trent, William P., 20, 54.
Trinity Church, 5.
Tuckerman, H. T., 179.
Tuilleries, The, 41.
Turenne, Marshal of France, 128.
Tyler, John, 257.

Vail, 265.
Valdevielso, Mexican Minister to Spain, 301.
Van Alen, Congressman, 335.
Van Buren, John, 231.
Van Buren, Martin, 22, 208, 221, 222, 223, 231, 233, 243, 249, 250, 257, 333.
Vanderlyn, John, 42.
Van Ness, Judge William P., 7, 64, 71, 231, 335.
Van Nesses, The, 73.

354

Van Wart, Sarah (See Sarah Irving).
Van Warts, The, 88, and *passim.*
Vatican, The, 35.
Velletri, 24.
Venice, 35.
Veraguas, Duke of, 198.
Verplanck, Gulian C., 106.
Vesuvius, 40.
Victoria, Duchess of (wife of Espartero), 271.
Victoria, Queen, 107, 260, 261, 272.
Virgil, 24.
Voltaire, 124.

Wainwright, Bishop, 237.
Wales, Irving's Journal of the Tour in, 34.
Wallenstein, 144.
Walpole, Horace, 28, 29, 92.
Walton, Izaac, 111.
War of 1812, 21, 73, 78, 85, 89.
War of Independence, 3.
Warner, Charles Dudley, 49.
Washington, George, 8, 12, 77, 237, 239, 261, 341.
Weber, Carl Maria von, 54, 141, 145, 150.

Webster, Daniel, 222, 230, 242, 250, 257, 280, 284, 292, 295, 339, 340, 341.
Welleses, The, 263.
Wellington, Duke of, 123, 216, 217, 220.
Wemyss, Captain, 129.
West, William E., 175, 183.
Whittier, John G., 20, 341.
"Wild Huntsman, The," see Irving, Writings of.
Wildman, Colonel, 222.
Wilkie, Sir David, 185, 199, 220, 337.
Wilkins, Martin, 47.
William IV, 216, 220.
William I, King of the Netherlands, 218.
Willis, Nathaniel Parker, 328, 335.
Wilson, a Scotch painter, 26.
Wilson, Henrietta, 173.
Winkelmann, Johann, 33.
Winthrop, Robert C., 337.
Wollstonecraft, Mary, 61.
Wordsworth, William, 261.
"World Displayed, The," 14.
Wren, Sir Christopher, 111.

Ximenes, Mateo, 207, 266.

Zurbano, General, 281, 298.

355

A NOTE ON THE TYPE IN
WHICH THIS BOOK IS SET

The type in which this book has been set (on the Lino-type) is Caslon Old Face, a faithful and authentic re-production from the original patterns of William Caslon I. Historically considered, Caslon's old face types are the most important contribution the English speaking world has ever made to the art of typography. No other face has ever attained to so lasting and general a popularity. Caslon's types were made to read. Even their apparent imperfections contribute to this effect being, in fact, the result of a deliberate artistry which sought above all else for legibility in the printed page.

SET UP, PRINTED AND BOUND BY THE
VAIL-BALLOU PRESS, BINGHAMTON,
N. Y. · PAPER MANUFACTURED BY
W. C. HAMILTON & SONS, MI-
QUON, PA., AND FURNISHED
BY MARQUARDT, BLAKE &
DECKER, NEW YORK. ·